Day Hikes in Washington State

90 Favorite Trails, Loops, and Summit Scrambles

Don J. Scarmuzzi

WEST
MARGIN
PRESS

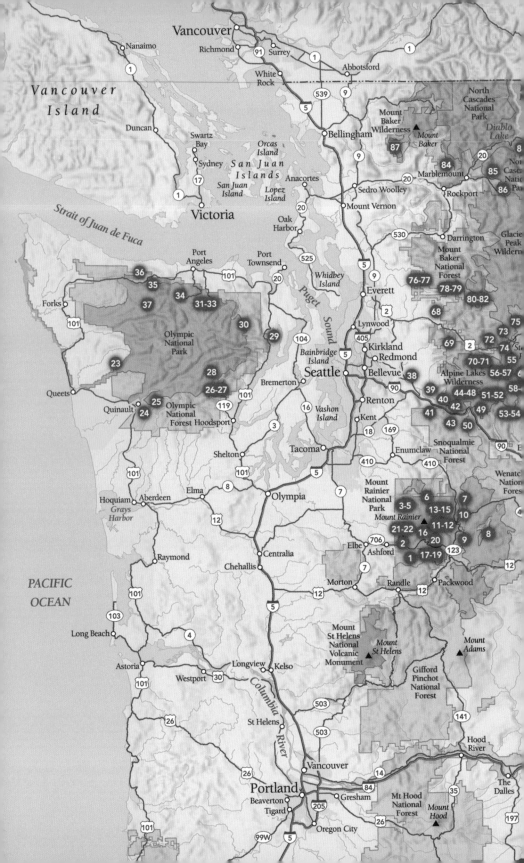

CONTENTS

PREFACE

Like *Day Hikes in the Pacific Northwest*, this follow-up provides options for most lake and loop hikes to continue to summits or lookout sites! Read each crazily detailed hike (and trailhead directions) in advance and only proceed from the first goal to the next if you are adept, following closely the levels of difficulty for each segment of your hike. *Day Hikes in the Pacific Northwest* is still a great resource for hikes around the Mount St. Helens, Goat Rocks, and Mount Adams regions in Washington, and more; however, in this volume, local connoisseurs will see these treks in a new light, and visiting adventurists will find them purely gratifying.

More than ever people want to connect with something tangible and breathe in some fresh air (barring smoke from seasonal fires), with Washington State providing plenty of magnificent natural places to explore. However, the best advice I can give is to avoid prime time on Saturdays and Sundays, drive farther out than the usual hour or so, and skip congested trailheads with a backup plan ready. Parking hassles and overcrowded trails can be a problem on weekends, whereas weekday outings offer more solitude. To park at many trailheads, hikers must pay a day-use fee, which may be covered by a Northwest Forest Pass or Discover Pass (unless it's a State or National Park). Both passes can be obtained for one day ($5 to around $12 per vehicle) or one year ($30 to $35) and are available online, at ranger stations, and at many retail outlets. It's always helpful to look up your hike online for particulars on payment at the trailhead and to make sure trails are open. A trail may be inaccessible due to landslides, flooding, road closures, fires, or snow, or for wildlife protection. (For National Fire Situational Awareness: https://maps.nwcg.gov/sa/#/%3F/46.1107/ -121.7664/7.) Another piece of advice: when you park your car before a hike, be sure to conceal all valuables. Out of sight, out of mind!

Each hike begins with essential information about elevation, distance, duration (including short breaks), difficulty level, and trip reports that point out tidbits like what parking pass is needed, the restroom sitch (outside virus times), and what wildlife you may encounter. Elevation information includes the highest point (or points) of a hike, as well as the maximum vertical gains you will experience. Difficulty level is broken up into five categories: **easy** (short, little elevation change, sometimes paved, ideal for families and novices); **moderate** (more elevation change, navigating tree roots, rocks); **strenuous** (longer hike, steeper, switchbacks, drop-offs); **very challenging** (quite long, sustained steep climbs for thousands of feet, bushwhacking, scrambling, GPS device recommended); and **expert only** (punishing steeps, exposed cliffs, free climbing possible, traction required at times, route-finding).

For the sake of brevity, several abbreviations are used: **TH** (trailhead), **FR** (Forest Road), **CG** (campground), **ft** (feet), **mi** (mile), **AWD** or **4WD** (all-wheel drive, four-wheel drive), **PCT** (Pacific Crest Trail 2000/Pacific Crest National Scenic Trail), **MLH** (Mountain Loop Highway), and **BYOTP** (bring your own toilet paper). Also note the following terms: A **switchback** is a spot in a trail that zigzags sharply, whether once or a hundred times. A **shoulder** is a rise or small ridge. **Exposure** refers to an individual's level of risk of falling where a tumble would be fatal. A trail section described as **airy** is exposed to some degree, with drop-offs; exercise extreme caution in such areas. **Gendarmes** refer to spiked pinnacles or spires blocking a ridgeline, borrowing their meaning from medieval French soldiers standing guard. Distances on the maps given are approximate.

Hiking with the right gear is critical. A dry, warm hiker is a happy hiker! Bring some, if not all, of the following on your day hike (see page 289): a friend, layers, backup rain gear, dry socks, a hat, sunscreen, water and purifier, food, flashlight or headlamp, map, GPS, compass, charged phone, first-aid kit with an emergency blanket, hand sanitizer, toilet paper, wipes, lighters, knife, insect repellent, whistle— and a sense of humor. No drones were used in creating this guidebook!

Finally, as hiking rules and recommendations evolve, give others space, say hello in passing, and wear a face mask when warranted. Although the information was accurate at the time of printing, the author and publisher are not responsible for your personal safety based on descriptions here. Take care of each other and stay safe. "Nature has been for me, for as long as I remember, a source of solace, inspiration, adventure, and delight; a home, a teacher, a companion." —Lorraine Anderson

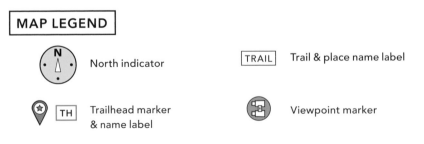

| MAP LEGEND |

North indicator

Trailhead marker & name label

TRAIL   Trail & place name label

Viewpoint marker

Find Silver Lake from hike 30, page 94.

MOUNT RAINIER

ELEVATION: 5685 ft; vertical gain of 1400 ft

DISTANCE: 3.5 mi round-trip

DURATION: 2 hours or so round-trip

DIFFICULTY: Moderate (steep at times, drop-offs near summit block, brief)

TRIP REPORT: The weathered lookout was built in 1929 and is usually open to the public except in winter (restoration project closes lookout into 2022). Wildflowers are ablaze during July and August, and the view from the pillar of a summit above the forested ridge showcases Mount Rainier National Park with other Cascade volcanoes unfolding S. This popular and narrow route will make distancing from others difficult, but that doesn't mean you should abandon your dreams and goals. Be considerate when passing, communicate, and step off trail when possible yielding to uphill traffic. No fee or restroom.

TRAILHEAD: High Rock/Greenwood Lake TH at Towhead Gap. From Seattle, take I-5 S and other routes into WA-706 E for 80 mi to Ashford. Continue on WA-706 E from the Rainier Basecamp Visitor Information (clean restrooms behind) 2.5 mi, turn right at a National Forest marker on Kernahan Rd (FR-52, closed in winter) 4.5 mi, turn right on FR-84 (gravel, well traveled, narrow, 2WD okay) 6.5 mi, and fork right on FR-8440 for 2.5 mi, curving over the saddle at Towhead Gap (4300 ft) and finding the TH at right with parking on the sides.

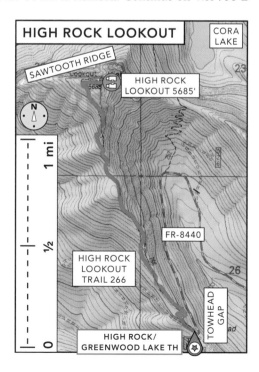

From Portland, take I-5 N to exit 68 (Morton/Yakima), turn right onto US-12 E for 30 mi, and turn left on WA-7 N in Morton (speed trap) 16 mi to Elbe. Turn right on WA-706 E 7 mi to Ashford, and follow as above (95 mi, 2½ hours from Seattle; 150 mi, 3 hours from Portland).

Hikers accumulate for grand views of Mount Rainier near High Rock Lookout before it closed in late 2020 for a well needed on-site restoration.

ROUTE: Begin by hiking NW on High Rock Lookout Trail 266 (signed) up the SE ridge of High Rock through fir and hemlock, with 2 quick switchbacks continuing steadily (trillium, bear grass, avalanche lilies, huckleberries in fall) while enjoying micro-breaks in the pitch over the steepening yet pleasant track. After another switchback (steps) and a turn up through the forest, Mount Rainier pops into full view (unimpeded, with Goat Rocks, Mount Adams) as you leave the sheer ridgeline traversing NW up 0.25 mi (lupine, paintbrush, others) over to the W ridge of High Rock. Turn right (E, opposite spur to cliff edge) slogging up Trail 266 (steep, narrow, roots) 100 yards before you see the lookout on the aptly named Sawtooth Ridge.

Be cautious, especially with young children, ascending the final 100 ft of very steeply sloped rock slabs surrounding the lookout and summit area (no more solid trail) as you scrutinize the nearby pillars en route. Lower peaks along jagged Sawtooth Ridge continue NW and you can see a bit of Cora Lake almost 1900 ft directly below, the Tatoosh Range across the valley in front of Mount Rainier, and Goat Rocks and Mount Adams to the SE, with Mount St. Helens to the SW. Enjoy the lighting at different times of the day and year, as you'll surely wish to return!

ELEVATION: 4292 ft at Lake George, 5485 ft on Gobblers Knob, 5475 ft on Mount Beljica; vertical gains of 1450 ft for Lake George, 2600 ft for Gobblers Knob, 3400 ft for Mount Beljica (3850 ft for both summits)

DISTANCE: 3.75 mi mountain bike/hike to Round Pass; 1 mi hike to Lake George, 10 mi round-trip; 2.5 mi hike to Gobblers Knob, 12.5 mi round-trip; 5.75 mi hike to Mount Beljica, 20 mi round-trip for both summits from the TH

DURATION: 2–3 hours riding/hiking to Lake George, 1½ hours more to Gobblers Knob, 3 hours to Mount Beljica; 7–10 hours round-trip for both summits from TH

DIFFICULTY: Mix of strenuous for Lake George and Gobblers Knob (easy mountain bike/hike to Round Pass, steady to Lake George, steep summit block, drop-offs, well-signed) and very challenging beyond Goat Lake (very long, steep summit, route-finding, drop-offs)

TRIP REPORT: Along Mount Rainier National Park's SW boundary are these outings tempting you to push further, up to Gobblers Knob Fire Lookout or perhaps into Glacier View Wilderness down to Goat Lake or up to Mount Beljica. Because of road washouts closing easier access to all but avid hikers and bikers, families with young

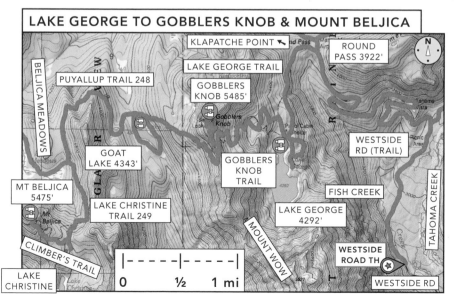

LAKE GEORGE TO GOBBLERS KNOB & MOUNT BELJICA

KLAPATCHE POINT — nd Pass — ROUND PASS 3922'

N

BELJICA MEADOWS

PUYALLUP TRAIL 248

LAKE GEORGE TRAIL

GOBBLERS KNOB 5485'

Gobblers Knob

WESTSIDE RD (TRAIL)

GOAT LAKE 4343'

GOBBLERS KNOB TRAIL

MT BELJICA 5475'

FISH CREEK

TAHOMA CREEK

LAKE CHRISTINE TRAIL 249

LAKE GEORGE 4292'

CLIMBER'S TRAIL

MOUNT WOW

WESTSIDE ROAD TH

LAKE CHRISTINE

0   ½   1 mi

WESTSIDE RD

children have a more tranquil option to visit Lake George. Follow current eMTB laws if riding electric and be respectful, especially while passing pedestrians. Adventurists might ride as far as Klapatche Point as an add-on or option to delve further into the park (18-mi round-trip with very brief hiking option to see Denman Falls). Wildlife sightings may include black bear and cougar. Entrance Stations are within the National Park (yourpassnow.com), and there is no on-site restroom, with an outdoor privy at Lake George.

TRAILHEAD: Westside Rd TH. From Seattle, see High Rock Lookout on page 11 for directions for 80 mi to Ashford. Continue on WA-706 E from the Rainier Basecamp Visitor Information (clean restrooms behind) for almost 6 mi to the Nisqually Entrance. Continue up Paradise Rd E 0.75 mi, then fork left on Westside Rd (gravel, potholes) almost 3 mi to the barricade with pull-in parking on right.

From Portland, take I-5 N to exit 68 (Morton/Yakima), turn right on US-12 E for 30 mi, turn left on WA-7 N in Morton (speed trap) 16 mi to Elbe. Turn right on WA-706 E for 7 mi to Ashford, and follow as above (90 mi, 2 hours from Seattle; 145 mi, 2½ hours from Portland).

ROUTE: Begin walking or biking N past the barricade and gate on Westside Rd (Trail) soon across Fish Creek (solid bridge), then ascend NE along Tahoma Creek within the floodplain (great shot to Mount Rainier). After 1.5 mi move W up turns through cedar and fir less than 1 mi passing the Tahoma Vista Picnic area on a sharp left turn. Climb steeper through the forest (thick with berry bushes), winding around 1.5 mi NW up to Round Pass (3922 ft), with a bike rack and Lake George Trail on your left. About 100 ft farther on your right is a brief spur N to a notable Marine Memorial Airplane Crash Monument. Take Lake George Trail (accurate signage) easily hiking W then S almost 1 mi through the tall old forest up to subalpine blue-green Lake George beneath rugged Mount Wow. The first spurs left (S) head to the privy, campground, and locked patrol shelter, with swimming options nearby.

For Gobblers Knob and more, continue right (W) from the junctures leaving Lake George steeper up 8 turns on Gobblers Knob Trail for 1 mi (through meadows, wildflowers, passing a tarn in the forest) including 3 more quick switchbacks to a juncture near a saddle. For the lookout, hike sharply right (NNW) up Gobblers Knob Trail about 0.5 mi farther steadily up 10 tight switchbacks (wildflowers), winding around to the signage at the (locked) lookout. From the decks and small summit enjoy the in-your-face views of Mount Rainier and its countless glaciers over a few growing trees. Mount Wow dominates along the connecting ridge and farther S are High Rock, Goat Rocks, and Mount St. Helens. See a corner of Lake George toward Mount Rainier and a slice of Goat Lake SW toward Mount Beljica, with Glacier View Summit NW!

For Goat Lake and Mount Beljica, hike S from the lookout juncture 150 ft up over the small saddle (5125 ft) on Puyallup Trail 248, then about 1 mi down (views,

2 steep switchbacks, leaving National Park into Glacier View Wilderness) to Goat Lake. Spurs head left (SSE) from the flats to circumnavigate the tree-choked colorful lake (4343 ft). Return to Lake George and Round Pass or work up Trail 248 steeper W and NW, then undulate without difficulty around a ridge moving SW (slightly overgrown) narrowly to the next key intersection in the woods above Beljica Meadows (1.25 mi from Goat Lake or opposite to Glacier View TH).

Turn left (S) onto Lake Christine Trail 249 for Mount Beljica steady easy up (beautiful ancient forest, slightly overgrown) 1 mi to a wide saddle. Descend the other side SSW 150 ft to an unsigned juncture finding the solid climber's trail with blazes (ribbons/trail markers/painted rectangles) right (W), and follow it 0.5 mi to the peak where it begins mellow then becomes super-steep for the last bit (carefully). See Mount Rainier towering immensely behind Gobblers Knob (appears lower) and look to a corner of Beljica Meadows far below!

Mount Wow from the inviting shoreline at Lake George!

3 SPRAY PARK

ELEVATION: 6450 ft; vertical gain of almost 2000 ft for Parks Overlook

DISTANCE: 4.25 mi up, 8.5 mi or so round-trip, including Spray Falls and spurs

DURATION: 2 hours up, 3–4 hours round-trip

DIFFICULTY: Strenuous (steep at times, family-friendly, options, brief easy snow crossings July to August)

TRIP REPORT: On the quiet side (except on weekends) of Mount Rainier's NW slopes is the Mowich Lake TH, which is only open mid-July through mid-October, so check ahead for road and trail conditions. Mowich Lake is the portal to the backcountry and some of the most attractive wildflower-laden meadows on the enormous volcano, with numerous ponds, waterfalls, and little summits within the alpine environment. Some families return from Spray Park (6.5 mi round-trip, 1300 ft vertical gain) skipping the overlook. Wildlife sightings may include marmots, mountain goats, and black bear. Entrance Stations are within the National Park (yourpassnow.com), and there are on-site restrooms.

TRAILHEAD: Mowich Lake TH. From Seattle, take I-5 S and other routes to WA-165 S, driving 50 mi to Carbonado. Continue 3 mi on WA-165 S, crossing the Fairfax Bridge (Carbon River) 0.5 mi farther, fork right on Mowich Lake Rd 11.5 mi (gravel after 1.5 mi, potholes, washboard, 2WD okay, AWD preferred, closed in winter) to the Entrance Station, then drive almost 5 mi more to the end of the road at Mowich Lake Campground (very small, walk-in, not lakeside) with pull-in parking on the sides.

From Portland, take I-5 N to exit 127 (Puyallup), merge onto WA-512 E for 11.25 mi, stay right for WA-167 N/WA-410 E (Yakima) for 1 mi, stay right onto WA-410 E for 12 mi, turn right on WA-165 S to Carbonado for 6.5 mi, and follow as above (65 mi, 2½ hours from Seattle; 180 mi, 3½ hours from Portland).

ROUTE: Leave Mowich Lake (left of outhouse) on the Wonderland Trail that encircles the mountain, but only for 0.25 mi S. Descend 2 switchbacks (steps) plus 2 steeper turns before crossing a log bridge to an accurately signed juncture (Spray Park 2.8 mi). Continue left (SSE) on Spray Park Trail, which undulates easily (cedar, fir, hemlock). Cross two more bridges (see Fay Peak over Lee Creek from first one), move up steps a bit steeper briefly, and then walk down and up (switchback) to cross the bottom of a scree field. Hike ESE very steeply up several S-turns (steps) to Eagle Cliff Viewpoint (1.5 mi from TH). Take the viewpoint spur 40 ft, *not* "100 ft" right (S, old

Spray Falls either whets the appetite or serves as dessert before/after the beautiful meadows above within Mount Rainier National Park!

wooden rails, 4950 ft). Look up the canyon to North Mowich Glacier, Mowich Face, Sunset Ridge, and Liberty Cap under the sleeping giant!

Walk cautiously up less than 0.5 mi E across some very steep terrain (and over a mossy little creek), reaching the signed spur path for Spray Falls (lighting improves later in the day). Walk right (ESE) almost 0.25 mi for the falls (across nice-looking Grant Creek), soon crossing a scree slope to boulder-laden Spray Creek. The 354-ft cascading waterfall is partly obscured when the creek level is high, and hopping rocks over it for that perfect shot is too dangerous for most. The safer tease view isn't bad, as the large majestic waterfall twists up higher and often lives up to its namesake!

From Spray Park Trail hike N up 12 steep, tight switchbacks for less than 0.5 mi to the bottom of Spray Park in the lower meadows. Walk NE on easier terrain for less than 0.25 mi (thinning fir, bear grass), crossing Grant Creek again. Continue NE (wide, gravel, wildflowers), leaving the trees over a small bridge and then move steadily NNE up a few switchbacks and turns. You'll arrive at a nondescript intersection in Spray Park (5750 ft) near a widening expanse of the creek within the meadows (3.25 mi from TH including spurs). Heather, heliotrope, lupine, paintbrush, and other foliage dominate the landscape with several tarn ponds (choice reflections) worth exploring from spurs (some closed for restoration). Observing W and NW are Hessong Rock and Mount Pleasant above the colorful grassland!

Continue 1 mi to the high point of Spray Park Trail to a bench (and rise) that could easily be called Parks Overlook. You'll keep right (NE) on the wider Spray Park Trail (instead of crossing the creek onto spurs) up steadily 0.5 mi, passing an even more stunning meadow (far-reaching views, gobs of wildflowers) near neighboring tarns. You'll walk up steps and cross snow patches (until late summer), passing an unsigned juncture (6250 ft) for Knapsack Pass Trail that heads left (NW) less than 0.5 mi up around the NE ridge of Mount Pleasant en route to Knapsack Pass (Hessong Rock to Mount Pleasant Loops on page 19). Keep SE where the trail is steeper above the tree line 0.25 mi to a junction on a rocky bench as you traverse the last 75 ft to the crossroads near a huge cairn before Spray Park Trail descends thousands of feet NNE to the Carbon River. Take the narrow unsigned climber's trail steeply right (SE) instead 100 ft or so and call it a day from the boulders anywhere on the broad rise. From Parks Overlook atop and between Spray, Mist, and Seattle Parks, lounge within the grandeur near the path that continues past the surreal wildflower-blanketed landscape to Echo and Observation Rocks under Mount Rainier. North in the distance the Stuart Range, Glacier Peak, North Cascades, and even Mount Baker can be spotted!

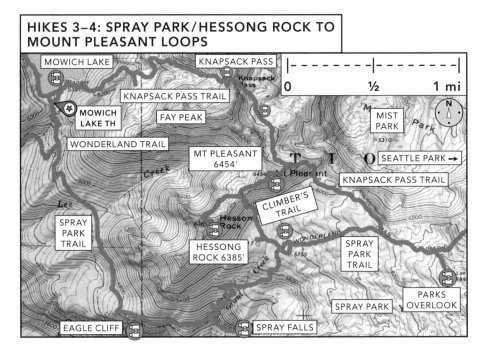

HIKES 3–4: SPRAY PARK/HESSONG ROCK TO MOUNT PLEASANT LOOPS

HESSONG ROCK TO MOUNT PLEASANT LOOPS

ELEVATION: 6385 ft on Hessong Rock, 6454 ft on Mount Pleasant; vertical gains of 2300 ft for both summits on Spray Park (clockwise) loop, 2600 ft for both summits via Knapsack Pass (counterclockwise) loop

DISTANCE: Around 4 mi to Hessong Rock or Mount Pleasant directly, 9 mi round-trip for both summits via Spray Park loop, 6.75 mi round-trip for both summits via Knapsack Pass loop

DURATION: 5–7 hours round-trip

DIFFICULTY: Strenuous (steep ups/downs, route-finding, Class 2, traction/ice axe required through July)

TRIP REPORT: Less traveled are two fantastic loop options that leave the crowds in Spray Park for the more challenging summits above on the same little ridge. Then you continue either into the top of Spray Park or across a wide scenic bench above Mist Park en route to Knapsack Pass before descending to the valley at Mowich Lake (largest within Mount Rainier National Park). August into October works best, when most of the snow (nearly 55 ft per year) finally melts off Mount Rainier's N slopes. Wildlife sightings may include black bear. Entrance Stations are within the National Park (yourpassnow.com), and there are on-site restrooms.

TRAILHEAD: Mowich Lake TH. See Spray Park on page 16 for directions (65 mi, 2½ hours from Seattle; 180 mi, 3½ hours from Portland).

ROUTE: See Spray Park on page 16. You'll head 3.25 mi up Spray Park Trail to a nondescript intersection within a big clearing in Spray Park (5750 ft). Take the path left (NW) off the main trail (no sign) immediately across a small creek. You'll soon pass a tiny pond (from another brief spur left/W). Stay on the climber's trail past smaller tarns, continuing steeply NW (grasses, wildflowers) then even steeper straight up with turns to the visible saddle between Hessong Rock and Mount Pleasant (0.5 mi from Spray Park Trail).

Turn left (SW) from the wide saddle more than 0.25 mi for Hessong Rock first as both summits include steep travel on narrow but obvious tracks. You'll quickly leave the ridgeline right (W), traversing down under the N side of the rocky summit block over a gently sloped scree- and/or snow-covered bench. Head SW up the low side of a wide but steep rocky ramp briefly, then climb left (SE) very steeply with better footing

Cliffs near Hessong Rock to Mount Pleasant and Spray Park!

for a few feet to the nearby boulder-covered peak (cautiously). You'll see Spray Park in its entirety, the top of Spray Falls, Tillicum Point, Echo and Observation Rocks, and of course Mount Rainier! Look N to neighboring Fay Peak and Mother Mountain with Mount Pleasant to the NW along the adjoining ridge. Return to the main saddle sensibly.

Mount Pleasant is less than 0.25 mi from the saddle, following the footpath NE up the ridge crest. Easily bypass rocky obstacles right (S) of the ridgeline for most of the solid bushwhack (grasses, wildflowers, handful of trees) becoming steeper and rockier to the peak. On a clear day, you can see up to North Cascades but the local scenery is certainly the highlight! Return by the same route (8.5 mi round-trip) or continue for the more amusing loops. Avoid descending the N ridge from the summit and instead take the easier NE ridge (slightly right), working steeply down less than 0.25 mi over the crest (faint rocky climber's trail) to a junction (6200 ft). The easier (clockwise) option takes you right (SE) less than 0.5 mi for Spray Park on Knapsack Pass Trail (steep at first) down past tarns to Spray Park Trail. Then you turn right past several more tarns through the wide meadow, traveling 0.5 mi SW to the end of the loop in Spray Park.

For the counterclockwise loop, turn left (NW) from the NE ridge juncture onto Knapsack Pass Trail over a rocky and/or snow-covered wide treeless bench for 0.75 mi to Knapsack Pass. You'll stay near the path, passing small tarns as the beauty stuns from the top of Mist Park; see majestic Mother Mountain ridge through Fay Peak to Mount Pleasant! The route becomes rockier and a bit steeper with large gendarmes near the hidden pass (more evergreens) where subalpine Mowich Lake is revealed. Enjoy superlative views near and far and begin descending Knapsack Pass Trail W, which is steady and steep (1.25 mi to TH) down scree and then becomes a thin and fairly unmaintained path (very few trees and turns). Fay Peak looms left as you stay on the main path (western pasqueflower, others into late August), passing a wider expanse in the creek (with small cascade), then move SW easily past the Ranger Station nearest the deep-blue clear lake to the TH.

5 TOLMIE PEAK

ELEVATION: 5959 ft (5939 ft at Tolmie Peak Lookout); vertical gain of around 1500 ft

DISTANCE: 3 mi to true summit from Tolmie Peak TH, 6.25 mi round-trip max, more than 7 mi round-trip from Mowich Lake TH

DURATION: 1½–2 hours up, 3–4 hours round-trip

DIFFICULTY: Mix of moderate for Eunice Lake or the lookout (steeper at times, brief, family-friendly, well-signed, rocky, ups/downs, mosquitoes and bees near lakes into August) and strenuous for true summit (narrow ridgeline, drop-offs)

TRIP REPORT: Take delight in this incredible day hike mid-July through September with minimal effort! Some people return from unspoiled Eunice Lake (4 mi round-trip, 500 ft vertical gain) with Tolmie Peak Lookout (closed but surrounding decks open) providing one of the very best views of Mount Rainier from any of the National Park's remaining lookouts. Wildlife sightings may include deer, elk, and black bear. Entrance Stations are within the National Park (yourpassnow.com), and there are restrooms at Mowich Lake TH (outdoor privy near lookout).

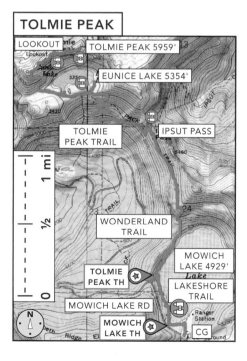

TRAILHEAD: Tolmie Peak TH or Mowich Lake TH. See Spray Park on

From Tolmie Peak Trail, Eunice Lake and Mount Rainier never disappoint!

page 16 for directions to a curve at the signed Tolmie Peak TH (or continue more than 0.25 mi to Mowich Lake TH). Park on the left side of the road and don't forget to display your pass (65 mi, less than 3 hours from Seattle; 180 mi, 3½ hours from Portland).

ROUTE: From Mowich Lake TH, take the signed Lakeshore Trail a few feet toward the colorful calm lake and turn left (N) on Wonderland Trail (shares Lakeshore Trail 0.75 mi), navigating trees, roots, and rocks (with side paths, see Mount Rainier) less than 0.5 mi to the spur coming from Tolmie Peak TH.

From Tolmie Peak TH, walk NE down the spur trail (tree roots) 100 ft, turning left (NNE) onto Wonderland Trail. Walk more than 0.25 mi easily along the tree-surrounded brilliant lake (no more lakeside viewpoints), then leave the water, climbing N (thick forest, steep steps) with a switchback before crossing over a tiny saddle descending a few steps. Continue N up easily (mid-sized trees) to a signed fork near Ipsut Pass (1 mi from Tolmie Peak TH). Wonderland Trail moves straight to Ipsut Pass (NNE, easily 100 ft farther, worth checking out) before descending. Head left (NW) down Tolmie Peak Trail with 2 moderate switchbacks into steeper gravel and past more impressive rock walls. Hike up a few feet and then climb (steps, 1.5 mi from Tolmie Peak TH) very steeply up 5 switchbacks N to the Eunice Lake basin.

You'll see the sheer rocky S face of Tolmie Peak and the lookout on the subsummit before arriving to a signed juncture at Eunice Lake. One of a few spurs heads right (NE, almost 2 mi from Tolmie Peak TH) 100 yards to a sandy beach area showcasing the crystal-clear blue-green water, where you may be tempted to take a chilly dip on a warm day! Move W down the narrower Tolmie Peak Trail through flatter meadows while passing the lake (heliotrope, paintbrush, lupine), then climb WNW into taller trees up steep steps to a switchback (0.25 mi from lake signage). Hike NE, steeply ascending the next rocky switchback, then move into the woods, going W sharply up steps to switchback 3, where you continue NE (more steps) to the high ridge at a tiny saddle juncture in a clearing. Take the main trail right (NE, rocky, semi-steep, fewer trees) along the high ridge to the intact lookout. Nearby to the NW are Mount Howard, Arthur Peak, and Green Lake, with the Carbon River gorge to the N, and Castle Peak, Mother Mountain, and others to the SE. You'll see waterfalls streaming down from Mount Rainier's many glaciers!

For Tolmie Peak, walk 30 ft E of the lookout (privy left down steeply into dense trees), continuing ENE along the narrowing ridgeline (bushwhack path). Move right (S) of the crest a bit (brush), then follow the thinly tree-covered rocky ridge (steep, loose for the final 40 ft) to the top. From the best perch of the day, look N to the Stuart Range, Mount Baker, and Glacier Peak, and then S to Mount St. Helens!

6	WINDY GAP TO NATURAL BRIDGE

ELEVATION: 5820 ft near Windy Gap, 5400 ft at Natural Bridge; vertical gain of 4500 ft total

DISTANCE: 7.5 mi to Natural Bridge from Ipsut Creek Campground TH, 15 mi round-trip; plus 5 mi (each way) required mountain biking or walking from Carbon River Entrance to Ipsut Creek Campground TH, 25 mi round-trip total

DURATION: Around 4 hours hiking to Natural Bridge from Ipsut Creek Campground, 7–9 hours round-trip (plus ½–2 hours each way to Ipsut Creek Campground from Carbon River Entrance)

DIFFICULTY: Very challenging (fairly easy walk or mountain bike ride, then steadily steep, switchbacks, exceptionally long from official TH, ups/downs, GPS device recommended)

TRIP REPORT: The least visited trails (except by locals) within Mount Rainier National Park are found tucked away on the Carbon River just NW of the giant volcano. The valley floor receives surprisingly little snow in winter, making it a delightful year-round option for enthusiasts! Many people use Ipsut Creek Campground TH as their base if not

From scarely photographed Natural Bridge to Lakes Ethel and James!

attempting Natural Bridge as a day bike-n-hike or to hike to other destinations. Wildlife sightings may include deer, elk, mountain goats, and black bear. Wilderness Permit required for camping and obtained online or at Carbon River Ranger Station. National Park fee required (yourpassnow.com), and outhouses are located at both THs.

TRAILHEAD: Carbon River Entrance. See Spray Park on page 16 for directions to the Fairfax Bridge (Carbon River) near Carbonado. Follow WA-165 S for 0.5 mi farther, fork left onto Carbon River Rd 5 mi to Carbon River Ranger Station, then go 2.5 mi more along the river corridor to the end at a small parking area in the trees (all paved but bumpy during last miles; 70 mi, 2 hours from Seattle; 175 mi, 3½ hours from Portland).

ROUTE: Begin by going E, past the gate on the old road converted into the gradual Carbon River Trail (fun with eMTB, check local laws) up the river canyon (rocky, sandy) painlessly through the woods exactly 5 mi (finishing SE) to Ipsut Creek Campground. Stash or lock your bike at the convenient bike parking across from the outhouses.

Hike Wonderland Trail (closer to Ipsut Creek) S, briefly passing a juncture (Wonderland Trail spur moves right up creek past nearby Ipsut Falls, 87 ft high). Walk left (SE) instead, up the Carbon River 2 mi (easy, dense forest, log bridges) to the Northern Loop Trail crossroads, passing another juncture in a clearing at the river crossing (closed Wonderland Trail spur). The sign there correctly states Windy Gap is 4.6 mi away as you stay left (ENE) carefully across the first of two solid log bridges over the Carbon River and Spukwush Creek. A collapsed bridge between the river and creek over the rocky bed is easily bypassed (best chance all day to see Mount Rainier). Then walk left (NW) from the crossroads (opposite Wonderland Trail) in the woods on Northern Loop Trail (40 mi long total) as you amble down a bit before climbing 27 switchbacks E through the alluring forest canopy (large Douglas fir, pitch varies). The route mellows (views) from the top of the turns traversing ESE under the perpendicular Yellowstone Cliffs.

Fork left from Yellowstone Cliffs Camp (5.25 mi from Ipsut Creek Campground) up the slightly overgrown main path (across super-steep wildflower-covered slopes) with cliffs and Tyee Peak to your left, and Crescent Mountain to the right. After 1 mi and 14 more tight switchbacks (ENE, then SE) you'll reach a juncture for Tyee Peak left (N), but continue straight (E) on Northern Loop Trail briefly to Windy Gap. You'll pass nice-looking small lakes with great angles of jagged Crescent and Sluiskin Mountains towering above the superb landscape approaching the next intersection on the E side of the gap!

Traverse 0.5 mi left (NNE) on Natural Bridge Trail across rock fields to another signed juncture (faded rough path left not recommended). Head right (NNE) as you notice the burn area SE to NE from Redstone Peak to nearby Lake James and Lake Ethel while descending 10 tight switchbacks quite steeply to the tiny viewing area above Natural Bridge. Be mindful of the rough terrain in the trees. Walking on Natural Bridge itself is forbidden and getting that perfect picture through the arch to the lakes is unfeasible because of the sheer rock surrounding the area. This rare adventure is still completely worth the effort from Windy Gap in one of Mount Rainier's most remote expanses! Climb 420 ft back to the top of the gap before the long trek to the TH.

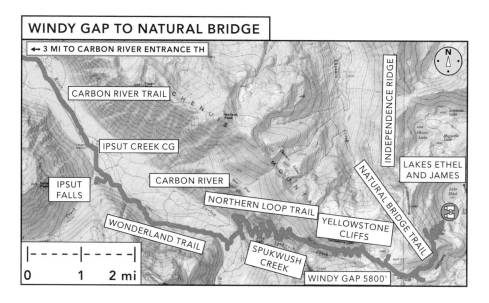

WINDY GAP TO NATURAL BRIDGE

← 3 MI TO CARBON RIVER ENTRANCE TH

CARBON RIVER TRAIL

IPSUT CREEK CG

CARBON RIVER

IPSUT FALLS

NORTHERN LOOP TRAIL

WONDERLAND TRAIL

SPUKWUSH CREEK

INDEPENDENCE RIDGE

NATURAL BRIDGE TRAIL

LAKES ETHEL AND JAMES

YELLOWSTONE CLIFFS

WINDY GAP 5800'

0   1   2 mi

N

ELEVATION: 6856 ft; vertical gain of 2900 ft

DISTANCE: Almost 5 mi up, 10 mi round-trip no loop, 11 mi round-trip loop

DURATION: 2½–3 hours up, 4–6 hours round-trip

DIFFICULTY: Strenuous (steadily steep with breaks; steeper/rockier loop option on Bullion Basin Trail, easier clockwise, GPS device helpful)

TRIP REPORT: Norse Peak, opposite Crystal Mountain Resort, is the highest point in Norse Peak Wilderness. The former lookout site NE of Mount Rainier has far-reaching views in every direction, provides plenty of solitude, and lies within a much dryer climate than areas W of the bulbous volcano. Most people ascend and descend the N route, but feel free to tack on a clockwise loop for more of a workout and continuously wonderful views! Wildlife sightings may include hawks, deer, elk, and mountain goats. No fee or restroom.

TRAILHEAD: Halfcamp TH. From Seattle, take I-5 S to exit 154A (left, Renton), for I-405 N to exit 4, and merge onto WA-169 S (Enumclaw) for 27 mi. Turn left on WA-410 E (Chinook Pass Hwy in Enumclaw, some parts closed in winter) for 32 mi, turn left on Crystal Mountain Blvd for 4 mi, and find Gold Hill Rd on the left (dirt, big yellow gate, no signage). Use the pullouts on either side of Crystal Mountain Blvd without blocking the gate, which could be open or closed.

From Portland, take I-5 N to exit 68 (Morton/Yakima), turn right on US-12 E

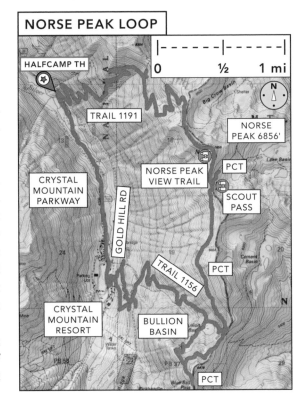

for 69 mi, then turn left on WA-123 N for 16 mi and enter Mount Rainier National Park at 2.5 mi (rougher, narrower; check ahead for road conditions, closed mid-November until Memorial Day). Turn left at Cayuse Pass on WA-410 W for 8 mi, turn right on Crystal Mountain Blvd for 4 mi, and park as noted on previous page (80 mi, 2 hours from Seattle; 180 mi, more than 3 hours from Portland).

ROUTE: For the primary direct route (clockwise loop), walk past the gate SE up Gold Hill Rd less than 0.25 mi with Norse Peak Trail 1191 (empty signboard) on a switchback left; take it NNW (passing Horse Camp Trail at left) less than 0.50 mi. Climb 11 switchbacks ENE steadily (wide, views after 2 mi from TH), then traverse 0.75 mi E and S (easier) in and out of thinning trees and passing an unsigned juncture (Goat Lake Trail) straight/right (S) up 3 switchbacks (stay off trails that are closed for restoration), past skunk cabbage, trillium, and other wildflowers. Ascend 6 more switchbacks NE (larger meadows, rutted route) before walking S, just below the high ridge (more than 4 mi up, sparse trees) up to a ridge juncture leaving Trail 1191; you'll see the sizable Big Crow Basin N of Norse Peak.

Keep right (S) on Norse Peak View Trail crossing the saddle to the W side, then traverse the narrow track (wide, open slopes). The top of Mount Hood can be spotted to the right (S) of Goat Rocks and Mount Adams, then once you're on the main ridge, the Stuart Range is seen NNE with the Olympics NW! Cross to the left (E) side again from the summit block, finishing easy turns SSE to the wide rock- and wildflower-covered old lookout site. There is a short rocky wall on top to break the wind; otherwise the breeze is welcome to keep the flies at bay and cool you down. There are several beautiful basins to the E with rolling green slopes (smattering of evergreens), and Crystal Mountain lies SW, overpowered by Mount Rainier. The immense Emmons Glacier (just right of Little Tahoma, left of Steamboat Prow) is the largest of the volcano's 26 glaciers holding the largest surface area (4.3 square mi) of any glacier in the contiguous United States!

Return by the same route or continue S for the loop down Norse Peak View Trail (few tight trees) past an opening left with illuminating views of Basin Lake in Lake Basin. The narrow path (open terrain, steeper, rockier) eases S to a wide saddle known as Scout Pass (with horse post), where PCT 2000 intersects the summit route (5.25 mi from TH on clockwise loop). Turn right onto the PCT, traversing S below the high ridge almost 1.5 mi to a juncture (crosses steep slopes, more difficult with snow coverage). It's around an hour from the summit to the unsigned juncture where the route moves right (W) from the fork (opposite PCT with a longer option) down the abrupt, loose, and suddenly rocky Bullion Basin Trail 1156 with only 1 switchback taking you 0.25 mi into Bullion Basin (right of old tarn) through a colorful little meadow!

Turn right (NW) from the more official-looking trail area juncture (opposite spur left to PCT near Blue Bell Pass and Crown Point) on Trail 1156 down 1.5 mi (wider, easier, more trees) as you hear Silver Creek cascading before crossing it (solid

From Norse Peak over Snoqualmie Mountain to one gigundous volcano!

bridge). The route becomes steeper after 2 switchbacks (roots, rocks, dust), then after switchback 5 the path will narrow (looser rock) before leveling SSW to the pretty little creek crossing. Walk up a tad from the bridge, then continue steeper very briefly SSW to gravel Gold Hill Rd E. Now you have options: either follow the wide, easy road down right to a five-way intersection, or cross it to the slightly shorter, steep, and rocky Trail 1156, meeting the road again momentarily. There, a sign indicates Bullion Basin Trail, the base area for Crystal Mountain Resort (pointing left, SW down Gold Hill Rd E), and Silver Creek and Henskin Lake Trails. You could turn right (N) on Gold Hill Rd E through dense forest 2.5 mi directly to the TH. Or for more views (0.5 mi briefer), you could finish along Crystal Mountain Blvd. Either way, take Gold Hill Rd E down right (N) toward the northern TH only 0.75 mi. Turn sharply left (SW, briefer route) through thick brush on narrow South Trail easily a few feet to a vague junction on the lowest switchback of a rough jeep trail. Continue right/straight (SSW) momentarily down to a corner of the gravel road that empties onto the visible Crystal Mountain Blvd (small sign: Crystal Mountain Outfitters-Horseback Rides). Turn right (N) less than 2 mi for a pleasant walk through the valley (watching for traffic) to the TH.

ELEVATION: 7766 ft; vertical gain of 4400 ft

DISTANCE: 6.25 mi up directly, 12.5 mi round-trip no loop, 13 mi round-trip summit loop

DURATION: Around 3 hours up, 6–7 hours round-trip

DIFFICULTY: Very challenging (steadily steep, loose scree, route-finding, easy Class 2/3 scrambling, ups/downs, traction helpful with snow before mid-July)

TRIP REPORT: Mount Aix (pronounced Aykes) is the most prominent peak in the rain shadow E of Mount Rainier still within the Cascades. It also lies within the William O. Douglas Wilderness rising above the Mount Baker–Snoqualmie National Forest and provides stupendous views of Mount Rainier, including the oversized Emmons Glacier! Try mid-June through October for this surprisingly difficult trek. Wildlife sightings may include hawks, mountain goats, and black bear. Northwest Forest Pass required, and there is no restroom.

TRAILHEAD: Bumping Rd TH. From Seattle, take I-5 S to exit 154A (left, Renton), for I-405 N to exit 4, merge onto WA-169 S (Enumclaw) for 27 mi, turn left on WA-410 E (Chinook Pass Hwy in Enumclaw, some parts closed in winter) for 63 mi,

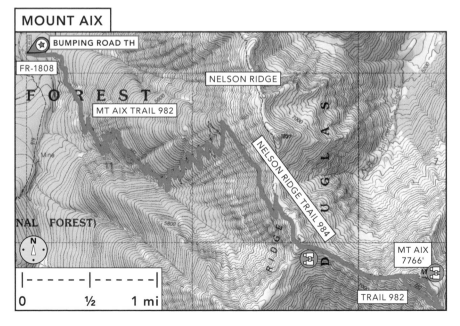

Pacific Lupine and the less-visited scramble to the juggernaut Mount Aix!

turn right on signed Bumping River Rd (FR-1800, no signal) for 10 mi then into gravel for 3 mi more. Turn left on rougher FR-1808 (Deep Creek Rd, potholes, rocky, high-clearance 2WD, AWD preferred) for 1.5 mi, turn left on the narrow driveway, and park to find the signed TH just beyond.

From Portland, take I-5 N to exit 68 (Morton/Yakima), turn right on US-12 E for 69 mi, then turn left on WA-123 N for 16 mi and enter Mount Rainier National Park at 2.5 mi (rougher, narrower; check ahead for road conditions, closed mid-November until Memorial Day). Turn right at Cayuse Pass on WA-410 E for 22 mi, turn right on Bumping River Rd, and follow as above to the tiny parking area (120 mi, 3 hours from Seattle; 200 mi, 3½–4 hours from Portland).

ROUTE: Take signed Mount Aix Trail 982 (free self-issue Wilderness Permit) almost 0.25 mi E as the path steepens 5 mi ESE up more than 35 switchbacks to a major saddle on Nelson Ridge. After the first longer set of tight switchbacks N (old-growth forest, tiny creek feeds), views appear as you traverse steep, grassy slopes SE before another long set of switchbacks NE (at 3 mi up). You finish by going SE, traversing the easier Trail 982 (scree, narrow, loose, eroding in places, drop-offs) and the final 6 switchbacks to a signed juncture on mostly treeless Nelson Ridge (7150 ft).

Hike Trail 982 right (SSE) from the saddle (opposite Nelson Ridge Trail) 0.25 mi moving W of a rocky ridge bump for your first perspective of the formidable Mount Aix; see Bumping Lake to the NW! Walk ESE 0.25 mi down to the next saddle (wildflowers) before hiking upward, leaving the ridgeline (Mount Aix's W ridge) just a few feet right (SE) to the unsigned juncture with Mount Aix Summit Trail (more difficult direct route/clockwise loop). For the somewhat easier option (0.75 mi farther), continue straight (SE, Trail 982) under the summit block briefly (scree) to the next ridge saddle, then hike steeply left (NW) from the faint juncture up the SE ridge, following Mount Aix Summit Trail between gendarmes to the very top (description later includes clues, watch for mountain goats).

For the direct route (less than 0.25 mi) from the first summit juncture, take the fork left (Mount Aix Summit Trail) much steeper E, clambering up the rocky SW slope just S of the high W ridge. Follow the thin path up the loose slope, then scramble carefully between big black rock fins to the peak. After enjoying views of the big volcanoes and Mount Daniel (with the Stuart Range), continue with the clockwise loop by hiking SE from the old lookout site. If snow persists on the N side of the ridge, you may have to descend (S) below the gendarmes, then work very carefully over the steep rocky slope back to the SE ridge. Either way, work your way between the large gendarmes down the ridgeline, finishing to the easier Trail 982 on the saddle. Turn right (NW), traversing cautiously to the end of the summit loop.

9 | SHRINER PEAK LOOKOUT

ELEVATION: 5834 ft; vertical gain of 3425 ft

DISTANCE: 4.25 mi up, 8.5 mi round-trip

DURATION: 2½ hours up, 4–5 hours round-trip

DIFFICULTY: Strenuous (steadily steep, dusty, quiet, not much shade on a hot day)

TRIP REPORT: This locked two-story lookout (built in 1932) in Mount Rainier National Park has open decks providing unmatched views of the great volcano, especially around sunrise through only a handful of trees! Try June through summer for wildflowers, or late September into October for fall colors, huckleberries, and cooler temps, which means fewer bugs! No fee or restroom.

TRAILHEAD: Shriner Peak TH. From Seattle, take I-5 S to exit 154A (left, Renton), for I-405 N to exit 4, merge onto WA-169 S (Enumclaw) for 27 mi, turn left on WA-410 E (Chinook Pass Hwy in Enumclaw, some parts closed in winter) for 40 mi, and stay right/straight on WA-123 S (check ahead for road conditions) for 7.5 mi.

Reach a tiny, paved nondescript pullout on the right (W) 100 ft before the signed TH on the E side of WA-123.

From Portland, take I-5 N to exit 68 (Morton/Yakima), then turn right on US-12 E for 69 mi, turn left on WA-123 N for 8.5 mi and enter Mount Rainier National Park at 2.5 mi (rougher, narrower; check ahead for road conditions, closed mid-November until Memorial Day). The small TH is right (E, colorful kiosk opposite a hiker symbol) at a tiny pullout with paved parking 100 ft farther left (90 mi, 2 hours from Seattle; 150 mi, 3 hours from Portland).

SHRINER PEAK LOOKOUT

WA-123

SHRINER PEAK LOOKOUT 5834'

SHRINER PEAK TH

P A R K

SHRINER PEAK TRAIL

N

½ mi   ¼   0

ROUTE: Begin up Shriner Peak Trail (huge trees on 2 quick mossy switchbacks) as you traverse the steeper slope steadily SE then NE (fir, hemlock, cedar), moving around a shoulder (easier, around 1.5 mi up), then ascend 8 switchbacks N (ferns, flora encroaching at times, smooth track). You'll see Mount Rainier from switchback 6 (2.5 mi up) as you turn up the nose of the more open and wider SW shoulder for the final steeper switchbacks (first set). Enjoy wildflowers through the meadow (few shorter trees) with the best view yet toward the E slopes of the heavily glaciated Mount Rainier beyond nearby Double Peak and the Cowlitz Chimneys!

Clouds burning off Mount Rainier from the top of the switchbacks on Shriner Peak Trail.

Continue past a few boulders (see up forested ridge to Shriner Peak) then traverse left (NNE) up into the woods (easier) almost 0.5 mi (below, W of ridgeline). Climb 6 rutted switchbacks (steeper, narrower) N to the apex as you finally see the lookout for the last 100 ft. From the old lookout's thin decks or the nearby plateau, you'll have an excellent panorama including Double Peak again NW between the Chinook Creek and Ohanapecosh River valleys! Explore the summit meadow, including the spur 100 yards SSE to nearby camps (and privy) near another viewpoint!

10 CRYSTAL PEAK

ELEVATION: 6596 ft; vertical gain of 3100 ft

DISTANCE: Less than 4 mi up, 7.75 mi round-trip

DURATION: 2–2½ hours up, 3–4 hours round-trip

DIFFICULTY: Strenuous (steadily steep, switchbacks, well traveled, drop-offs near top, busy on summer weekends)

TRIP REPORT: See six big Cascade volcanoes on a clear day from the old lookout site, not to be confused with nearby Crystal Mountain Resort. Best July into August for the full complement of wildflowers! Wildlife sightings may include deer, elk, and mountain goats, which roam the upper slopes into late fall before the snow arrives. No fee or restroom.

TRAILHEAD: Crystal Peak TH. From Seattle, take I-5 S to exit 154A (left, Renton) for I-405 N to exit 4, merge onto WA-169 S (Enumclaw) for 27 mi. Turn left on WA-410 E (Chinook Pass Hwy in Enumclaw, some parts closed in winter) for 36 mi and reach ample pull-in parking at right and the nondescript TH at left (E, small hiker symbol).

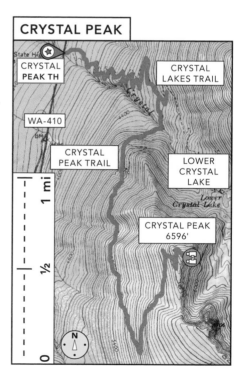

CRYSTAL PEAK

CRYSTAL PEAK TH

CRYSTAL LAKES TRAIL

WA-410

CRYSTAL PEAK TRAIL

LOWER CRYSTAL LAKE

Lower Crystal Lake

CRYSTAL PEAK 6596'

From Portland, take I-5 N to exit 68 (Morton/Yakima), turn right on US-12 E for 69 mi, then turn left on WA-123 N for 16 mi and enter Mount Rainier National Park at 2.5 mi (rougher, narrower; check ahead for road conditions, closed mid-November until Memorial Day). Turn left at Cayuse Pass on WA-410 W for 4 mi and look for pull-in parking at left (80 mi, 1½ hours from Seattle; 170 mi, 3 hours from Portland).

ROUTE: Take signed Crystal Lakes Trail into the forest N, crossing Crystal Creek, then continue steeply 1 mi E (great shade, thick hemlock, fir) up 15 true switchbacks (plus S-turns). The route eases less than 0.5 mi SE as you make your way to a signed junction where you turn right (S) on Crystal Peak Trail (opposite Crystal Lakes, 2.25 mi more to summit). After crossing Crystal Creek again, look toward the colossal volcano (above White River valley, Goat Island Mountain in front, Little Tahoma Peak just left) as the landscape changes (brush, snags, flora, fewer trees, steeply sloped meadows). Vibrant lupine, paintbrush, tiger lilies, phlox, and others dazzle in summer, and there are huckleberries in September.

After you reach a switchback 1.5 mi above the Crystal Lakes junction, traverse left (NE) a bit steeper with 2 more switchbacks up to the cliffy edge of the NW ridge (scant lookout site remains). Turn right (ESE) much more steeply, moving cautiously, briefly to the mostly treeless, flatter summit area. You'll see blue-green Upper Crystal Lake down in the beautiful subalpine basin to the E under Silver King and Threeway Peak. Rocky Chinook Peak is higher, SE along the connecting ridge with Mount Adams in the background.

Upper Crystal Lake gleams under Silver King and Three Way Peak from Crystal Peak.

11 | OWYHIGH LAKES TO TAMANOS MOUNTAIN

ELEVATION: 5280 ft at Owyhigh Lakes overlooks, 6790 ft on Tamanos Mountain; vertical gains of around 1700 ft, 3300 ft max

DISTANCE: Around 3.75 mi to adjoining overlooks for Owyhigh Lakes, 7.5–8 mi round-trip; almost 5 mi to primary summit, 10 mi round-trip

DURATION: 1½ hours to lakes; 3 hours to summit, 5–7 hours round-trip

DIFFICULTY: Mix of moderate to lakes (pleasant grade, family-friendly, smooth, mosquitoes near water) and very challenging soon after (longer, super-steep, loose rock, drop-offs, route-finding, scrambling, easy Class 2/3 to true summit)

TRIP REPORT: Tamanos Mountain rises unassumingly thousands of feet above the Fryingpan Creek, White River, Shaw Creek, and Wright Creek valleys as the trail to it moves past Owyhigh Lakes (pronounced OH-wye-high) up a very steep hillside to a scenic saddle before the summits for close-up views of the Sarvant and Fryingpan Glaciers, hanging under Little Tahoma Peak and Mount Rainier! The shallow clear lakes (no swimming) are surrounded by wildflower-covered meadows with overlooks to jagged Governors Ridge. Wildlife sightings may include deer, elk, mountain goats, and black bear. Entrance Stations are within the National Park (yourpassnow.com), and there is no restroom.

TRAILHEAD: Owyhigh Lakes TH. From Seattle, take I-5 S to exit 154A (left, Renton) for I-405 N to exit 4,

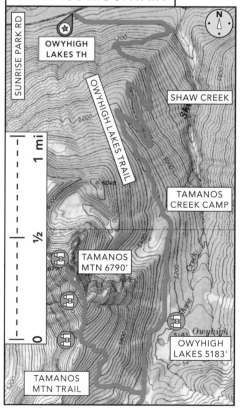

OWYHIGH LAKES TO TAMANOS MOUNTAIN

SUNRISE PARK RD

OWYHIGH LAKES TH

OWYHIGH LAKES TRAIL

SHAW CREEK

1 mi

½

0

TAMANOS CREEK CAMP

TAMANOS MTN 6790'

OWYHIGH LAKES 5183'

TAMANOS MTN TRAIL

merge onto WA-169 S (Enumclaw) for 27 mi. Turn left on WA-410 E (Chinook Pass Hwy in Enumclaw, some parts closed in winter) for 36 mi, and fork right on Sunrise Park Rd/White River Rd for 3.5 mi (1.25 mi to White River Entrance). The signed TH is at left with pull-in parking at right (eight spots) just past Shaw Creek.

From Portland, take I-5 N to exit 68 (Morton/Yakima), turn right on US-12 E for 69 mi, then turn left on WA-123 N for 16 mi and enter Mount Rainier National Park at 2.5 mi (rougher, narrower; check ahead for road conditions, closed mid-November until Memorial Day). Turn left at Cayuse Pass on WA-410 W for 3.5 mi (views), and turn left on Sunrise Park Rd for 3.5 mi as above (85 mi, 2 hours from Seattle; 330 mi, 3 hours from Portland).

ROUTE: Take Owyhigh Lakes Trail 0.5 mi E (easy, huge old-growth trees, down a tad) then up steeper (lush, mossy) before climbing a shoulder S for 6 steady switchbacks 1.75 mi (Douglas fir, hemlock, red and yellow cedar) over rustic footbridges across tiny creeks. Leave the shoulder on a longer traverse S with persistent shade (wildflowers, more roots) as you cross a log bridge over Tamanos Creek (3 mi up) 100 yards farther, passing Tamanos Creek Camp (signed, left). Continue down S along the easier grade another 0.25 mi (thinning forest, views), then leave most of the thick cedar through meadows (lupine, paintbrush, and aster late July into September) to an obvious wider expanse within a wide old avalanche chute covering Owyhigh Lakes Trail. There are two little natural rock bench areas that entail Owyhigh Lakes overlooks (few trees between them), the second one at 3.75 mi from the TH. See across the blue-green waters of the smaller neighboring lakes up scree fields to the protuberant and rocky Governors Ridge with Barrier and Buell Peaks SE. For the lakes side trip, look for bushwhack paths through thick grass down a few yards.

Stay S for Tamanos Mountain or the scenic saddle through meadows blanketed with lupine and paintbrush (great shot to Cowlitz Chimneys ahead) less than 0.25 mi to the next intersection just out of the woods at a broad saddle/meadow (5350 ft, no signs, more than 4 mi from TH). Fork right (W) onto Tamanos Mountain Trail 0.25 mi super-steeply up tight turns (narrow, smaller trees, overgrown) to a higher, steeply sloped larger meadow (skunk cabbage), continuing to labor very steeply N (tons more wildflowers). Finally, bend left a bit (WNW) directly up the super-steep meadow (rutted path fades) to the saddle S of Tamanos Mountain (6260 ft, around 4.75 mi from TH). See Cowlitz Chimneys (above glaciers) to nearby Mount Rainier hovering over Goat Island Mountain (just W across Fryingpan and Wright Creeks). There's a consolation summit mini spur left (S) from the saddle 100 yards easily to a superb viewpoint!

For the summits, hike steeply N more than 0.25 mi up the wide S ridge of Tamanos Mountain on narrow Tamanos Mountain Trail as you ascend the grassy slope, hugging a thin line of small trees on the ridgeline. The landscape becomes rockier to

The overlooks, near pristine Owyhigh Lakes under Governors Ridge, are easily accessed by most!

the treeless rounded top of the primary summit where most people stop. There's plenty of room to spread out for those not continuing! For the peak 100 yards away (no signs, 0.25 mi round-trip bonus), begin roughly past the only true obstacles (two rocky little gendarmes), keeping left (W) of the high ridge with a quick choice. Either take the slick rocky climber's trail down a bit then up steeply (and carefully) to the ridge crest just past the black rocky outcrop, or scramble the more solid rock just W of the crest (Class 3, no trail), hugging the subsummits (brush) more excitingly a few feet to the same point on the high ridge. Continue NW along the ridgeline (drop-offs) or the looser bailout path left (W) only 30 ft or so off-ridge. Then from the crest, walk over larger rock on or slightly left (W) moving right (E) before heading straight over flatter dark boulders to the end of the high ridge at the apex. You'll get a sweet bird's-eye view above the valleys from Goat Island Mountain to Sunrise Visitor Center under Sourdough Mountains as well as Panhandle Gap W above the Sarvant Glaciers!

ELEVATION: 6000 ft at Summerland, 6800 ft at Panhandle Gap; vertical gains of 2200 ft and 2950 ft (plus around 350 ft with Indian Bar overlooks), respectively

DISTANCE: 9 mi round-trip for Summerland; 6 mi to Panhandle Gap, 12 mi round-trip (plus 2.5 mi round-trip with Indian Bar overlooks)

DURATION: 2 hours up; 3 hours to the gap, 5 hours round-trip (plus 2 hours round-trip with Indian Bar overlooks)

DIFFICULTY: Strenuous (very long, steadily steep, popular, lingering snow or ice near gap into August when traction/ice axe required)

TRIP REPORT: Summerland is one of the most picturesque areas along the 93-mi Wonderland Trail encircling Mount Rainier, and the region becomes accessible for only a few months a year! Reaching that basin's steep lush meadows may be enough for many families, while a more dramatic landscape evolves to Panhandle Gap or great overlooks (6600 ft) of both the Indian Bar valley and Ohanapecosh Park! Wildlife may include marmots, mountain goats, and black bear. Entrance Stations are within the National Park (yourpassnow. com), and there is no restroom.

TRAILHEAD: Summerland/ Fryingpan Creek TH. From Seattle, take I-5 S to exit 154A (left, Renton) for I-405 N to exit 4, merge onto WA-169 S (Enumclaw) for 27 mi, turn left on WA-410 E (Chinook Pass Hwy in Enumclaw, some parts closed in winter) for 36 mi, then fork right on Sunrise Park Rd/White River Rd for 4 mi (1.25 mi to White River Entrance).

SUMMERLAND TO PANHANDLE GAP

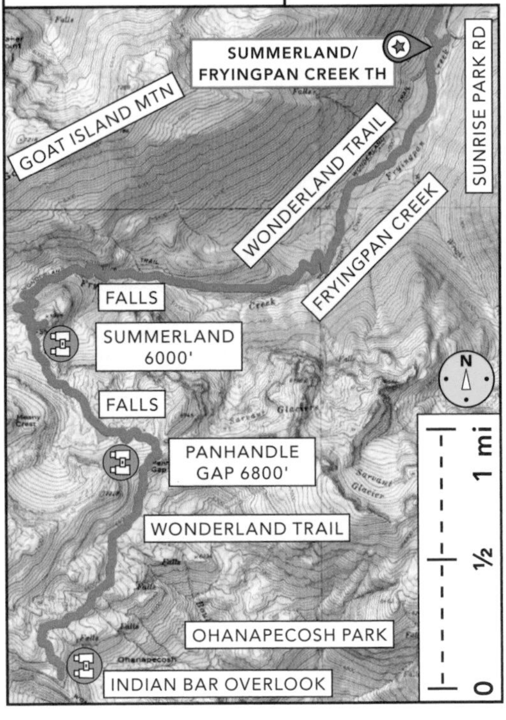

SUMMERLAND/ FRYINGPAN CREEK TH

SUNRISE PARK RD

GOAT ISLAND MTN

WONDERLAND TRAIL

FRYINGPAN CREEK

FALLS

SUMMERLAND 6000'

FALLS

PANHANDLE GAP 6800'

WONDERLAND TRAIL

OHANAPECOSH PARK

INDIAN BAR OVERLOOK

1 mi

½

0

Banshee Peak and Cowlitz Chimneys across Ohanapecosh Park from Indian Bar overlook!

The TH is on the left (W, past Fryingpan Creek) with pull-in parking at right that fills quickly (only park where legal).

From Portland, take I-5 N to exit 68 (Morton/Yakima), then turn right on US-12 E for 69 mi, then turn left on WA-123 N for 16 mi and enter Mount Rainier National Park at 2.5 mi (rougher, narrower; check ahead for road conditions, closed mid-November until Memorial Day). Turn left at Cayuse Pass on WA-410 W for 3.5 mi (views), turn left on Sunrise Park Rd, and follow as on previous page (85 mi, 2 hours from Seattle; 330 mi, 3 hours from Portland).

ROUTE: Take Summerland Trail 100 ft or so heading straight (SW) from the signed juncture onto Wonderland Trail. You traverse quite easily 1.5 mi along the W side of Fryingpan Creek (few decent-sized trees) with the path steepening across smaller mossy creeks (footbridges). Then ascend 4 switchbacks and a turn (SW, near main creek) before easing W straight up the wildflower-lined valley. Walk steeply and narrowly after a switchback, then cross Fryingpan Creek (3 mi up). This bridge and others are removed and replaced each spring as they wouldn't survive the harsh winters, and without them the route would be impassible! A cool waterfall is heard dropping within a tiny slot canyon below the log footbridge. Follow the narrower, boulder-filled Wonderland Trail WSW uphill gradually (high brush, huckleberries) before leaving the creek (almost 4 mi up) for 8 true switchbacks S, winding steeper (woods) less than 0.5 mi to Summerland's colorful and mostly treeless basin, complete with views of the mountain, a hut, an outdoor privy, and several choice campsites for which you must reserve ahead. Wildflowers include paintbrush, lupine, glacier lilies, partridge foot, marigolds, and more. Return or hike to the glacial ponds, the gap, or the overlooks.

Head right (S, Wonderland Trail) leisurely across large, steeply sloped meadows and minor feeds, then begin to ascend the steps on the steep hillside, entering the rock and scree world (cairns) toward another basin after crossing a decent creek (log bridge). Continue with better footing approaching a couple of turquoise ponds (leveling) in the upper basin. Watch waterfalls rip down from melting glaciers as you walk E, past the ponds. The route becomes a bit steeper, crossing a small rocky saddle (faraway views of Stuart Range) SW to nearby Panhandle Gap (great views)!

For Indian Bar overlooks, stay fairly high from the saddle SSW on rocky Wonderland Trail around 1 mi across a fun traverse undulating down to the far shoulder crest (E of Ohanapecosh Glaciers, patches of green, tiny water crossings), as you hike more steeply up momentarily, then down across a slightly larger creek before moving up again easily. Walk down across scree then hike up the cairned creek (melting snow) very steeply and briefly before contouring more easily over the last hills to the shoulder. Follow this wide shoulder S down 100 yards to a couple obvious, flatter viewpoints under 6600 ft (unofficial, Indian Bar overlooks). Observe the vast valley, steep slopes, and creek feeds left (E) within Ohanapecosh Park (mountain goats grazing) and the route 1.5 mi or so down to Indian Bar (Wauhaukaupauken Falls, just out of sight). On the right (W) is the massive cliff band with glaciers and subsequent waterfalls leading up to the ridge of Whitman Crest below Little Tahoma.

13 | FREMONT LOOKOUT

ELEVATION: 7181 ft; vertical gain of 800 ft

DISTANCE: 2.75 mi one way, 5.5 mi round-trip

DURATION: More than 1 hour one way, 2½–3 hours round-trip

DIFFICULTY: Moderate (steady, wide, rocky, popular, well-signed, drop-offs, more difficult with snow, traction required into August)

TRIP REPORT: From the highest parking lot in Mount Rainier National Park at Sunrise Visitor Center (6400 ft) you still have more than 8000 ft between you and the top of the Cascade's highest volcano, although most of the trails from Sunrise are actually family-friendly and suitable for the adventure seeker in all of us! Check ahead

Fremont Lookout is one of four (out of eight original) lookouts within the National Park.

for trail and road conditions as the road to Sunrise is usually open from mid-July through September or October, depending on snow coverage. Wildlife sightings may include marmots, mountain goats, and black bear. Entrance Stations are within the National Park (yourpassnow.com), and restrooms are present.

TRAILHEAD: Sunrise Visitor Center. From Seattle, take I-5 S to exit 154A (left, Renton) for I-405 N to exit 4, merge onto WA-169 S (Enumclaw) for 27 mi, turn left on WA-410 E (Chinook Pass Hwy in Enumclaw, some parts closed in winter) for 36 mi, and fork right on Sunrise Park Rd/White River Rd for 15 mi (1.25 mi to White River Entrance), winding steeply to the end at a large parking lot. There is a captivating view of Mount Adams and countless summits, including a great look down to Sunrise Lake, from the overlook area (Sunrise Point) on the final switchback in the road with parking in the center. It's one of the most scenic switchbacks anywhere!

From Portland, take I-5 N to exit 68 (Morton/Yakima), turn right on US-12 E for 69 mi, then turn left on WA-123 N for 16 mi and enter Mount Rainier National Park at 2.5 mi (rougher, narrower; check ahead for road conditions, closed mid-November until Memorial Day). Turn left at Cayuse Pass on WA-410 W for 3.5 mi (views), then turn left on Sunrise Park Rd for 15 mi and follow as above (95 mi, 2 hours from Seattle; 180 mi, 3½ hours from Portland).

ROUTE: Begin right of Sunrise Visitor Center (W end of lot, NW corner, left of restrooms) 75 ft NW across a maintenance road, then go 200 ft more (rock-lined spur, passing Sunrise Picnic Area) to a helpful kiosk/sign at a juncture. Keep straight (N) very briefly up the wide rocky path (steps) to a signed fork (less than 0.25 mi from TH). Walk left (NW) onto Sourdough Ridge Trail up easily more than 100 yards heading left (W, same trail) from the next juncture along the mostly open ridgeline (see Glacier Peak and Mount Baker) as the dusty route steepens before easing to the next juncture on a little saddle (Huckleberry Creek Trail right). Stay left (W) on Sourdough Ridge Trail, traversing the steeper slope S of the crest down a tad (see subalpine Shadow Lake below and distant waterfalls under Little Tahoma Peak), past a few small pines. Move up (nifty rock work, wildflowers) through a scree field to the fenced-in and protected Frozen Lake (water source for Day Lodge) on a sizable saddle. Arrive to a signed major five-way intersection just SW of the lake (1.5 mi from TH).

For Fremont Lookout, turn sharply right (NNW) onto Fremont Lookout Trail rising steeper above Frozen Lake more than 1.25 mi as you traverse the steep slope upward below and just W of Mount Fremont's three little summits out to the point where the decent lookout (locked) still resides. Hike along small pines and low flora past the middle summit (highest, brief scramble SSE), rounding the corner N (finally see lookout), as you keep to the scree and pumice trail across steep terrain (lingering snow and ice). Mountain goats frequent these slopes down into colorful Berkeley Park. Views from Fremont Lookout stretch from the Stuart Range to North Cascades and the Olympics! Skyscraper Mountain is SW, with Mount Rainier hulking across Berkeley Park and Burroughs Mountain. A few small lakes dot the valleys with wildflowers enveloping the fabulous landscape August to September. Return the same way or see Skyscraper Mountain and Burroughs Mountain hikes on pages 43 and 46 and map on page 44 for loop options from Frozen Lake.

Sunrise Lake from Sunrise Point on the final switchback driving to the TH.

ELEVATION: 7078 ft; vertical gain of 2000 ft (including Shadow Lake loop)

DISTANCE: 4 mi up, 8–9 mi round-trip

DURATION: 2–3 hours up, 4–5 hours round-trip

DIFFICULTY: Strenuous (steady, wide, busy on weekends, ups/downs, steeper summit block, drop-offs near top)

TRIP REPORT: Enjoy smashing views from the parking lot with wildflowers lining Berkeley Park (late July to August), then rise to an even more scenic pass en route to superior vistas for aspiring summiteers! Tack on a brief loop from Frozen Lake past Shadow Lake, finishing along the scenic cliffs far above the White River valley. Wildlife sightings may include marmots, mountain goats, and black bear. Entrance Stations are within the National Park (yourpassnow.com), and restrooms are present.

TRAILHEAD: Sunrise Visitor Center. See Fremont Lookout on page 40 for directions (95 mi, more than 2 hours from Seattle; 180 mi, 3½ hours from Portland).

ROUTE: See Fremont Lookout on page 40 for the description 1.25 mi to a signed major five-way intersection SW of Frozen Lake. Savor the views from the saddle, including Skyscraper Mountain, and continue straight (W) down Wonderland Trail gradually, then steeper (dustier) around a sweeping turn (smaller pines) to a large open meadow in Berkeley Park. Reach a signed juncture (2.25 mi from TH),

The full scope of Burroughs Mountain under Little Tahoma and Tahoma is incomparable!

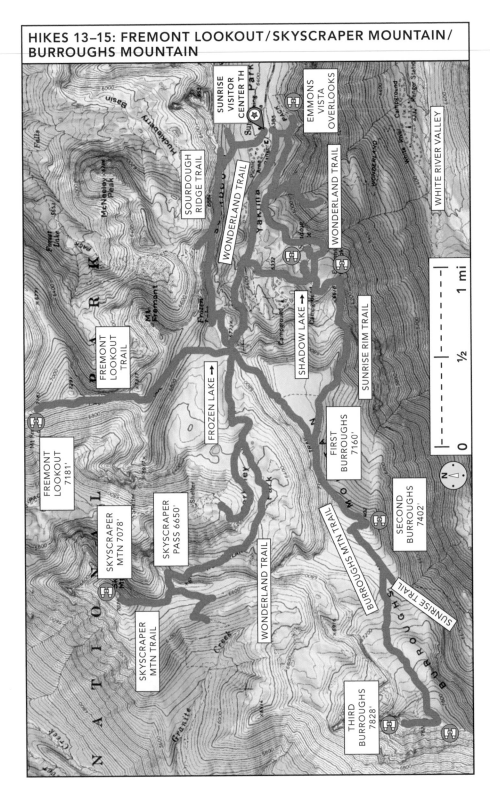

continuing left (SW, opposite Northern Loop Trail) on Wonderland Trail almost 0.75 mi over a small hill and down traversing W (under Burroughs Mountain) to a decent creek. Cross the fetching wildflower-lined creek then ascend the meadow NW (brighter paintbrush, others, see Mount Fremont Lookout), passing smaller trees from the rockier trail to Skyscraper Pass (6650 ft, almost 3.5 mi from TH) with outstanding views above the park to all three summits of Burroughs Mountain, Little Tahoma Peak, and the big mountain behind!

Traverse W 100 yards (narrower) across lingering snowfields (late July into August) or scree up to an unsigned juncture above a saddle and S ridge of Skyscraper Mountain. Turn right (N) off Wonderland Trail onto fainter Skyscraper Mountain Trail (unsigned, almost 0.5 mi more) down a bit over the wide saddle before working steeply just left (W) of the ridgeline (rocky, bushes, tiny trees), with the trail becoming even steeper (tight turns, switchbacks) to the small top. See Burroughs Mountain and Steamboat Prow up the Winthrop and Emmons Glaciers to Mount Rainier; then pan W across the West Fork White River valley to several waterfalls and to Vernal Park, then N to nearby Grand Park up to the Stuart Range and Glacier Peak!

For the lollipop loop from the Frozen Lake intersection (less than 2.5 mi more), follow signage straight down Wonderland Trail 0.5 mi ESE to the next juncture descending easily then steeply (looser rock, dirt, lingering snow until late July) next to a tiny creek within a rockier gully under First Burroughs Mountain. The terrain evolves (mostly grasses, wildflowers), easing to the juncture (sign/kiosk) where moving left (E) heads 1 mi up Sunrise Park Rd (closed to vehicles, boring) to the TH. Turn right (S) instead along the slightly narrower Wonderland Trail, which takes you easily less than 0.5 mi, passing the Sunrise Camp junction (outhouse left) a few feet to the next juncture. Keep left (E) on Wonderland Trail (opposite Burroughs Mountain Trail) 100 yards, passing the first lake spur to another in 100 yards (across a small wooden bridge at Shadow Lake's outlet). Take this spur 35–100 ft left along the right (E) side of the water for the best reflections into the pretty blue-green pool (no swimming).

Continue E then N on Wonderland Trail (taller trees, then views through a meadow) as you undulate NE with ease, crossing a babbling brook before reaching a signed juncture (0.75 mi from Shadow Lake). Hike left (SE, opposite Wonderland Trail down steeply to White River Campground) onto Sunrise Rim Trail, traversing effortlessly upwards 0.25 mi or so for a surprise view far down to a bright green lake under the glacier-engulfed volcano! Almost 0.25 mi farther is a juncture nearest the TH with Emmons Vista Overlooks existing right down a few stone steps from a spur to a partially obscured viewpoint and info kiosk, with the last overlook (much improved) down the spur a few feet farther. Keep left (N) on wider Sunrise Rim Trail from the overlook's juncture instead 100 yards up to the parking lot.

15   BURROUGHS MOUNTAIN

ELEVATION: 7828 ft on Third Burroughs; vertical gain of 2200 ft total

DISTANCE: 4.25 mi directly, 8.5–9.5 mi round-trip (with Shadow Lake loop)

DURATION: 2–2½ hours up directly, 4–5 hours round-trip

DIFFICULTY: Mix of moderate for First or Second Burroughs or the lower loops (not steep, wide, rocky, busy, more difficult with snow and ice when traction required late July into August) and strenuous for Third Burroughs (steeper, narrow, no shade, scree, drop-offs, ups/downs)

TRIP REPORT: Most stop at First or Second Burroughs Mountain, but the more amazing experience lies ahead from the upper slopes of Third Burroughs Mountain, so close to Mount Rainier that its adjoining ridge connects to Steamboat Prow and Camp Schurman, the second most popular climber's camp! See Fremont Lookout on page 40 and Skyscraper Mountain on page 43 for more info. Entrance Stations are within the National Park (yourpassnow.com), and restrooms are present.

TRAILHEAD: Sunrise Visitor Center. See Fremont Lookout on page 40 for directions (95 mi, 2 hours from Seattle; 180 mi, 3½ hours from Portland).

ROUTE: See Fremont Lookout on page 40 for the description 1.5 mi to a signed major five-way intersection SW of Frozen Lake. Hike Burroughs Mountain Trail from the saddle WSW more than 1.25 mi to Second Burroughs, passing the flatter First Burroughs halfway. The first bit is steeper, covering an even steeper slope (lingering snow or ice, use traction or hike elsewhere locally). Pass a signed juncture on First Burroughs (return loop option left, E on Sunrise Rim Trail past Shadow Lake), descending slightly before hiking up the treeless rocky ridge steadily SW to Second Burroughs Mountain (near a stone bench, 7402 ft, 2.75 mi from TH) on another plateau with outstanding vistas of the behemoth volcano and Fremont Lookout the other way (N).

For Third Burroughs, continue with a solid switchback taking you SW steeply down toward a saddle (400 ft to regain) between summits. Fork right before the lowest point (Sunrise Trail dives steeply left) onto narrower Burroughs Mountain Trail (unsigned, 1 mi farther), slogging WSW up rocks and pumice (much steeper) before cruising more easily through the center of the broad, striking landscape. Ascend what remains of a wide, lingering snowfield (tracked out, easy) or scree field trail quite steeply and briefly directly to the nearby narrow S ridge of Third Burroughs Mountain, then head right (N) up steeply (larger boulders, rocks), passing the first (more popular) of two high points. Continue 100 ft to the N twin summit for the full flavor of the Winthrop, Inter, and Emmons Glaciers! Look to the continuation of the high ridge S past St. Elmo Pass to Steamboat Prow then down to Mount Ruth (climber's camps between). To the N are Skyscraper Mountain, the West Fork White River valley, Vernal Park, Sluiskin Mountain, and Grand Park. Be respectful as sound travels over the rocks, echoing loudly.

From First Burroughs Mountain, turn right (ESE, 2.5 mi to TH) for the loop on Sunrise Rim Trail, traversing down painlessly past larger rocks (see a glacial lake far below). Cross a steep scree field E along the cliff band, far above the White River valley to one of three Emmons Vista Overlooks on a switchback (rock-walled circle). Walk less than 0.25 mi N down the easier wide dirt trail to the next clear juncture W of and above Shadow Lake. Continue straight (E) from the sign onto Wonderland Trail, and walk down briefly to the lake's outlet spur, taking it left a moment (see the end of Skyscraper Mountain hike on page 45 for the remainder, 1.5 mi farther to TH).

Glacial flour from melting ice flowing down record setting Emmons Glacier paints the lake in the White River valley!

ELEVATION: 5935 ft at Mildred Point, 6520 ft on Van Trump Park Summit; vertical gains of 2500 ft and 2900 ft, respectively; nearly 3500 ft for both small high points

DISTANCE: 4 mi to either high point, 8.25 mi round-trip; 10.25 mi round-trip for both

DURATION: More than 2 hours to either high point, 5½–7 hours round-trip for both

DIFFICULTY: Strenuous (long for both high points, mosquitoes until September, difficult creek crossings until late July, Van Trump Park steeper)

TRIP REPORT: Breathtaking views and waterfalls, expansive wildflower-covered meadows, babbling brooks, adjoining high points, and ample exercise all help make these prodigious day hikes more than enjoyable from the SSW slopes of Mount Rainier! Wildlife sightings may include hawks, eagles, marmots, mountain goats, and black bear. Entrance Stations are within the National Park (yourpassnow.com), and there is no restroom.

TRAILHEAD: Comet Falls TH. From Seattle, take I-5 S and other routes into WA-706 E for 80 mi to Ashford. Continue on WA-706 from the Rainier Basecamp Visitor Information (clean restrooms behind) for almost 6 mi to the Nisqually Entrance. Continue up Paradise Rd E, winding 10 mi to the TH and the parking at left with fewer than 20 spots, which fill quickly on weekends.

MILDRED POINT TO VAN TRUMP PARK SUMMIT

From Portland, take I-5 N to exit 68 (Morton/Yakima), turn right on US-12 E for 30 mi, then turn left on WA-7 N in Morton (speed trap) for 16 mi to Elbe. Turn right on WA-706 E for 7 mi to Ashford, and follow as on the previous page (100 mi, 2½ hours from Seattle; 150 mi, 2½–3 hours from Portland).

ROUTE: Take signed Van Trump Park Trail less than 0.5 mi NE steeply (woods), then cross Van Trump Creek (solid bridge), continuing 1 mi (steadily steep) N along the E side of the creek (cascades) including up 11 switchbacks NW (see a fraction of Van Trump Falls, five-tiered, 190 ft, down left). Climb 4 more turns N 0.5 mi easier rounding the corner to Bloucher Falls (three-tiered, 124 ft) tumbling down Van Trump Creek East Fork at your right. Cross the creek to a switchback (first of 18, plus steep stairs) and spur in the woods; you should go left for a full look at Comet Falls (four-tiered, 462 ft, loses steam into autumn) up the creek lined with green grass then evergreens to the top of the tall narrow rock amphitheater! Resume the steeper switchbacks N 1 mi to the intersection for either Van Trump Park or Mildred Point.

Keep left (WSW) on Van Trump Park Trail from the signed intersection/fork near Van Trump Park (less than 3 mi up) 0.5 mi to the juncture for Mildred Point by descending 7 switchbacks (avalanche lilies, lupine), moving across Van Trump Creek (log bridge), then heading up 2 switchbacks to the signage. See Upper Comet Falls (35 ft high, usually twin falls) from the rocky creek bed, and if the log bridge is covered by rushing water (early July) you should take the user trail right of the creek (E side)

Bloucher Falls is a delightful bonus as you cross the footbridge over Van Trump Creek East Fork!

instead heading N adjacent the water up meadows briefly to good-enough views and call it a day as others have. Turn right (N) from the juncture 0.5 mi up Mildred Point Trail through meadows (wildflowers, few trees), encroaching the deeply rutted narrow route to a sign at the end of the maintained trail. Continue a couple hundred yards (carefully) as the rocky bushwhack path traverses NNW (left, below tiny high point) the last few feet down the narrow shoulder to a boulder-covered bluff above Kautz Creek canyon with 360-degree views (trail continues). See several dignified waterfalls up to the many glaciers under Point Success!

From the intersection above the creek, turn left (NNE) on Van Trump Park Trail (signed End of Maintained Trail 0.3 mi) briefly through the lower meadows littered with lupine, paintbrush, western pasqueflower, and bistort, continuing 1 mi or so to the high point. Hike without difficulty (NE, steps, unmaintained) over a rockier area, ascending the steepest pitch of the day (snowy into August) up the wide grassy shoulder. There's a wider spot on the trail (embedded boulders) to catch unsurpassed vistas of Mount Rainier past a nice double waterfall. Work your way more easily to the little summit 100 ft higher.

17 | EAGLE PEAK TO CHUTLA PEAK

ELEVATION: 5958 ft on Eagle Peak, 6000 ft on Chutla Peak; vertical gain of 3500-plus ft for both summits

DISTANCE: 3.75 mi to Eagle Peak directly, around 8 mi round-trip for both summits

DURATION: 2 hours to Eagle Peak first, 4–5 hours round-trip for both summits

DIFFICULTY: Mix of very challenging for Eagle Peak Saddle (super-steep switchbacks, more difficult when wet or snowy when traction required) and expert only for summits (scrambling, drop-offs, exposure, fairly solid rock, Class 4/5)

TRIP REPORT: The summit spires (intimidating from all angles) farthest W in the Tatoosh Range are best attempted as a pair from tiny Eagle Peak Saddle, where people not summiting stop for the tortured exercise and stellar views (5750 ft; 3000 ft vertical gain). The summits are only to be attempted by seasoned hikers and July into October is the best time to go. Some even snowshoe most of the route to the saddle in winter until the trees give way to either a fun zone for winter sports or an avalanche

The snowy N face of Wahpenayo Peak in July to Mount Adams from Chutla Peak.

zone, depending on conditions under the summits. Entrance Stations are within the National Park (yourpassnow.com), and there is no restroom, though there are some nearby within Longmire National Historic Landmark District.

TRAILHEAD: Eagle Peak TH. See Mildred Point to Van Trump Park Summit on page 48 for directions to the Nisqually Entrance. Continue up Paradise Rd E, winding 6 mi to Longmire Museum and National Park Inn. Turn right on Longmire Rd (second entrance) for 0.25 mi slowly (past Dead End sign, employee housing), winding up over the sweet wooden suspension bridge (Nisqually River). Find the signed TH at left in 50 ft (couple spots on each side) and more parking 150 ft farther at Longmire Campground Community Center (95 mi, 2 hours from Seattle; 150 mi, 2½ hours from Portland).

ROUTE: You can see Mount Rainier from the TH near the river. Begin rising steadily steeply more than 2 mi E up Eagle Peak Trail (large old-growth Douglas fir, cedar) for 21 or so switchbacks (plus turns) before crossing a mossy creek (footbridge). Then hike less than 1 mi with 3 moderate switchbacks NE to a faint rocky intersection on another switchback in a clearing (old cairn, 5000 ft, Wahpenayo Peak route straight). Keep left from the switchback on Eagle Peak Trail a long 0.5 mi NE to Eagle Peak Saddle by clawing up the crazy steep slope (into forest, rockier) and ascending steep meadows (paintbrush, bear grass, lupine, aster, lilies) up 14 tight switchbacks total (few steps) to the saddle, where you see Chutla Peak and four Cascade volcanoes!

For Eagle Peak, less than 0.25 mi away, turn left (N) up the climber's trail on the ridgeline (roots, brush) moving just right (E) of the rock obstacle a few feet to the main

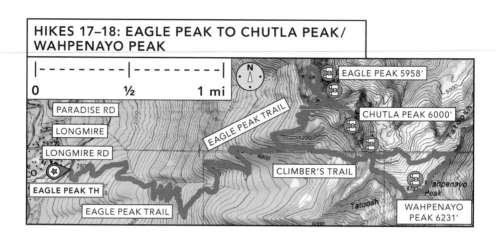

HIKES 17–18: EAGLE PEAK TO CHUTLA PEAK/WAHPENAYO PEAK

summit crux with two options. For the difficult direct route, free climb 35 ft straight up the rock face on the highest ridge with a few great choices (solid holds, Class 5, keeping three points of contact with Mother Earth). Then scramble left (N) up the ridgeline (a bit easier), passing a little fake summit 50 ft to the nearby boulder-covered peak (room for one at a time). See other towers NNW to Eagle Peak–North Peak. Return counterclockwise (loop) on the more traveled route. The primary option from the main crux moves down left (W) of the vertical summit block traversing the path 100 ft N as you hug the rock wall without trouble (see cairn). Then turn right (SE) past some very steep bouldering up the rocks only 10–15 ft before angling right (S) along a narrow ramp 75 ft (W, under highest ridge). Use caution across the exposed cliffy section (drop-offs, good holds) at the final tougher move, rounding the corner (better tread, brushy) to the nearby peak.

From Eagle Peak Saddle, hike past the old End of Maintained Trail sign more than 0.25 mi SE to Chutla Peak (Class 4). Walk E easily through a few trees along the ridge as the path (technically Eagle Peak Trail) narrows, down-climbing some boulders 7–10 ft SE steeply to the gravelly trail and continuing down to a lower saddle (just right, S of a ravine, huge drop-offs for remainder). Then climb very steeply E (thick brush, branches, roots, rocks) up the narrow ridgeline (don't compete with mountain goats, be extra careful on summit block), grinding SSE (solid ground) before finishing somewhat more easily and reaching the summit, which pokes above the last trees. See the entire Nisqually River valley and most of the Tatoosh Range (and Mount Adams). Toward Mount Rainier are the Tahoma, Kautz, Wilson, and Nisqually Glaciers with several far-off waterfalls!

18 | WAHPENAYO PEAK

ELEVATION: 6231 ft; vertical gain of around 3500 ft

DISTANCE: 4–4.25 mi up, 8.25 mi round-trip

DURATION: 2½–3 hours up, 5–6 hours round-trip

DIFFICULTY: Very challenging (steep switchbacks, no signs, route-finding, scrambling, drop-offs, solid rock, Class 3/4, mosquitoes June into July, summit loop option, traction required through July)

TRIP REPORT: This less traveled goal modestly holds some of the best views within the entire saw-toothed Tatoosh Range opposite the gargantuan volcano! It is best late July to September when snow is nearly gone. Wildlife sightings may include hawks, eagles, marmots, pica, deer, mountain goats, and black bear. Entrance Stations are within the National Park (yourpassnow.com), and there is no restroom, though there are some nearby within Longmire National Historic Landmark District.

TRAILHEAD: Eagle Peak TH. See Mildred Point to Van Trump Park Summit on page 48 and Eagle Peak to Chutla Peak on page 50 for directions (95 mi, 2 hours from Seattle; 150 mi, 2½ hours from Portland).

Gendarmes along the preferred NE ridge route of Wahpenayo Peak toward the Pacific Northwest's highest mountain (14,411 ft).

ROUTE: See Eagle Peak to Chutla Peak on page 50 for the description up Eagle Peak Trail 3 mi semi-steeply to a faint rocky intersection on a switchback (5000 ft, old cairn). Continue straight/right (E) from the switchback onto the unmaintained climber's trail traversing through a meadow, trees, thick brush, and tall bear grass 0.5 mi to the Wahpenayo Peak–Chutla Peak saddle (5600 ft). You'll cross rock fields then turn left (E) super-steeply straight up the last couple hundred feet (difficult when wet, snowy, icy), passing a good-sized rock monolith nearest the saddle.

The clockwise summit loop (preferred, 0.75 mi up) is described below. For the direct route (more difficult, 0.5 mi up, partly obscured to begin), hike right (SE) very steeply (faded climber's trail, grass, brush, few pines) just left (E) of the ridge crest a short distance before steeply regaining the WNW ridge of Wahpenayo Peak. Stay on or just left (E, a few feet) of the ridge for the remainder of the way to the peak. There are a few rocky high points en route but keep scrambling (occasional tight brush) then bouldering solid rock (carefully, drop-offs) as the route/ridge steepens, turning NE to the actual summit over flatter-sloped rock (see end for more detail).

For the clockwise loop from the Wahpenayo Peak–Chutla Peak saddle, leave the ridge after walking left a few feet, moving down to the right (E) a hair to the creek bed. Easily follow the faint climber's trail E through the meadow 100 yards or so (teeny tarns, to around 5480 ft), then begin to bushwhack (fading path) much steeper right (S, toward the summit) up a narrower grassy and rocky gully in the center of the picturesque basin (wildflowers), gaining around 250 ft in elevation. Clamber left (E), traversing semi-steeply more than 100 yards (grass, rock, few trees) up through a nearby weakness, making a beeline right (SSE, steeper, briefly) for the summit's NE ridge (juncture, continues down too). Turn right (SW, drop-offs) 0.25 mi farther up the pronounced rocky ridgeline climber's trail to the top (see Plummer, Pinnacle, Unicorn, and Boundary Peaks, and The Castle). The straightforward scramble becomes increasingly steep as you near the summit block (exposed sections) and climb the rock up the crest or close to it. From the flatter rock on the summit (fairly safe), look to distant waterfalls and other surprises!

Finish the clockwise loop (direct route) SW slightly left (S) of the ridgeline down a Class 3/4 pitch judiciously (steep rocky cliffs, okay holds), then find the climber's trail moving narrowly easier over the top of a little fake summit. Descend 2 switchbacks (more brush), continuing NW on or just right (E) of the crest, passing avalanche lilies and others near the super-steep path. The track becomes defined where you leave the ridge right (E, small saddle) for good a few feet, traversing steeply left (NW) to the main saddle.

PINNACLE–CASTLE–PLUMMER PEAKS TRAVERSE

ELEVATION: 6562 ft at Pinnacle Peak, 6460 ft at The Castle, 6370 ft at Plummer Peak; vertical gains of 1700 ft, 1600 ft, and 1500 ft, respectively; almost 2500 ft for all three summits

DISTANCE: 1.75 mi to Pinnacle Peak, more than 2.5 mi to The Castle, 2 mi to Plummer Peak, 6 mi round-trip for all

DURATION: ½ hour to Pinnacle Saddle then 1 hour or more to each peak, 5–6 hours round-trip for all

DIFFICULTY: Mix of moderate for Pinnacle Saddle or Plummer Peak (steady, sometimes steeper, crossing scree fields, snow and ice covered late July into August when traction required), very challenging for Pinnacle Peak (very steep, rocky, slight exposure, fairly solid, drop-offs, Class 3), and expert only for The Castle (highly exposed, rope not mandatory, loose rock and pumice, airy summit block, Class 4/5)

TRIP REPORT: If the Pacific Northwest's highest volcano weren't in the picture, the Tatoosh Range would still be a major attraction and a force to be reckoned with! There's a dozen named peaks in the serrated range that attract mountain goats, hikers, climbers, and well-equipped and experienced skiers in winter, providing all a real alpine adventure without having to trek several miles before the scenery explodes! Visit Pinnacle Saddle alone (5950 feet, 2.5 mi round-trip, 1000 ft vertical gain) or each peak within your skillset. Entrance Stations are within the National Park (yourpassnow.com), and there is no restroom.

PINNACLE–CASTLE–PLUMMER PEAKS TRAVERSE

REFLECTION LAKE TH

STEVENS CANYON RD

×5556

5226×

PINNACLE PEAK TRAIL

5600

½ mi

¼

0

Pinnacle Glacier

PINNACLE PEAK 6562'

THE CASTLE 6460'

Pinnacle Peak

PINNACLE SADDLE

5800

6000

PLUMMER PEAK 6370'

TRAILHEAD: Reflection Lake TH. See Mildred Point to Van Trump Park Summit on page 48 for directions to the Nisqually Entrance. Continue up Paradise Rd E, winding for 15.25 mi to a juncture. Turn right on Stevens Canyon Rd (toward Ohanapecosh Visitor Center and Campground) for 1.25 mi to find the signed TH right and pull-in parking left facing Reflection Lakes (100 mi, 2½ hours from Seattle; 160 mi, 3 hours from Portland).

ROUTE: Begin S across the road up Pinnacle Peak Trail 0.5 mi next to irrigation ditches (wooden steps, wildflowers, steadily easy) with a couple turns becoming rockier (thinning forest, tiny creeks, cascades). Cross scree fields over slightly steeper terrain, continuing up 4 switchbacks S, then work past a small cave (steep spur left) to Pinnacle Saddle (1.25 mi up). Goat Rocks Wilderness can be spotted left (N) in front of Mount Adams and much of the Tatoosh Range can be made out, especially Pinnacle Peak left (NE) and Plummer Peak right (SW).

Hike left from the saddle for the tougher climbs NE to Pinnacle Peak (almost 0.5 mi up) and The Castle (1 mi away). Pass both trails right (from 6050 ft and 6235 ft, last small pines, bushes) toward The Castle, keeping left (NE) for Pinnacle Peak, first up the nearby rough SW ridge (rugged, cairned). Options once you're above the tree line (no clear trail) lead you very steeply NE up the rocky slope just right (E) of the ridge crest where you scramble N even steeper up the left side of the narrowing super-steep gully (check holds, larger rock more stable than smaller rocks and volcanic pumice) to its top near the larger-than-expected summit cap. Finish right (ENE) easier but mindfully along the wider high ridge a few more feet (drop-offs, rocks, brush) up to the larger boulders on the peak. Make noise and wait for goats to pass in order to prevent altercations. See the living postcard in Mount Rainier across Reflection and Louise Lakes and the entirety of the Tatoosh Range panning W from Eagle (double rounded), Chutla, Wahpenayo (larger cone), Lane (standalone pillar), Denman (lesser), and Plummer Peaks, with The Castle just E and Foss, Unicorn, Boundary, and Stevens Peaks (connecting ridge E) to complete the range!

Carefully descend the same route, perhaps even turning around to face the mountain from the steeps in the gully. Go back to the tree line and follow the first rocky spur path S 100 yards toward the visible Castle traverse trail, turning left (ENE) on it. Contour across the steep slope (rocky, grassy, wildflowers) under the sheer S face of the SE ridge belonging to The Castle's slightly lower SW spire. Lingering snow and ice covering the traverse up might force you down around the sheerer S face from a thin alternate spur, which then moves super-steeply up on or just left of possible snowfields N to the saddle between the towers. If no snow or ice, take the primary trail narrowly N a moment along the S face past a tiny landing (small pine brush) as you contour a few feet more around (or climb rocks directly) to the actual ridgeline or just right (E, somewhat exposed) approaching the small saddle between towers under the summit. Work your way NE around the right (E) side to a 30-ft-high or so vertical rock

The Tatoosh Range's Pinnacle Peak and The Castle from friendlier Plummer Peak!

wall comprising several steeples. One of the first options is a low Class 5 move left off the main bushwhack path under and just right of a set rope. The tough route funnels NW into a very brief and tight chimney a few feet to the highest ridge near the peak; make sure to check all holds. The preferred Class 4 climb is farther, near the E end of the wall, and has a few more choices left of another fixed rope (up right). Try slightly left up the wide rocky gully without difficulty, working right (NNE) when possible cautiously toward the rope (Class 5 route), but move left (NNW) straight up a few feet just before the ridgeline. Then scramble slowly 50 ft or so left (SW, easier) from the wafer-thin high ridge crest or just right (N, considerable exposure) along the towers to the highest tiny point (quite airy and thrilling). There's a great view down to Louise Lake and to Pinnacle Glacier under the neighboring peak! Make your way cautiously SW back to Pinnacle Saddle.

For Plummer Peak from Pinnacle Saddle (almost 0.5 mi away), take the unsigned climber's trail W 100 ft up to a fork on Plummer Peak's NNE ridge crest (6000 ft). You could take the dirt trail right (W), traversing more than 100 ft (potential narrow snowfield to cross until August) to another juncture, turning sharply and steeply left (SE) up over snowfields back toward the wide ridgeline. The preferred option from the first fork is to stay left (SW) up the rockier section, briefly following the ridgeline path SSW steeply (easily) past old snags, boulders, and small pines approaching the summit. Plummer Peak is as rewarding as any in the range and with plenty of room from the flat summit to spread out. Then you might even find a brief glissade for some of the descent!

ELEVATION: 4542 ft at Bench Lake, 4679 ft at Snow Lake (4700 ft at pond past Snow Lake); vertical gain of around 500 ft total

DISTANCE: 2.5 mi round-trip total

DURATION: 1½–3 hours round-trip with dawdling

DIFFICULTY: Moderate (brief but very steep ups/downs, narrow, solid trails, crossing snow possible until August near Snow Lake basin)

TRIP REPORT: Hike the E edge of the famed Tatoosh Range to a remarkable lake basin then subalpine Bench Lake bordering a cliff that drops more than 1000 ft into Stevens Canyon. Camp, swim, fish, or just enjoy the fabulous views and reflections of Mount Rainier and others into the colorful smaller lakes that are worth exploring! Entrance Stations are within the National Park (yourpassnow.com), and there is no restroom, though there is an outdoor privy at Snow Lake Camp.

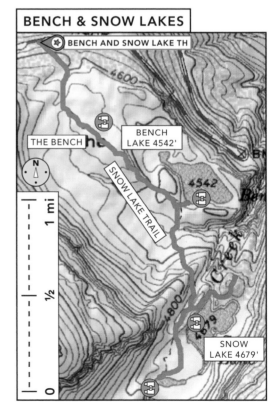

TRAILHEAD: Bench and Snow Lake TH. See Mildred Point to Van Trump Park Summit on page 48 for directions to the Nisqually Entrance. Continue up Paradise Rd E, winding for 15.25 mi to a juncture. Turn right on Stevens Canyon Rd (toward Ohanapecosh Visitor Center and Campground) for 2.75 mi to find the signed TH and a small lot with 10 spots or so on the right (100 mi, 2½ hours from Seattle; 160 mi, 3 hours from Portland).

ROUTE: Take Snow Lake Trail (accurate signage) 0.25 mi SE, undulating upward and becoming steeper (steps, few trees, high brush) before easing over the plateau meadow known as

Stevens and Unicorn Peaks from The Bench in Mount Rainier National Park.

The Bench. Look to the pillars of Unicorn and West Unicorn Peaks up right with Stevens Peak straight ahead! Continue more easily up and down (shot down to the extension of Bench Lake's W side) before descending steeper turns then leveling to a fork (unsigned post, less than 0.75 mi from TH) for the Bench Lake spur (described last here).

    Continue right (S) down Snow Lake Trail soon across a short log bridge then climb super-steeply SE up S-turns (steps) and at least 2 solid switchbacks discreetly over the highest point of the hike (4730 ft). Move down 2 steep switchbacks which flatten then roll more easily S as you enter Snow Lake basin (0.25 mi from Bench Lake spur), arriving to the signed juncture with Snow Lake Camp spur on the left (NE, over outlet to camp/privy). Keep right (S) of lakeside viewpoint spurs as you look to the striking abrupt N shoulder of Unicorn Peak developing (above the lake) up to the Tatoosh Range's tallest summit! Continue SW briefly for the enticing pond, passing the End of Maintained Trail sign across a minuscule creek before finding the solid path promptly left of the boulder field. Wander past small trees 150 ft through the flat open meadow, walking SW a few feet more (dense brush, larger trees, narrower) to the shore of the colorful pond (extension of Snow Lake as Unicorn Creek narrows between bodies of water). Hear a small cascade emanating near the inlet while staring up the rock and snowfields to Unicorn Peak!

    From the juncture for Bench Lake, turn right (ENE) steeply down the spur twisting 100 ft (woods, narrow) to the pretty water. Walk a bit right to the S side of the cliff-lined lake for that picture-perfect reflection of Mount Rainier if it decides to show!

21 | SKYLINE LOOP TRAIL TO PANORAMA POINT

ELEVATION: 7050 ft at the highest point (Pebble Creek intersection); vertical gain of around 1850 ft

DISTANCE: 6 mi round-trip loop

DURATION: 2½–4 hours round-trip

DIFFICULTY: Strenuous (very busy, mostly above tree line, rocky, steep briefly at times, family-friendly, ups/downs, well-signed, traction required October into August)

TRIP REPORT: The celebrated loop hike on the ominous volcano begins from Paradise Jackson Visitor Center (open May into October). July into September are the most visited months when wildflowers are proliferous, waterfalls are plentiful below giant glaciers, and trails are boundless with wonder, providing truly inspirational panoramic views all day! The road is plowed in winter (tire chains required) from Paradise to the Nisqually Entrance and beyond for those who enjoy snowshoeing or cross-country skiing even though Panorama Point itself is in an avalanche zone while other tracks remain popular! Wildlife sightings may include hawks and other birds, marmots, deer, and black bear. Entrance Stations are within the National Park (yourpassnow.com), and restrooms are present with an outhouse at Panorama Point.

TRAILHEAD: Paradise Jackson Visitor Center. See Mildred Point to Van Trump Park Summit on page 48 for directions to the Nisqually Entrance. Continue up Paradise Rd E, winding for 17.25 mi to the few parking areas that fill early on weekends, especially the closest at the Visitor Center near Paradise Inn. There are also a few spots along Paradise Rd E as the road turns to one way 2 mi down to Stevens Canyon Rd a few feet from Paradise Rd E (100 mi, 2½ hours from Seattle; 160 mi, 3 hours from Portland).

ROUTE: Between Paradise Picnic Area and Paradise Inn, there are so many trails loaded with activity that it can be a bit confusing near the TH area (with mapped kiosks). From the lower lots, walk briefly N up Alta Vista Trail and turn right (E) on Avalanche Lily Trail briefly as it turns into Skyline Trail at the Visitor Center. From the closest lot (including roadside parking), begin left of the Climbing Information Center (and Paradise Ranger Station) and right of Paradise Jackson Visitor Center (maps available) up a few steps then 50 ft (or any spur) to the first of at least 30 junctures on Skyline (Loop) Trail!

Follow the less chosen but arguably more preferred counterclockwise loop (see Camp Muir on page 63 for direct route to Panorama Point, clockwise), walking right (NE, paved) on Skyline Trail almost 0.25 mi, passing a juncture (left, Waterfall Trail) 0.25 mi steeper N for Myrtle Falls Viewpoint. Turn right (E) down the steeply paved spur (steps) 75 ft to the railed-in overlook of the waterfall (framed between trees) as it spreads out, cascading 72 ft down the rocks with the bridge over Edith Creek above and Mount Rainier behind! Continue NNE on Skyline Trail, crossing the footbridge over the creek (into gravel) to a major fork (0.5 mi from TH) where you could hike left (NE) on Golden Gate Trail to meet Skyline Trail again as a scenic shortcut (saves 1 mi). For this you would walk NE up the straightaway through active Edith Basin (western pasqueflower, lupine, paintbrush, and bistort), ending with 5 easy switchbacks (shot to Golden Gate Falls) and a few turns ENE to the intersection.

Continue E on Skyline Trail (from fork, primary route), traversing up and down some easily (wildflowers, few trees) with views of the nearby distinguished Tatoosh Range. The going becomes rockier past two creeks before moving up a bit steeper. Curve S briefly then climb 5 moderate switchbacks E, passing a juncture in the flats (less than 1.5 mi from TH, right for Lakes Trail, also known as Mazama Ridge Trail). Keep straight (E) steadily up the rock-lined Skyline Trail over the crest of a wide rise (built-in steps), continuing N briefly past Stevens Van Trump Historical Monument (small rockwall viewpoint) to another signed junction. Walk left (NW) on Skyline Trail into photogenic meadows, holding two quick creek crossings (lush, wildflowers, flora). Move a bit steeper SW (rocky steps), climbing another rise (see Mount St. Helens) NW up steeper rock steps, then pass a bench near a small cascade, moving up steep stone steps to easier ground (lingering snowfields nearby). Move N up more steep steps, passing the intersection with Golden Gate Trail (loop shortcut left, almost 2.5 mi from TH on primary route).

From the shortcut intersection,

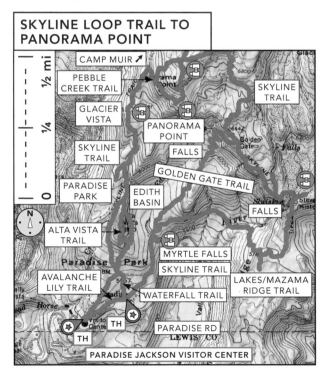

SKYLINE LOOP TRAIL TO PANORAMA POINT

The resplendent scene from Alta Vista Viewpoint and Edith Basin to the Tatoosh Range!

hike Skyline Trail steeply N up the rocky rise (steps) into a widening meadow easier (lingering snow under Panorama Point), then continue up the lusher basin (marmots) NW on steeper and rockier terrain past the usually closed Low Skyline Trail (left, 3 mi from TH on primary route, 0.5 mi farther to top of trail). Continue N on the (High) Skyline Trail steeply (loose rock, scree, dusty) up 3 quick switchbacks then soon another switchback before traversing W easier from the top of the basin (well under Paradise Glaciers and McClure Rock). Move painlessly up 2 more switchbacks on the last bit SW to the Pebble Creek intersection.

From the Pebble Creek intersection, see the climber's trail up Pebble Creek Trail (technically down a few feet then) toward Camp Muir. Keep left (S, counterclockwise loop) instead more than 0.25 mi easily down rocky Skyline Trail to Panorama Point. Look across Nisqually Glacier to Wilson Glacier Falls under Wilson Glacier! You'll pass a few feet left (E) of a small bump (Panorama Point on maps) as you see down (S) to the large rocky (or snowy) moraine bench usually loaded with spectators that is the National Park's official location. Move down 2 steep switchbacks; just above signed Panorama Point (6800 ft) is a cool stone and mortar outhouse built into the rocky hillside with a couple spurs leading to it. If you're lucky, the clouds have burned off the Cascade's highest stratovolcano and the nearby sawtooth Tatoosh Range can be seen directly S across the valley with so much more! And farther up Mount Rainier are the Muir Snowfield and Nisqually Glacier to Point Success.

Turn right (SW) from the signage if facing Panorama Point on Skyline Trail (3.75 mi on longer counterclockwise loop) 0.25 mi down 2 switchbacks and steep stone steps to the land of vegetation and wildflowers traversing NW past Pebble

Creek Trail (right) steeper to a rocky switchback. Descend left (S) from the top of the shoulder (constant views) 0.25 mi steeper (past brief loop options for Glacier Vista), then move down steps (steadily steep) over the astounding landscape slightly left (E) of the wide shoulder skipping junctures (including one right for Dead Horse Creek Trail almost 1 mi from Panorama Point). Continue S easily through a lush narrow meadow with a small creek ending down stone steps (low pines) to a crossroads near Alta Vista at a paved square/viewing area (5 mi on longer counterclockwise loop). You'll be able to see Mount Adams over the Tatoosh Range!

It's around 0.75 mi S to the Visitor Center from the viewing area with paved Skyline Trail moving right (SW) around the hill known as Alta Vista. For Alta Vista options, take the fork left from the viewing area onto Alta Vista Trail (gravel) a few feet to a fork. The flatter path with the same name continues left around the E side of the bump with the better option (slightly longer) taking you right from the fork steeply 100 yards narrowly to the top with only a few trees blocking views W. From Alta Vista Viewpoint, continue S as the path becomes paved (views E into Edith Basin) down a little wildflower-covered meadow then 2 fairly steep switchbacks SE to a juncture with the flatter Alta Vista Trail. Move right (SSW) a few feet to the Skyline Trail crossroads. For the lower lots stay on Alta Vista Trail SW following signage 0.75 mi and for the Visitor Center head left (SE) briefly and quite steeply down paved Skyline Trail. Cross Waterfall Trail, then take any trail down abruptly to the visible TH area.

22 | CAMP MUIR

ELEVATION: 10,100 ft; vertical gain of around 4800 ft

DISTANCE: 4.25 mi up directly, 8.5–9.5 mi round-trip

DURATION: 3½–5 hours up, 7–10 hours round-trip

DIFFICULTY: Expert only (high altitude, glacier travel, rapidly changing conditions, cornices develop into September, sustained steeps, traction highly recommended, GPS device and trekking poles helpful, glissading possible)

TRIP REPORT: Named after John Muir, who summited Mount Rainier in 1888, this popular climbers camp also attracts day hikers looking to push themselves for indescribable payoffs above or in the clouds! Go for a bluebird day late July into September and be extra cautious from the snowfield around boulder islands or rocks where holes develop. Watch for occasional crevasses that widen around September near Anvil Rock, where running water can be heard below icy patches. See Skyline

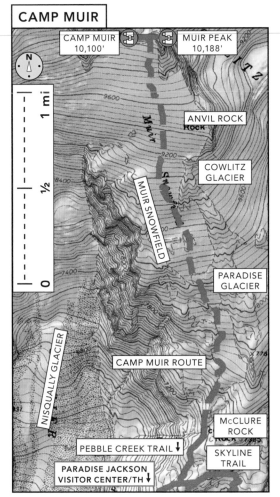

CAMP MUIR

CAMP MUIR
10,100'

MUIR PEAK
10,188'

N

1 mi

9600

ANVIL ROCK
Rock

9200

COWLITZ
GLACIER

8400

MUIR SNOWFIELD

½

7400

PARADISE
GLACIER

0

NISQUALLY GLACIER

CAMP MUIR ROUTE

X 778

McCLURE
ROCK

PEBBLE CREEK TRAIL ↓

SKYLINE
TRAIL

PARADISE JACKSON
VISITOR CENTER/TH ↓

See also map on page 61.

Loop Trail to Panorama Point on page 60 for clues in Paradise Park. Entrance Stations are within the National Park (yourpassnow.com), and restrooms are present with privies at Camp Muir.

TRAILHEAD: Paradise Jackson Visitor Center. See Skyline Loop Trail to Panorama Point on page 60 for directions (100 mi, 2½ hours from Seattle; 160 mi, 3 hours from Portland).

ROUTE: For the direct route through Paradise (or clockwise Skyline Loop Trail) to the high Skyline–Pebble Creek Trail intersection (for Camp Muir), hike steeply N straight up Skyline Trail (paved to begin, well-signed) 1.5 mi from the crossroads above the steps behind Paradise Jackson Visitor Center (steeper at times, with log/stone steps, rockier through creek-filled meadows) to the Pebble Creek Trail intersection above Glacier Vista (views). Turn left (NE, bypassing Panorama Point) on Pebble Creek Trail steeply 0.25 mi to the Pebble Creek intersection. Continue straight/left (NE, leaving Paradise Park) over and down some on Pebble Creek Trail 0.25 mi as you cross Pebble Creek (rock-hop easily) with the rocky path petering out 100 yards farther near the headwall of the Muir Snowfield (W of McClure Rock). It's 2 mi farther and almost 3000 ft up to sanctuary at Camp Muir.

Hike N steeply over rocks, pumice, boulders, and patchy snow (no more set trail) until the Muir Snowfield becomes solid. Keep in mind, especially on the descent, that there are cliffs and hidden cornices to avoid just E of McClure Rock all the way to aptly named Anvil Rock near Camp Muir. These rocky protrusions are important landmarks during sudden whiteouts as the route steepens N to Anvil Rock and beyond following the center of the snowfield, more or less, over the track. You finally see the

Day hikers labor up to Camp Muir, Mount Rainier's highest basecamp.

stone and wooden structures at Camp Muir ascending the last feet NNW super-steeply with the Cowlitz Glacier right, the Nisqually Glacier left, and the Tatoosh Range behind you (S) looking miniature!

From the saddle at basecamp, see the continuation of the climbing route N across the top of the glacier (dotted with tents and climbing teams practicing maneuvers) over to Cathedral Rocks. Straight up NW is the rocky spine (Cowlitz Cleaver, Beehive) surrounded by the Nisqually Cleaver, Disappointment Cleaver, Gibraltar Rock, and Cadaver Gap. Camp Muir is the second highest (to Mount Adams) nontechnical hike in the whole state. Investigate the area's Ranger Station, warming hut, bunked huts, and the highest outhouses in Washington!

Muir Peak (10,188 ft) is the crumbling point just E of the saddle that makes for a fun scramble most people miss or skip. Walk right (E) behind the highest funky stone bunkhouse, finding the climber's trail very steeply 100 ft or so up loose stones then larger more solid rock (few choices), hugging the boulders the final 30 ft to the tiny airy top (best perspective of the day)! Continue SE steeply down 35 ft (somewhat easier), reaching a small flat landing (safe viewpoint between summit pinnacles) with a rock barrier blocking wind. Gaze down the Cowlitz Glacier and Muir Snowfield simultaneously!

Return to camp and head S down the Muir Snowfield. There are several brief glissading options as conditions allow (usually below Anvil Rock, remember pants or garbage bag, etc). Finish in Paradise Park either with a loop down Edith Basin on Golden Gate Trail or a visit to nearby Panorama Point, Glacier Vista, or Alta Vista Viewpoint from Skyline Trail en route to Jackson Visitor Center.

OLYMPIC PENINSULA

SAMS RIVER (QUEETS CAMPGROUND) LOOP TRAIL

ELEVATION: 320 ft; vertical gain of around 100 ft

DISTANCE: 3 mi round-trip loop

DURATION: 1½–2 hours round-trip loop

DIFFICULTY: Moderate (muddy and overgrown in places, fairly family-friendly, wide)

TRIP REPORT: Olympic National Park is a phenomenal treasure and a geological wonder to behold from all angles! Here we skip the bustling Hoh Rain Forest for more mild weather just S in the peaceful Queets River valley. Many people stay at the rustic but charming Queets Campground if making the long drive. This description has you begin at Queets Ranger Station (clockwise). Wildlife sightings may include owls, bald eagles, river otters, coyote, fox, elk, cougar, and black bear. National Park fee is required (yourpassnow.com) most times, and a small pit toilet is present at the nearby campground.

TRAILHEAD: Queets Ranger Station or Queets River TH. From Seattle, take I-5 S to exit 104 (Aberdeen/Port Angeles) onto US-101 N for 5.5 mi, stay left onto WA-8 W for 21 mi, then onto WA-12 W (Elma) for 20.5 mi. Cross the bridge over Wishkah River (Aberdeen) onto US-101 N for 53 mi. Turn right on signed FR-21 (W Boundary Rd, no RVs, 2WD okay), following small signs—Upper Queets Valley (Highway 101 signs on return)—almost 11 mi (into unpaved on curve at 8 mi), then turn right in the valley on signed Queets River Rd (gravel/dirt) for 2 mi to Queets Ranger Station (left, small parking area). For Queets River TH, continue for 1 mi more on narrow Queets River Rd (passing CG loop spurs) with pull-in parking at left (four spots).

From Portland, take I-5 N to exit 88 (Tenino), turn left on US-12 W for 25 mi, turn left in Elma, and merge to stay on US-12 W for 20.5 mi to Aberdeen, and follow as above (170 mi, 3½ hours from Seattle; 200 mi, 4 hours from Portland).

ROUTE: From Queets Ranger Station TH, walk right of the usually closed small building just left of the old sign that says Sams Loop Tr—Pets, Weapons, Vehicles, & Bicycles Prohibited on Sams River Loop Trail and head into the woods NE (impressive hemlock, spruce, mossy flora, ferns), moving narrowly down a few feet toward the Queets River. Move through a long meadow (smattering of trees), then follow the riverbank (cautious with young ones, almost 0.5 mi from Ranger Station, see

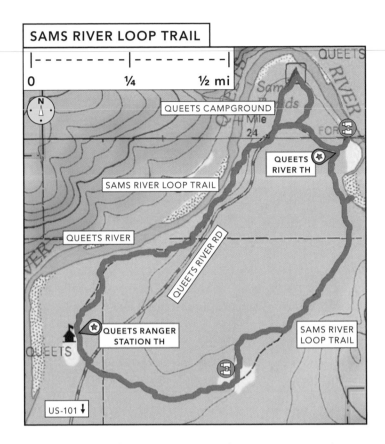

SAMS RIVER LOOP TRAIL

|—————————|—————————|
0   ¼   ½ mi

QUEETS CAMPGROUND

QUEETS RIVER TH

SAMS RIVER LOOP TRAIL

QUEETS RIVER

QUEETS RIVER RD

QUEETS RANGER STATION TH

SAMS RIVER LOOP TRAIL

US-101

Kloochman Rock upstream). Continue NE up the uneven section (narrow, wet tree roots) before paralleling closer to the main road, then walk down a bit crossing 30 ft over a bog (mossy log bridge) near the river. Soon work over a large downed tree easily before the flat narrow trail winds pleasantly E away from the water to Queets River Rd (1 mi from Ranger Station, signed Trail Follows Rd 0.25 mi on ground pointing left).

Follow Queets River Rd left (NNE) 100 ft, keeping right (SE, past CG loop) along the quiet narrow road briefly to Queets River TH (kiosk), watching for gigantic second- and third-growth Sitka spruce rising up quickly among the ancient stumps of the behemoths that were cut long ago. From the kiosk, a map denotes the unmaintained Queets River Trail with a ford over the wide rushing river to a once-visited mammoth Douglas fir (felled).

Walk right (SW) from Queets River TH above the riverbank where Queets and Sams Rivers meet (watch for wildlife) on Sams River Loop Trail (younger thin trees) as you saunter next to Sams River, soon heading SE narrowly past ferns atop lush green undergrowth (large spruce, vine and bigleaf maple). Stroll down a bit before leveling with a teaser shot NE up the Queets River valley to the top of the snow-covered Mount Olympus Massif before you move SW away from Sams River at 0.5 mi from Queets

Sunlight pierces the canopy on the Olympic's most secluded easy trail, albeit a damp one, with owls hooting and songbirds singing!

River TH (1.75 mi from Ranger Station). Navigate the muddy trail SW (ferns proliferate) 0.5 mi as the forest opens somewhat with everything covered in moss. The route is simple, though the area floods in spring. Pass alder and apple trees into the first of a few little meadows for the next 0.25 mi, with a great chance to see some large elk if you're quiet. Pop over a lovely tiny stream as the path WSW disappears with trail signs on both ends of the meadow. Continue briefly into the next meadow then into the forest W (muddier, slightly rougher) across a couple fallen trees before easing NW through the flats (ferns, younger spruce, hemlock). At more than 1.5 mi from Queets River TH (2.75 mi from Ranger Station on clockwise loop), cross a slippery log bridge over a slow-moving creek (shallow, mossy) within a pretty setting. The trail dries to nearby Queets River Rd where you turn right (N) 40 ft to Queets Ranger Station.

TRIP REPORT: The Quinault Rain Forest Loop Drive (more than 30–mi plus spurs) takes visitors to several roadside attractions including waterfalls, wildlife-viewing meadows, beachside vistas, and brief walks (around 10 mi total, all family-friendly) through ancient temperate rainforests and along the beautiful Quinault River to Pony Bridge! Each location is listed as its own subhike to keep it simple, following the counterclockwise tour. June to September are prime while off-season and winter months hold more solitude with Lake Quinault Lodge and mercantile remaining open. Lake Quinault lies mostly outside Olympic National Park (within Olympic National Forest) and there's a hauntingly elegant stateliness wafting throughout the lake valley. The silky, calm dark water reflects the rugged local mountains and provides multiple access points primarily from the S side. You'll admire gigantic old-growth Douglas fir, cedar, spruce, and hemlock with moss-lined creeks and the canopy dripping from the 11 ft of rain the region receives each year. Check www.olympicnationalparks.com/ or www.fs.usda.gov/detailfull/olympic/home/?cid=fseprd716032&width=full.

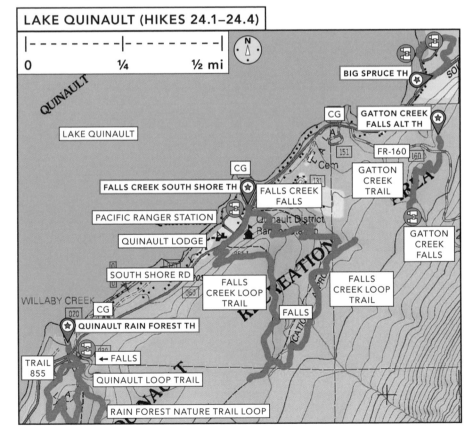

LAKE QUINAULT (HIKES 24.1–24.4)

0   ¼   ½ mi

N

QUINAULT

BIG SPRUCE TH

LAKE QUINAULT

CG

GATTON CREEK FALLS ALT TH

151   FR-160   160

CG

GATTON CREEK TRAIL

FALLS CREEK SOUTH SHORE TH

FALLS CREEK FALLS

Cem

131

PACIFIC RANGER STATION

Quinault District Ran

QUINAULT LODGE

GATTON CREEK FALLS

SOUTH SHORE RD

FALLS CREEK LOOP TRAIL

FALLS CREEK LOOP TRAIL

WILLABY CREEK

020   CG

FALLS

QUINAULT RAIN FOREST TH

TRAIL 855

← FALLS

QUINAULT LOOP TRAIL

RAIN FOREST NATURE TRAIL LOOP

24.1   RAIN FOREST NATURE TRAIL LOOP

ELEVATION: 330 ft; vertical gain of around 150 ft total

DISTANCE: Less than 0.75 mi round-trip loop including Willaby Creek Falls

DURATION: Less than ½ hour round-trip

DIFFICULTY: Easy (wide, muddy, brief ups/downs, mostly fenced, drop-offs)

TRAILHEAD: Quinault Rain Forest TH. From Seattle, take I-5 S to exit 104 (Aberdeen/Port Angeles) onto US-101 N for 5.5 mi, stay left onto WA-8 W for 21 mi, then onto WA-12 W (Elma) for 20.5 mi. Cross the bridge over Wishkah River (Aberdeen) onto US-101 N for 41.5 mi (milepost 125), turn right on South Shore Rd/ FR-93400 for almost 1.5 mi, and turn right (opposite Willaby Campground) into the lot signed for Rain Forest Nature Trail.

From Portland, take I-5 N to exit 88 (Tenino), turn left on US-12 W for 25 mi, turn left in Elma, merging to stay on US-12 W for 20.5 mi to Aberdeen, and follow as above (150 mi, 2½ hours from Seattle; 185 mi, 3 hours from Portland). Northwest Forest Pass required, and flush toilets are present.

ROUTE: Take Quinault Rain Forest Nature Trail 855 right (SW, from kiosk) on a counterclockwise interpretive loop (instead of following sign pointing left). Before turning SSE on the easy ascent, observe towering old-growth fir, cedar, hemlock, and spruce lining the wide gravel path (ample moss, ferns)! Move up 4 turns within the first 0.25 mi easing N to a fork (kiosk, wooden fence), then keep left (N) 0.25 mi on Quinault Loop Trail along the mossy fence steepening (see Willaby Creek in ravine below) down to the final signed juncture (TH left). Continue N 150 ft down steeper steps (Quinault Loop Trail) under the pretty South Shore Rd bridge to the visible footbridge (or just before) for a look at Willaby Creek Falls (15 ft, plus cascades). Climb back to the juncture and turn right (SW) down Trail 855, briefly passing one more enormous tree at right (partly wrapped by viewing deck) 100 ft shy of the parking lot.

24.2 FALLS CREEK LOOP

ELEVATION: 365 ft; vertical gain of around 200 ft

DISTANCE: 2.25 mi round-trip loop including Falls Creek Falls

DURATION: 1 hour max round-trip

DIFFICULTY: Easy (simple creek crossings, ups/downs, tree roots)

TRAILHEAD: Falls Creek South Shore TH. Drive almost 1 mi right (NE) from Quinault Rain Forest TH along South Shore Rd and find pull-in parking on the left before crossing Falls Creek (no signage, seven spots, 2.25 mi from US-101). No fee or restroom, and additional parking with restrooms exists at the Pacific Ranger Station (Quinault Office) before the TH.

ROUTE: For Falls Creek Falls (12 ft high) under the nearby road bridge, walk N down 1 switchback from the path directly in front of the TH parking. It's 75 ft to the bench and interpretive sign on the creek's bank. Watch the water flowing down the mossy rocks gently into a clear turquoise pool. The best viewpoint, however, is from the other side of the creek at the corner of Falls Creek Campground near a pretty sweet campsite! Walk along the main road over the bridge 100 ft to the campground driveway, or drive briefly and walk as close as possible without intruding on others.

Beautifully clear Falls Creek Falls tumbling down rocks under the road bridge are worth a quick look!

Take Falls Creek Loop Trail (sharing Quinault Loop Trail, unsigned) across South Shore Rd (from primary TH) SE over the wide boardwalk (and smaller footbridge) up 4 steeper switchbacks within the first 0.25 mi. Ease up 2 more switchbacks (more open forest), then work down the wide gravel trail parallel to the water (thick flora) as you cross Falls Creek. Ascend 2 switchbacks SE easily, keeping right (SSW, opposite Gatton Creek Trail) on the narrower loop trail 0.25 mi up (passing cute Cascade Falls, 20 ft high). Hike over the bridge above the falls, continuing SW pleasantly down the dirt path to Falls Creek again (footbridge, more than 1 mi from TH). Instantly reach the next juncture and move right (SW, opposite Quinault Loop Trail past Cedar Bog) to Quinault Lodge on Falls Creek Loop Trail, undulating N down (gravel, easy) far above Falls Creek less than 0.75 mi (woods) with a few turns nearest South Shore Rd (across from lodge). Walk right (NE) on the road 100 yards (past mercantile, Ranger Station, and museum) to the TH.

24.3 GATTON CREEK FALLS

ELEVATION: 380 ft (350 ft at bridge/viewpoint); vertical gain of only 60 ft

DISTANCE: More than 0.5 mi round-trip from Alt TH

DURATION: 15 minutes round-trip

DIFFICULTY: Easy (gravel, wide, ups/downs, quite brief from Alt TH)

TRAILHEAD: Gatton Creek Falls Alt TH. Drive left (NE) from Falls Creek South Shore TH for 0.5 mi along South Shore Rd (past main TH across from Gatton Creek Campground), turn right immediately after crossing the bridge over Gatton Creek on FR-160 (no sign, confusing numbers posted, gravel/dirt, one-lane, 2WD okay) for less than 0.5 mi, and find the signed TH right with parking on the sides. No fee or restroom.

ROUTE: With so many incredible areas in the Quinault Rain Forest, shorten this mundane jaunt from the main TH and cut to the chase from the alternate TH. Take Gatton Creek Trail right (SW) over the bridge and then go down 2 switchbacks, across another bridge (tiny creek), and then up 2 switchbacks (see across valley, very few larger trees). Ease S as you hear the lengthy 60-plus-ft cascade on Gatton Creek before arriving to the bridge/viewpoint over it. The waterfall loses much steam by summer's end but roars through the forest May to July, continuing under the bridge and beyond!

24.4 WORLD'S LARGEST SITKA SPRUCE

ELEVATION: 180 ft; vertical gain of 50 ft

DISTANCE: More than 0.5 mi round-trip with lakeside view

DURATION: Less than 10 minutes one way, ½ hour round-trip if lingering

DIFFICULTY: Easy (flat, short-lived, wide gravel trail)

TRAILHEAD: Big Spruce TH. From the beginning of FR-160 (at Gatton Creek), turn right (NE) on South Shore Rd for less than 0.5 mi and find parking on the right and the signed TH on the N side of the road (1 mi from Ranger Station, 2 mi from Quinault Rain Forest TH, almost 3.5 mi from US-101). No fee, and a portable outhouse is present.

ROUTE: Take the trail past the small sign for the world record's largest Sitka spruce down a bit, walking NE through a scant number of some big old trees (bog on left). Turn N into a clearing and see the gargantuan spruce just beyond the footbridge! From the tree (59 ft in diameter), wander 100 yards SW off-trail past a few camper trailers, directly toward a beachy area with sailboats, for terrific views across the lake NNW up to the tree-covered mountains, including Higley Peak.

Impressive record-holding spruce is just one of many lakeside attractions near Lake Quinault.

24.5 MERRIMAN FALLS

TRAILHEAD: Merriman Falls TH (unsigned). Continue NE from Big Spruce TH along South Shore Rd for 3.25 mi, slowing to limited pullouts on both sides (no signs, 4.25 mi from Ranger Station, more than 6 mi from US-101, 0.5 mi past Colonel Bob TH; see Colonel Bob Peak on page 80 for briefer route), with the falls visible right as you cross the bridge. No fee or restroom.

ROUTE: The landscape changes as you enter a lush emerald jungle of a rainforest and nearly miss the falls driving to the TH. Take the paths from either side of the bridge over Merriman Creek 30 ft or so to the base of the enchanting 40-ft waterfall! It's best seen from the right side of the bridge, however, where other little cascades are seen falling between moss-covered rocks under ancient logs into tiny pools!

Merriman Falls drops seductively through the verdigris forest.

24.6 BUNCH CREEK FALLS

TRAILHEAD: Bunch Creek Falls TH (unsigned). Drive 1.25 mi from Merriman Falls TH (see hike above) along South Shore Rd (NE then E) into gravel for 4 mi more to reach the pullouts before the bridge (9.75 mi from Ranger Station, 12 mi from US-101, just inside Olympic National Park). National Park fee required (yourpassnow.com) but free in winter (and probably for a brief visit anytime), and there is no restroom.

ROUTE: The best shot is again from the nearest (W) side of the bridge with no trails as you gaze up the narrow 60-ft cascade tumbling down a mossy fern-covered steep hillside! It's tough to find the best angle for this quaint but friendly waterfall.

Continue NE from Bunch Creek Falls TH on South Shore Rd almost 1 mi (potholes) to the dusty intersection for the Upper Quinault River Bridge with the option either to remain on the Quinault Rain Forest Loop Drive (left) or to hike to Pony Bridge (3–4 hours round-trip total, including drive).

24.7 PONY BRIDGE

ELEVATION: 1270 ft at the high point (900 ft at the bridge); vertical gain of more than 1000 ft total

DISTANCE: Less than 5.5 mi round-trip

DURATION: 2–3 hours round-trip

DIFFICULTY: Strenuous (muddy when wet, ups/downs, narrow and steeper at times, more difficult with snow or for young children, wildlife sightings may include deer, elk, and black bear)

TRAILHEAD: Graves Creek TH. Drive straight (NE) from the Upper Quinault River Bridge intersection on South Shore Rd onto Graves Creek Rd (gravel, narrow, potholes, rougher, 2WD high-clearance okay) for almost 2.5 mi, passing a low spot on the road (which historically floods May into July, so check conditions at nps.gov/olym/planyourvisit/current-road-conditions.htm). Continue for 3.25 mi, passing Graves Creek Ranger Station at right for another 0.25 mi with the small but wonderful Graves Creek Campground left (open year-round, check ahead in winter) and the TH almost 0.25 mi farther. There is parking on the sides (17 mi from Pacific Ranger Station, almost 19 mi from US-101). National Park fee required (yourpassnow.com) but free in winter, and an outhouse is present, though it may or may not be closed in winter.

ROUTE: Take East Fork Quinault River Trail (between kiosks) over the wide Graves Creek bridge less than 0.25 mi N to a signed fork, keeping left (NE, opposite Graves Creek Trail) promptly across another creek but this time cautiously over a potentially slippery log bridge. The hike is steadily easy up through the timeless Olympic Wilderness (small streams, tall trees, tons of ground cover) with the sun penetrating the canopy. Continue up a sweeping turn (1 mi from TH, steeper, rockier) hiking 0.5 mi NNE, then descend a bit past a little cascade (right) before the route begins undulating (views) and becomes fairly steep and rugged for the remaining 0.5 mi NE down to Pony Bridge. From a switchback on the rockier path (wood/rock steps) is a tease view of the snow-capped Olympics E through the trees. Hear the Quinault River through the mossy forest (fir, hemlock, cedar) as you trudge N toward it with occasional small streams running over the sopping-wet trail.

Reach the bank high above the dazzling blue-green river (2.5 mi from TH), sneaking up to Pony Bridge past huge trees near the mossy edge of the vertical rock walls that comprise the little slot canyon. Looking up the stunning river corridor from the bridge is a nearby small cascade (side creek), pouring down green rocks, that loses steam after spring like the river where salmon can be seen running in the fall! Feel free to cross the bridge and explore, being very cautious near ledges (no fencing). From the main trail over the bridge is a small, flat, open area (Pony Bridge Camp). Find ideal picnic spots left (S) down a few feet to a locale above a colorful pool, or move right (N then SE) from the camp up East Fork Quinault River Trail 100 ft or so to another great viewpoint near the edge. Incidentally, the Enchanted Valley is only 10 mi more one way!

Famed landmark makes for a great turnaround for those longing for an actual hike on the Quinault Rain Forest Loop Drive.

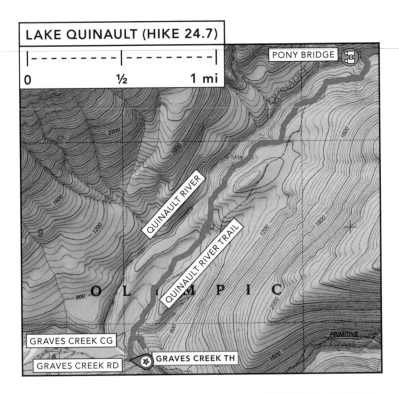

LAKE QUINAULT (HIKE 24.7)

| 0 | ½ | 1 mi |

PONY BRIDGE

QUINAULT

QUINAULT RIVER

QUINAULT RIVER TRAIL

O L Y M P I C

GRAVES CREEK CG

GRAVES CREEK RD

GRAVES CREEK TH

PRIMITIVE

Creek

24.8 BUNCH FIELDS WILDLIFE VIEWING AREA

TRAILHEAD: None officially, or choose the sides of the road. After returning from Graves Creek TH, turn right (N) on North Shore Rd across the Quinault River Bridge for the N side of the lake loop tour. First, feel free to park on either side of the bridge, then walk on it or the nearby banks to see fabulous views up and down the river. Watch for bears and eagles scrutinizing the river for salmon! Less than 0.25 mi N of the Upper Quinault River Bridge is a fork. Drive left (W) on signed North Shore Rd (gravel, narrow) as Bunch Fields opens at left. Pass a bridge to nowhere in the first sizable meadow and park where it is safe on the sides for wildlife viewing.

ROUTE: From your vehicle or thereabouts, see black-tailed deer, bald eagles, black bear, or the hefty Roosevelt elk if you're fortunate! From the end of the next meadow (driving W) is a small sign for Bunch Fields 0.75 mi from the North Shore Rd fork near the Upper Quinault River Bridge.

24.9 JULY CREEK PICNIC AREA & LOOP TRAIL

ELEVATION: 230 ft; vertical gain of around 100 ft total

DISTANCE: Less than 0.5 mi round-trip loop including spurs

DURATION: ½–1 hour round-trip max

DIFFICULTY: Easy (brief, wide, spur to log-filled beach slightly more difficult)

TRAILHEAD: July Creek Picnic Area. Continue SW on North Shore Rd from the westernmost Bunch Fields sign 6 mi, then onto the paved two-lane road for almost 4.5 mi more (passing Quinault Rain Forest Ranger Station). Find the TH and parking on the left (S, 3.25 mi from US-101 directly). No fee, and an outhouse is present.

ROUTE: Follow July Creek Loop Trail right of the outhouse for the picnic area and brief counterclockwise loop S toward Lake Quinault as you quickly arrive near some picnic tables and a grill down right with great views beyond a logjam. Head left (E) from the fork past a rather large tree that fell across the trail in 2018 with a large section removed. Continue NE past more giants to a juncture for the beach viewpoint. Walk right (NE) down the steeper unsigned spur 75 ft or so as it empties onto a beach loaded with smaller felled trees. Work your way right (E) carefully 50 ft to the water's edge for some of the best views all day. See Colonel Bob Peak rising slightly higher than the rest in the range SE and S across the pristine lake! Make your way back up the spur and turn right (N) on the loop trail 50 ft, passing signs indicating the day-use area. Turn left (SW) along the road 100 ft to the TH.

Drive left (SW) along North Shore Rd 3.25 mi to US-101 S, then turn left (SE) 2 mi, passing Amanda Park with a final chance to see Lake Quinault before continuing home safely.

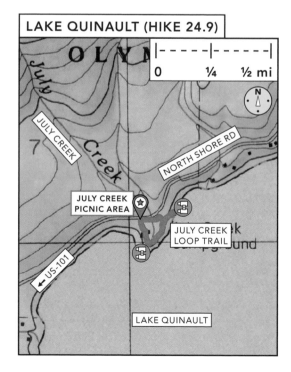

LAKE QUINAULT (HIKE 24.9)

ELEVATION: 4492 ft; vertical gain of around 3700 ft from Pete's Creek TH

DISTANCE: 4 mi up, 8 mi round-trip

DURATION: Almost 3 hours up, 5–6 hours round-trip

DIFFICULTY: Very challenging (steep, nearly 100 switchbacks, solid trail, slightly overgrown, ups/downs not bad, steeper summit block, drop-offs, traction/ice axe recommended until late July)

TRIP REPORT: The SW corner of Olympic National Park is home to this rough peak far above the Quinault River valley. The demanding day hike tops the old rainforest near a scenic high basin under the summit with transcendent views of the Colonel Bob Wilderness, the rugged Quinault Ridge, Lake Quinault, the Mount Olympus Massif, the Pacific Ocean, and Mount Rainier! Northwest Forest Pass required, and a vault toilet is present.

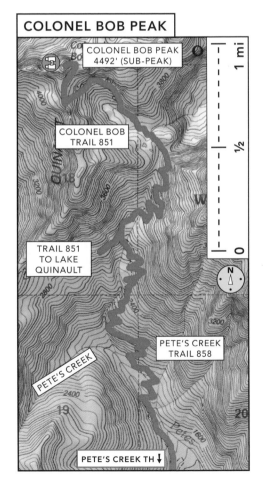

COLONEL BOB PEAK

COLONEL BOB PEAK 4492' (SUB-PEAK)

COLONEL BOB TRAIL 851

TRAIL 851 TO LAKE QUINAULT

PETE'S CREEK TRAIL 858

PETE'S CREEK

PETE'S CREEK TH ↓

TRAILHEAD: Pete's Creek TH. From Seattle, take I-5 S to exit 104 (Aberdeen/Port Angeles) onto US-101 N for 5.5 mi, stay left onto WA-8 W for 21 mi, then onto WA-12 W (Elma) for 20.5 mi. Cross the bridge over Wishkah River (Aberdeen) onto US-101 N for 28.5 mi, turn right (milepost 112, past Humptulips) on Donkey Creek Rd (FR-22) for 8 mi, and turn left for 10.75 mi on FR-2204 (small sign, one-lane, gravel, potholes after 1.5 mi) to find the TH on the left and a small parking area on the right.

From Portland, take I-5 N to exit 88 (Tenino), turn left on US-12 W for 25 mi, turn left in Elma, merging

From Colonel Bob Peak either the marine layer burns off revealing Lake Quinault, or you just get a whole lot of exercise!

to stay on US-12 W for 20.5 mi to Aberdeen, and follow as on previous page (155 mi, 3 hours from Seattle; 200 mi, up to 3½ hours from Portland).

ROUTE: Cross the road to the N side (instead of taking parking adjacent Trail 858.1 downhill) to begin left (NNW) up Pete's Creek Trail 858 (overgrown) with 5 steep switchbacks before a mini traverse, then 2 turns up to a rocky slide area. Move down slightly, crossing 12 ft over the slide, and continue to traverse NNW (old Douglas fir, Sitka spruce, cedar, hemlock) before descending across Pete's Creek (dry). Hike rocky Trail 858 (accurate 1 mi marker) N up 2 steeper turns, then walk down across a couple rocky creek beds (water running beneath) before climbing NE up 6 switchbacks sharply. Traverse (1.5 mi from TH) NW up the overgrown section, then climb 10 steep rocky switchbacks N, passing a small camp at left. Follow Pete's Creek N steeply (large trees) then even steeper up 8 new switchbacks (views, wildflowers), covering the super-steep open slope. Head into the woods up 4 more solid switchbacks to a signed intersection on another switchback (2850 ft, less than 2.5 mi up, opposite Lake Quinault).

Hike right (NNE) onto Colonel Bob Trail 851 steeply for 0.5 mi up 20 slightly overgrown switchbacks (trees), then walk easier down 2 switchbacks (views). Up the rockier trail, pass a small tarn and then descend 3 quick turns NW (more tarns) to a foggy juncture near a picturesque camping zone on Fletcher Creek, known as Moonshine Flats (3700 ft; see Gibson Peak SE and Colonel Bob Peak up through forest NW). Cross the wildflower-choked creek without difficulty by moving straight/left from the juncture.

Continue NW up 6 steep switchbacks on Trail 851 (lingering snow to high ridge), then traverse W steeply under a cliff band before grinding SW up 11 rocky switchbacks (roots). Work right (N) near a saddle under cliffs (E, difficult with snow and ice) for a few feet, find the trail NNE down a tad, then traverse up with 1 more switchback to the high ridge (views). Hike quite steeply W then SW up 11 brief switchbacks to the narrow rocky summit above all the trees (drop-offs). It's fairly safe on the slightly lower of the twin summits and home to a historic lookout site. The rough scramble ENE to the highest columns of Colonel Bob Peak would be quite an endeavor. The view of Lake Quinault over nearby Mount O'Neil and Wooded Peak is magical if you are blessed to have more sun than clouds!

26 | MOUNT ROSE LOOP

ELEVATION: 4301 ft; vertical gain of 3200 ft directly (plus 200 ft with loop)

DISTANCE: 3 mi up directly, 6.5 mi round-trip loop

DURATION: 2–2½ hours up, 3–5 hours round-trip

DIFFICULTY: Very challenging (steadily steeper than most, advanced hikers only, not crowded, 165–200 switchbacks/turns one way, impossible when wet, traction/ice axe required with snow near summit block December to April)

TRIP REPORT: Mount Ellinor's smaller sibling extending from its SW ridge is not to be overlooked or underestimated! Dozens of tight switchbacks and turns weave nearly straight up the mountain, including on both sides of a possible lollipop loop; and facing mostly S, the hike entices as early as May without requiring you to cross much snow, if any, while most of the Olympics trails are still concealed! The viewpoint from the summit boulders far above Lake Cushman holds better-than-expected vistas. Wildlife sightings may include mountain goats. No fee, and a portable outhouse is present.

TRAILHEAD: Mount Rose TH. From Seattle, take I-5 S to exit 104 (Aberdeen/Port Angeles) onto US-101 N for 5.5 mi to exit 101 (Shelton/Port Angeles), and continue onto US-101 N for 28.5 mi to Hoodsport (milepost 332). Turn left on WA-119 N (no signal) for 8.75 mi winding to a stop sign, turn left (past Big Creek CG) on WA-119/FR-24/N Lake Cushman Rd for more than 1.5 mi then gravel for 1 mi, turn right onto the signed TH driveway (one-lane) for 75 ft, and find pull-in parking at left with 12 spots or so and roadside spaces nearby on N Lake Cushman Rd.

High above Lake Cushman, Mount Rose entices hard-core hikers without the traffic from next door at Mount Ellinor!

From Portland, take I-5 N to exit 104 (Aberdeen/Port Angeles) onto US-101 N, and follow as on previous page (100 mi, 2 hours from Seattle; 160 mi, almost 3 hours from Portland).

ROUTE: Begin W on Mount Rose Trail 814 promptly over a couple bridges with pretty little cascades coming down the lush creeks. The flattest portion of the trail ends momentarily from a kiosk and yellow sign (noting burnt trees from 2006 fire) on the first switchback (of 18, first set). Climb N through switchback 6 (0.5 mi from TH, log bench) far above a creek passing larger fir and hemlock easily (smooth, wide), then after true switchback 12 (0.75 mi from TH) the route will steepen 0.25 mi through switchback 18 where you traverse SW steeply and briefly (thinning forest, few boulders) to the crest of a long shoulder (partial clearing to lake).

Hike right (N) quite steeply up 5 tight switchbacks on Trail 814 (burnt trees), passing an old sign (Mount Skokomish Wilderness, Olympic National Forest) on top of a newer sign: EL. 1990 (in ft, 1.25 mi from TH). Clamber 0.5 mi N super-steeply just E of another creek (roots, loose rock, steps) up tight turns (around 18 total), over the wide mossy shoulder with bear grass to a faint fork. The spur left (around 2600 ft) moves very steeply N up 2 switchbacks on the abrupt mossy hillside to the shoulder crest for easier walking and interesting views, and meets the main trail again (best saved for descent). Trail 814 ascends 2 switchbacks N from the (lower) fork steeply to the crest at the (upper) spur option where you continue N shortly to the signed Summit Loop intersection at an open area within the beautiful forest that used to be a Horse Camp (sign says EL. 3050, but it's actually 2950 ft, almost 2 mi from TH).

Hike the direct route left (NW) from the Summit Loop intersection (preferred clockwise loop, 0.5 mi briefer than counterclockwise, both from Trail 814) up 7 steep switchbacks before a micro-break on the curving shoulder, then continue very steeply and steadily W up 16 tight switchbacks at most (next set, more than 0.25 mi from intersection). Ascend 3 steep narrow switchbacks W (felled trees), moving more easily (wider track) past large Douglas fir (3500 ft) before climbing steeper again steadily WSW up tight turns (mossy boulders) within a dry wash. Continue WSW up 2 steep turns, then 10 tight switchbacks and steep turns (roots). Move along an easier stretch, then look for orange blazes near a few felled trees to cross (without difficulty) as you steeply rise SW up 10 more switchbacks. The top switchback (moving right) from some large boulders has a fallen tree on it that you must navigate, watching for the route (around 0.75 mi from loop intersection) to the main SE ridge of Mount Rose near the burn where there are fantastic views from Lake Cushman to Timber Mountain and Lightning Peak.

Follow blazes to the summit (especially with any snow around) as you push over a few felled trees and steeply climb 10 or so tight switchbacks NW (bear grass, paintbrush, boulders, burnt trees) like a mountain goat to the top! Just past the EL. 4300 sign is the small peak on top of the outcrop (drop-offs). From the boulders, look to Lake Cushman, the North Fork Skokomish valley, far left (SE) to Mount Rainier, and right (NE) past a few trees to rockier Mount Ellinor and Mount Pershing!

For the clockwise Summit Loop, walk left (NNE) 0.75 mi toward Mount Ellinor on Trail 814 along the tree-covered high ridge. Descend the steeper summit block (roots, rocks) 50 ft before easing down the gradual path (soft pine needles), briefly

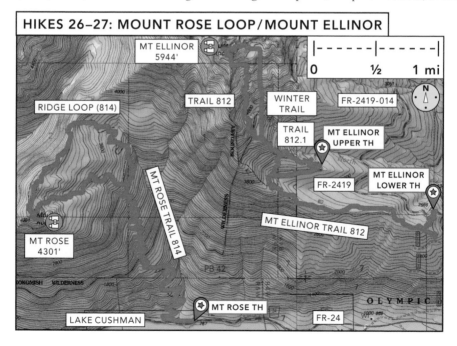

HIKES 26–27: MOUNT ROSE LOOP/MOUNT ELLINOR

passing a brushy saddle up to a ridge bump (small opening) then down steeper (just E of the ridgeline) before easing N back to the crest. You undulate NE steeply (narrowly) over the next two bumps (see left across Bear Gulch to rocky Copper Mountain) before diving off the ridge right (ESE).

Move E down 2 switchbacks (from felled tree), then duck under a fallen tree two times on a turn before descending around 10 switchbacks SE steeply. Pass a small Bear Hunter Camp 0.7 sign (left, no trail, defunct camp, 0.5 mi from high ridge) on another switchback, keeping right (S, Trail 814) steeply down (small logs, roots) with a creek crossing then 2 switchbacks. Soon after, hike down 3 additional switchbacks plus tight turns (views) and cross a tiny creek over double logs before descending 4 steep switchbacks S. Finally, move over another tiny creek (orange markers on large trees) to the Summit Loop intersection. Head left (S) almost 2 mi steeply to the TH.

27 | MOUNT ELLINOR

ELEVATION: 5944 ft; vertical gain of 3300 ft (2000 ft from Upper TH)

DISTANCE: More than 3 mi up from Lower TH, 6.25 mi round-trip (3.25 mi round-trip from Upper TH)

DURATION: 2–3 hours from Lower TH, 3–6 hours round-trip with lingering

DIFFICULTY: Strenuous (brief, congested, progressively steeper, solid trail when dry, glissade chute in spring when traction with ice axe helpful)

TRIP REPORT: One of the most rewarding hikes in the Olympics is this all-too-popular day trip, as you trudge up the occasionally mountain goat–lined steep slopes between your pillared rocky goal and nearby Mount Washington! Wildlife sightings may include chipmunks, marmots, mountain goats, cougar, and black bear. No fee or restroom at Mount Ellinor Lower TH; Northwest Forest Pass required, and a vault toilet is present at Mount Ellinor Upper TH.

TRAILHEAD: Mount Ellinor Lower TH or Mount Ellinor Upper TH. From Seattle, take I-5 S to exit 104 (Aberdeen/Port Angeles) onto US-101 N for 5.5 mi to exit 101 (Shelton/Port Angeles), and continue onto US-101 N for 28.5 mi to Hoodsport near milepost 332. Turn left on WA-119 N (no signal) for 8.75 mi winding to a stop sign, turn right on FR-24 (into gravel) for 1.5 mi, turn sharp left on FR-2419 (Big Creek Rd, washboard sections, narrow) for 4.5 mi, reaching the signed Lower TH with pull-in parking on the corner with 15 spots or so. For Upper TH, continue 1.75 mi, then turn

Nearby Mount Washington dwarfs hikers descending Mount Ellinor's rocky slopes.

sharp left (FR-2419-014) for 1 mi to the end.

From Portland, take I-5 N to exit 104 (Aberdeen/Port Angeles), then onto US-101 N, and follow as on previous page (110 mi, 2½ hours from Seattle; 160 mi, 3 hours from Portland).

ROUTE: The Upper TH begins around 1300 ft higher and cuts the overall mileage in half, and is not recommended considering the longer drive for most. You would take Upper Mount Ellinor Trail 812.1 less than 0.5 mi NW up steep switchbacks (fir, scree field) to the primary juncture with Trail 812.

From the Lower TH signage, follow Mount Ellinor Trail 812 (Lower Mount Ellinor Trail) across the dirt road S, passing the nearby kiosk on the second of 5 quick turns. Hike W (past Big Creek Camp Trail left, less than 0.25 mi up) easily up the wide ridge (big firs, pleasant grade) with 8 turns before you skirt the N side of the ridge (views), reaching the first of two junctures that bear right (E and SE, 1.5 mi up) to Upper TH. The primary one is 0.25 mi and 6 switchbacks farther NE (through steep forest).

Hike left (NW) from the Upper TH juncture (3860 ft) up the steeper S ridge of Mount Ellinor (Trail 812, worn track) with a turn then 15 switchbacks for almost 0.5 mi to the Winter Trail juncture (4350 ft) where you stay left (Summer Trail, 812). Ascend 11 switchbacks NW (mini clearing, views), then climb wooden steps steeply back into trees with 2 turns N (rocky, roots, wood steps) as the cliffy ridge breaks up somewhat. Enjoy the last micro-break with great views of the Cascades, the marine layer, Puget Sound, Hood Canal, and Cushman Lake! Climb the open rock field N (which is a snowfield until June most years) super-steeply (conveniently up stone stairs) to the treeless meadow above. Lumber up the visible path with wooden steps (rocky, grassy, lupine- and bear grass–covered steep meadow) to a notch in the saddle of the main ridge. Respect goats although hundreds have been relocated from the Olympics in recent years, lessening your chances of an encounter.

Hike very steeply 0.25 mi N up around 18 switchbacks (few scattered trees) past a few faint forks heading right (NE) toward Mount Washington. Keep left (W, Trail 812), winding up the final turns less than 100 yards to the boulder-laden apex of Mount Ellinor. Climb a few feet steeply but easily to the highest of the sharper rocks if you wish, but there are somewhat safer areas to hang out on as well. Watch for drop-offs while carefully investigating the summit block from different angles as you see N to Mount Pershing above Ellinor Lake (with Mount Olympus and more), W to nearby Copper Mountain, and NE along the craggy connecting ridge to Mount Washington!

28   LAKE OF THE ANGELS

ELEVATION: 4921 ft at lake, 5280 ft at saddle overlook; vertical gains of around 3500 ft for lake, plus 300 ft for overlook

DISTANCE: Almost 3.5 mi up, 7.5 mi round-trip (plus 1 mi round-trip for overlook)

DURATION: 3 hours up to lake, 6–8 hours round-trip total

DIFFICULTY: Very challenging (consistently very steep to lake basin and above it, not family-friendly, trekking poles recommended, tree roots, GPS device helpful, nearly impossible when wet, route-finding with snow until August)

TRIP REPORT: One of the most epic destinations within Olympic National Park is this ridiculously gorgeous high alpine basin between Mount Stone and even more prominent Mount Skokomish with Lake of the Angels as its centerpiece! The trail is named after Carl Putvin, a trapper who died in 1913 at only 21 while exploring the territory. One trail from the lake continues to a small saddle connecting the mountains above for jaw-dropping vistas! Wildlife sightings may include hawks, marmots, fox, deer, mountain goats, and black bear. No fee or restroom.

TRAILHEAD: Putvin TH. From Seattle, take I-5 S to exit 104 (Aberdeen/Port Angeles) onto US-101 N for 5.5 mi to exit 101 (Shelton/Port Angeles), and continue onto US-101 N for 42 mi. Turn left on FR-25 (Hamma Hamma River Rd, milepost

318) for 6.25 mi, turn right to stay on FR-25 into gravel at 1.75 mi (potholes), and go 3.75 mi more to the signed TH right with ample pull-in parking at left.

From Portland, take I-5 N to exit 104 (Aberdeen/Port Angeles), then onto US-101 N, and follow as on previous page (125 mi, 2½ hours from Seattle; 175 mi, 3 hours from Portland).

ROUTE: Take narrow Putvin Trail 813 (just W of Boulder Creek) N almost 0.5 mi (steadily steep, see cascades near mossy boulders) as you move steeper away from the water, heading W. Traverse only a bit easier (roots, rocks) as the trail commands your attention, crossing a ravine (at more than 0.75 mi up) to the visible trail (steep slope), then move down a switchback, crossing another ravine (with small creek possibly flowing) before walking up easier on the other side. Cross a third ravine (narrower, at 1 mi up), then hike steeper before easing W to an old road intersection (Boulder Creek Way Trail, 1.25 mi up). Turn left (SW) 75 ft down the old road to the signed Putvin Trail right (Lake of the Angels, 2 mi away) with the warm-up behind you!

Climb 5 tight switchbacks very steeply N, then hike NNW (micro-break) with the trail narrowing up 18 super-steep switchbacks and tight turns. Next, follow the nice tread up past a sign (Stoves Only...) in the middle of a tree on a spur E of Whitehorse Creek (3650 ft, almost 2 mi up). Continue N quite steeply (rockier) E of another creek feed, up several slightly overgrown turns (wildflowers, ferns, views, less trees), then hike tight turns and switchbacks to the bottom of the headwall (more than

Within the Valley of Heaven lies tough-to-reach Lake of the Angels under Mount Skokomish!

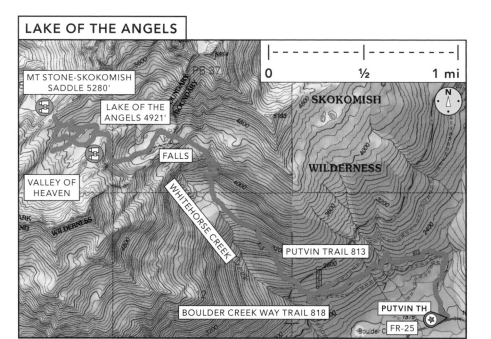

LAKE OF THE ANGELS

MT STONE-SKOKOMISH SADDLE 5280'

LAKE OF THE ANGELS 4921'

SKOKOMISH

FALLS

WILDERNESS

VALLEY OF HEAVEN

WHITEHORSE CREEK

PUTVIN TRAIL 813

BOULDER CREEK WAY TRAIL 818

PUTVIN TH

FR-25

2.25 mi up). The route steepens considerably (problematic if wet, icy, or snow covered) as you scramble Trail 813 NE away from the side creek ultra-steeply 30 ft or so up (thick roots, rocks, drop-offs), then judiciously pull yourself 25 ft over a steeply slanted rock slab where there's usually a fixed rope to pull yourself up. Move steeply up 2 switchbacks (see S over Jefferson Peak and Mount Pershing to Mount Rainier), lumbering to a faint fork on the mostly open slope at the top of the headwall (less than 2.5 mi up). See cairns and the orange arrow hanging from a tree pointing left (NW) toward Lake of the Angels.

Amble more easily NW (narrowly, trees) before moving down steeper briefly, then hike up steeply through a more open meadow (wildflowers, seasonal berries). Hear and see Whitehorse Creek Falls cascading below the basin belonging to Lake of the Angels. Enter a mostly flat, muddy, and rocky subalpine meadow (better views), heading WSW 100 yards, then move back into trees near the widening creek where the trail easily passes a tarn (Pond of the False Prophet) and other tarns in another flat clearing (spurs lead to camps). Walk right from the fork at the first tarn 75 ft, strolling left easily over an old log footbridge above the expanding creek (rocky mountains above), then continue briefly NW down a bit and across more flat meadows SW (tarns, tiny creek) on Trail 813. Soon, you move down from a small hill steeply to the right (W) through some trees a few feet into another little meadow (small sign Entering National Park, No Fires or Pets) at 4565 ft (3 mi from TH).

Begin the final grind less than 0.5 mi N to the lake basin, also known as the Valley of Heaven! In the first 0.25 mi hike WSW over Whitehorse Creek slyly before climbing very steep turns (last brush), followed by an easier traverse N toward the more obvious creek. It's all eye candy from there with several pillars of Mount Stone above. Turn W following Whitehorse Creek (past signage) through the flats 100 yards to Lake of the Angels (outlet, end of official trail). See Mount Skokomish and enjoy the splendor of the crystal-clear green lake with reflections of the quixotic boulder- and snow-covered landscape! Easily walk less than 0.5 mi around the small shallow lake in either direction from footpaths. The near side (left, E) is treeless with wildflowers. The right (W) side holds two parallel paths, one nearest the lake (smooth boulders, tiny cliff band) and one just above (N) on a small and fairly flat shelf (few trees, wildflowers, camping spots) with options from there either to continue around the lake, or head up the climber's trail toward Mount Skokomish, or up to the nearby saddle overlook.

For the beckoning overlook less than 0.5 mi away, cross the outlet of the lake near the logjam to the right (W), easily following the faint path around the N side. Hike right (NW) from the first immediate fork to the shelf and meadow just above the lake, holding the first of two routes to the saddle. The second is more of a bushwhack heading straight (SW) for an easier 100 yards farther before turning much steeper right (N) from a foggy juncture near a large rock. For the main route, fork right (NW) from the shelf, heading steeply WSW briefly. You'll reach another faint fork and rocky area in a clearing near a steeply sloped rock. Follow cairns right (N) from the fork (or go straight/W briefly to meet the bushwhack route), and move past the sloped rock a few feet without trouble, then climb the trail up the grassy hillside (wildflowers, mountain blueberries) very steeply. Meet the bushwhack route just before the saddle finishing NNW 100 yards or so as conditions may be cooler and windier than at the lake.

Lake of the Angels slips out of view from the partially tree-covered saddle where several flat boulders double as great picnic spots and overlooks. See North Cascades N of Mount Rainier, straight NE up to Mount Stone, NW to Mount Hopper, and the top of snow-covered Chimney Peak behind and between rugged Mount Duckabush and Mount Steel. Then look SW up the shoulder to the long steep glacier hanging under the majestic rocky massif of Mount Skokomish!

ELEVATION: 2804 ft on Mount Walker North Viewpoint; 2730 ft at Mount Walker South Viewpoint; vertical gains of 2000 ft directly for Mount Walker North Viewpoint, around 2200 ft for both viewpoints (no elevation change if driving to both upper THs)

DISTANCE: 2 mi hiking directly to Mount Walker North Viewpoint on Trail 894 from primary TH (plus 0.5 mi to Mount Walker South Viewpoint), 5 mi round-trip no loop; around 4.5 mi up Mount Walker Rd (FR-2730) to either viewpoint, 7.5 mi round-trip loop visiting both viewpoints

DURATION: 1–2 hours up directly, 3–4 hours round-trip for both viewpoints; 2 hours walking up Mount Walker Rd to Mount Walker South Viewpoint (first), 4–5 hours round-trip loop

DIFFICULTY: Strenuous (steadily steep Trail 894, narrow but well traveled, switchbacks, trekking poles helpful, traction required in winter, gentle grade on Mount Walker Rd, open to vehicles May to September)

TRIP REPORT: Busy late May into June when the especially colorful Pacific rhododendrons are blooming on the easternmost summit within the Olympic Peninsula. The steeper grind up the main trail breaks out of the forest near two separate old lookout sites, giving way to unique and contrasting vistas from Puget Sound and Seattle to Mount Constance within the Olympics. In winter with the road closed, a more peaceful direct route or loop can be enjoyed. Wildlife sightings may include hawks, grouse, and other birds, cougar, and black bear. No fees at THs, and restrooms are present at both upper THs.

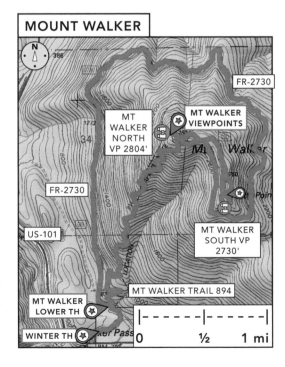

TRAILHEAD: Mount Walker Lower TH (and winter TH), or Mount Walker Viewpoints (upper THs). From Seattle, take I-5 S to exit 132B (for WA-16 W) in Tacoma for more than 0.5 mi, merge left onto WA-16 W (crossing Tacoma Narrows Bridge, no toll westbound) for 27 mi, then to WA-3 N (in Gorst) for 25 mi. Turn left over Hood Canal Bridge on WA-104 W for 11 mi and exit right for Center Rd (Chimacum/Quilcene). Turn right on Center Rd for 8.25 mi, turn left on US-101 S for 5 mi, turn left on Mount Walker Rd (FR-2730, gravel, brown signs for Mount Walker Viewpoint) past the nearby gate (closed in winter when you park before gate without blocking it) for only 0.25 mi, and find parking at left opposite the sign for the Lower (primary) TH. Continue 3.75 mi up FR-2730 (one-lane) for the upper THs to a signed juncture on the high ridge where turning left leads 100 ft to Mount Walker North Viewpoint parking circle (small), and turning right on FR-2730 leads 0.25 mi to Mount Walker South Viewpoint parking circle (small).

From Portland, take I-5 N to exit 104 (Aberdeen/Port Angeles) onto US-101 N for 5.5 mi to exit 101 (Shelton/Port Angeles). Continue on US-101 N for 60.5 mi, turn right on FR-2730, and follow as above (115 mi from Seattle, 2½ hours; 185 mi, 3 hours from Portland).

ROUTE: From the winter TH at the gate near US-101, walk 0.25 mi N along Mount Walker Rd to the primary TH on the right (before next gate, see end for winter route up road). For the direct route to Mount Walker North Viewpoint, take narrow Mount Walker Trail 894 briefly N (easy), then ascend 20 steep switchbacks and turns NNE (salal, Oregon grape) with Douglas firs blocking most views until the top of the steady but not unpleasant climb; there, increasingly more rhododendron will be blooming, showing a range of colors from pinks to purple and then some! You are dumped out to Mount Walker North Viewpoint from another switchback as you walk left within the open mound and fenced area, barely breaking out of the forest for the spectacle. Left (W) are distinctive Mount Constance, Warrior Peak, and others within the Olympic Range, and right (NE) past the tips of Quilcene and Dabob Bays and Puget Sound are Mounts Baker and Shuksan.

The trip would be incomplete without a visit to the South Viewpoint. Take the spur left (E) from Mount Walker North Viewpoint (opposite signed Trail 894) through the forest less than 100 ft (easy) over the inconspicuous summit to the parking circle. Continue E (thinning trees) passing the nearby signed juncture (Mount Walker Rd) as you amble over the high ridge before curving S (narrower) for 0.25 mi to the next traffic circle. Take either spur 100 ft S through a few trees to the smaller overlook area with a couple benches (short wooden fence, info sign). Closer to the SSW are tree-covered Mount Turner and Buck Mountain. Then look E over the bays, Hood Canal, and Puget Sound to Seattle, panning SE to Mount Rainier, Mount Adams, and Mount St. Helens! Return down either Trail 894 from the North Viewpoint or the main road from the high ridge juncture (easier but twice as long).

Social distancing becomes simpler on Mount Walker in winter with roads closed to vehicles!

For the clockwise loop (from winter TH), take Mount Walker Rd 1.5 mi N (traction with snow coverage helps), continuing 1 mi more NE then E up the steady incline (thick cedar, hemlock, very few views). The road bends SE then S (tall rhododendrons) as you pass a minor overgrown viewpoint on a wider curve, keeping S a bit longer. Bear W then N, easing under Mount Walker (fewer trees) as you approach the high ridge juncture. Head right for the South Viewpoint first.

ELEVATION: 5400 ft at Silver Lake, 6280 ft on Mount Townsend; vertical gains of 2300 ft for Silver Lake alone from Tubal Cain TH, 3300 ft for summit one way from Tubal Cain TH (3700 ft with Silver Lake too), around 4000 ft for loop (including Silver Lake)

DISTANCE: More than 4 mi directly to Silver Lake, 8.5 mi round-trip; 6 mi directly to the summit from Tubal Cain TH (via Silver Lakes Way Trail), 12 mi round-trip (8 mi or more to summit including Silver Lake, 14 mi round-trip); almost 10 mi round-trip loop (around 12 mi round-trip loop including Silver Lake)

DURATION: 2 hours to Silver Lake from Tubal Cain TH; 3½–4 hours to summit (5 hours to summit with Silver Lake first), 7–8 hours round-trip

DIFFICULTY: Mix of strenuous for Silver Lake from Tubal Cain TH (maintained trails, narrow, overgrown at times, briefly steep, family-friendly, trekking poles recommended) and very challenging for the summit/loop (long, very steep at times, popular S ridge route, ultra-steep for loop, rocky, very few drop-offs)

TRIP REPORT: The routes from the overly popular Mount Townsend THs are not listed here as we opt for a much-improved nature experience along Silver Creek to striking subalpine Silver Lake under majestic Hawk and Welch Peaks. Go-getters continue for views from Hood Canal farther into the Olympics. Even fewer diehards finish with a loop from the summit or subsummit down the wildly steep but scenic ridge to the less visited TH within the Silver Creek valley. Best late July to September to minimize the chance of running into snow, high water, mud, and bugs, and to maximize your time in the sun with an admirable wildflower show. No fees or restrooms, though there is an outhouse at Upper Dungeness TH 3 mi before the TH.

TRAILHEAD: Tubal Cain TH. See Mount Walker on page 91 for directions from Seattle to WA-104 W; stay on it more than 15 mi and keep right at fork, merging into US-101 N for 15.5 mi. Turn sharply left on gravel Louella Rd (no turning lane, easy to miss, signed for Dungeness Trail) for 1 mi, turn left on Palo Alto Rd (smooth gravel) for 5.5 mi, then fork right on signed FR-2880 for less than 0.25 mi, fork right (FR-2880, one-lane, gravel, steep) for 1 mi, passing Dungeness Forks Campground across the bridge over the Dungeness River (13.25 mi and 1 hour more). Continue (FR-2880) for 0.75 mi, then fork left into FR-2870 (signed for Dungeness Area Trails) for 2.5 mi, fork right (FR-2870) for 4.75 mi, and fork left (FR-2870, signed for Dungeness/Tubal Cain Trails) for 1.5 mi passing Upper Dungeness TH on the right after the bridges. Continue for about 3.5 mi to find a small parking lot at right signed for Tubal Cain Trail 840.

From Portland, take I-5 N to exit 104 (Aberdeen/Port Angeles) onto US-101 N 5.5 mi to exit 101 (Shelton/Port Angeles). Continue on US-101 N 90 mi and turn sharply left on Louella Rd, and follow as on previous page (140 mi, more than 3 hours from Seattle; 230 mi, 4½ hours from Portland).

ROUTE: From Tubal Cain TH, ignore Tubal Cain Trail (and others) and walk up the continuation of decommissioned FR-2870 around 150 ft, passing a signed juncture left (end of counterclockwise loop, Little Quilcene Trail 835). That grueling direct route to Mount Townsend up Dirty Face Ridge is not recommended in this direction (grades of 35–40%) and will make for a much briefer descent to end the day! Stay on the wide gravel road almost 1 mi SSE (good shot back to Tyler Peak) as you reach the trail sign left.

Begin S up maintained (narrow) Silver Lakes Way Trail, traversing effortlessly (E of Silver Creek, copious deadfall trailside) more than 1.25 mi to a faint juncture (old access trail) at a sizable (live) tree. Continue SSE 0.25 mi up through larger pines and fir (tons of roots, rocks, not bad when dry) as the route mellows back to Silver Creek, which is more like a babbling brook into August and September, as the mossy ground cover gives birth to tiger lilies, yarrow, and larkspur. Undulate through the forest (thick with undergrowth, avalanche lilies) to the flats by the lush creek. The route becomes super-steep 100 yards E up

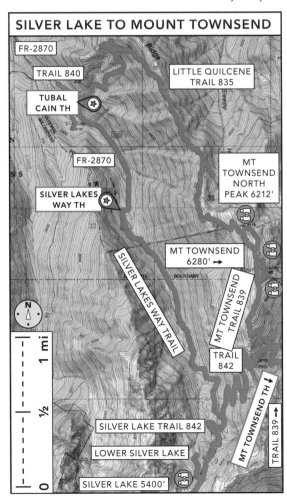

SILVER LAKE TO MOUNT TOWNSEND

FR-2870

TRAIL 840

TUBAL CAIN TH

LITTLE QUILCENE TRAIL 835

FR-2870

SILVER LAKES WAY TH

MT TOWNSEND NORTH PEAK 6212'

MT TOWNSEND 6280' →

SILVER LAKES WAY TRAIL

MT TOWNSEND TRAIL 839

TRAIL 842

MT TOWNSEND TH ↑

TRAIL 839 ↑

SILVER LAKE TRAIL 842

LOWER SILVER LAKE

SILVER LAKE 5400'

1 mi

½

0

Hikers make their way up the broad, wildflower-covered ridge to Mount Townsend surrounded by prominent Olympic peaks.

several tiny rocky turns before mellowing again as you go down (S, see Welch Peaks above). Cross Silver Creek (3 mi from Tubal Cain TH) to its W side in front of a mossy boulder, which is a simple hop from mid-July on but might require a 10- to 15-ft-long ford through rapid water May into July. Climb S steeply out of the creek bed following a rise easily and briefly before heading left back down to cross the creek again where possible. Walk with ease serenely through the flats (wildflowers) to the end of the trail as it breaks up near the intersection with Silver Lakes Trail 842 (unsigned, 3.25 mi from Tubal Cain TH).

For Silver Lake 1 mi away, continue right (SSW) on worn Silver Lake Trail 842 effortlessly up 5 switchbacks, including one crossing Silver Creek (where possible), as the route levels (fir, hemlock, wildflowers) to the N side of the lake at its tiny outlet. Explore spurs in either direction for ample views through the trees near the shore of the brilliant blue-green water! There's also the less traveled continuation of Trail 842 directly across the outlet down 300 ft (steep and narrow) for 0.25 mi (brushy, rocky) to Lower Silver Lake (much smaller). Great picnic locales are around Silver Lake from big boulders or from the wildflower-covered meadow S of the lake.

For Mount Townsend from the intersection area with Silver Creek Way Trail, head right/straight (NE) after the lake excursion on unsigned Trail 842 up 4 gentle switchbacks (thinning forest, see Silver Creek valley). Watch your step over loose gravel, crossing the relatively steep mountainside easily (wildflowers July into August) with even fewer trees up another switchback (look N to Strait of Juan de Fuca) before reaching a notch in the saddle between Welch Peaks and Mount Townsend (1.25 mi from Silver Lakes Way Trail). Take in the vistas, including Hood Canal and Mount Rainier, then continue NE down 4 quick switchbacks (larger trees) before traversing the steep slope briefly to the end of Trail 842 at a switchback on Mount Townsend Trail 839 (1.5 mi from Silver Creek Way Trail, 4.75 mi directly from Tubal Cain TH, 7 mi including Silver Lake).

Join the masses coming from the more popular TH keeping left (NW, onto Trail 839) for 0.5 mi up 7 moderately steep and steady switchbacks, passing colorful wildflowers (open terrain, see Mount Baker). Push steeper through switchback 8 to Mount Townsend's broad and nearly treeless S ridge before the trail eases. Hike rutted Trail 839 over loose gravel N for 0.25 mi (lupine, paintbrush, cobweb thistle, harebell, bistort, foxglove) to the clear summit spur juncture right. Take the spur steeper and narrower 100 yards NNE to the rock-covered climax (pretty safe) as you see down to Sequim, Port Townsend, Port Angeles, the Dungeness Spit, Seattle, the Hood Canal, Puget Sound, Salish Sea, Vancouver Island, the Strait of Juan de Fuca, and farther into the snow-capped Olympic range!

For the more difficult loop to Tubal Cain TH (3.75 mi away directly) or to check out Mount Townsend North Peak less than 0.5 mi away, walk N down the expansive Dirty Face Ridge following the path left from a nearby juncture (viewpoint spur) down a few feet to the main trail. Reach the Mount Townsend North Peak spur and take it or keep to Trail 839 just W of the high ridge as trails convene below the subsummit. For Mount Townsend North Peak (6212 ft), hike right (NNW) less than 0.25 mi up gravel easily to the boulders at the apex along the wide ridge and enjoy the somewhat more intense 360-degree panorama! Continue NW from the high point (mini loop, less than 0.25 mi to main trail) as you descend the path through rocky terrain, steeply hugging the scenic ridgeline 200 yards. The solid spur moves left (SSW) off the ridge quite steeply (scrubs) 100 yards or so to meet Trail 839 where you go right (E, just S of ridge).

Hike Trail 839 down 2 switchbacks through the wild landscape (scant trees, wildflowers) then head N through a rocky notch on the ridge crest (stone path) as the smooth but steep and narrow track reaches a junction (1.5 mi from Mount Townsend) on a switchback in the woods. Keep left (NW) from the switchback onto Little Quilcene Trail 835 down the ridgeline. The trail becomes easier for a moment, then you navigate the rocky ridge with brief ups/downs (second one steeper up 200 ft but with awesome views). The route narrows, easing a moment (overgrown with Oregon grape). At 1.25 mi from the rocky notch (above Trail 839 junction) the route steepens W of the ridge over the smooth trail, turning much tougher, rockier, and super-steep as you go NW to a switchback (less than 1 mi, 1000 ft, and ½ hour more to Tubal Cain TH). Descend ultra-steeply S (ferns, rhododendron, trees, few steps) with another solid switchback and continue SW (narrow, rocky) through the thick forest, following then crossing a mostly dry creek bed. Punishing Trail 835 is super-steep but doable for the final 200 yards to FR-2870 near the TH.

ELEVATION: 6434 ft on Maiden Peak, 6764 ft on Elk Mountain (6724 ft on West Elk Mountain); from Deer Park TH, vertical gains of 1535 ft for Maiden Peak, 2200 ft for Elk Mountain (2350 ft including Maiden Peak), more than 2500 ft for all; from Obstruction Point TH, vertical gains of 800 ft for Elk Mountain, around 1300 ft for all

DISTANCE: From Deer Park TH, almost 4 mi to Maiden Peak, 5.5 mi to Elk Mountain (6.25 mi to West Elk Mountain), 13.5 mi round-trip for all; from Obstruction Point TH, 2.25 mi to Elk Mountain, 4 mi directly to Maiden Peak, 9 mi round-trip for all

DURATION: From Deer Park TH, around 2 hours to Maiden Peak, 3–4 hours to Elk and West Elk Mountains, 6–8 hours round-trip for all; from Obstruction Point TH, around 1 hour to Elk and West Elk Mountains, 2 hours directly to Maiden Peak, 3–4 hours round-trip for all

DIFFICULTY: Strenuous to Maiden Peak (route-finding, scree, ups/downs, bushwhacking, steeper summit block), and very challenging for Elk and West Elk Mountains from Deer Park TH (long, much scree, route-finding, GPS device helpful, steep at times, bugs July into August)

TRIP REPORT: If you love to hike wide glacier-formed friendly ridges with magnificent views from the TH, then this is for you! Deer Park Rd takes people farther and higher than most into Olympic National Park's rain shadow NE of the Mount Olympus Massif. It rains 220 inches per year on Mount Olympus, but only 16 inches a few miles away in Sequim. Grand Ridge Trail (longest and highest continuous trail in the Olympics) runs 7.5 mi one way from Deer Park (with one of the best small campgrounds anywhere) to Obstruction Point TH at the beginning of Hurricane Ridge. Wildlife sightings may include ravens, hawks, eagles, the Olympic chipmunk, deer, cougar, and black bear. No fee, and a small outhouse is present.

TRAILHEAD: Deer Park TH (or Obstruction Point TH—see end of Route, and see Moose Peak to Grand/Badger Valleys Loop on page 104). From Seattle, take I-5 S to exit 132B (for WA-16 W) in Tacoma for more than 0.5 mi, and merge left onto WA-16 W (crossing Tacoma Narrows Bridge, no toll westbound) for 27 mi and onto WA-3 N (in Gorst) for 25 mi. Turn left over Hood Canal Bridge on WA-104 W for more than 15 mi, stay right at fork merging into US-101 N for less than 32 mi (35 mi to Port Angeles), turn right on Deer Park Loop for 0.5 mi, and turn right on Deer Park Rd for

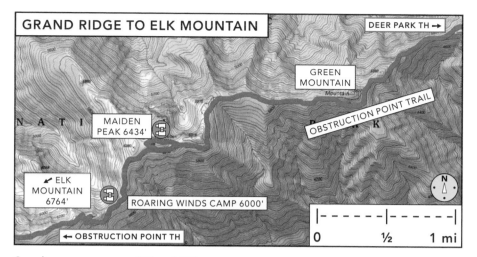

GRAND RIDGE TO ELK MOUNTAIN

DEER PARK TH →

GREEN MOUNTAIN

OBSTRUCTION POINT TRAIL

MAIDEN PEAK 6434'

ELK MOUNTAIN 6764'

ROARING WINDS CAMP 6000'

← OBSTRUCTION POINT TH

N

|- - - - -|- - - - -|
0   ½   1 mi

See also maps on pages 103 and 105.

16 mi (closed October to June, into gravel at 8.5 mi, one-lane at 10 mi, narrow, curvy, dusty, becomes steeper, washboard, 2WD okay, AWD preferred) to the signed TH fork. Drive right briefly down to the bottom of the side road and park on either side in the few pull-in spots (before the usually closed Ranger Station). The side road continues E up steeper rocky turns to Deer Park Rd closer to the CG.

From Portland, take I-5 N to exit 104 (Aberdeen/Port Angeles) onto US-101 N for 5.5 mi to exit 101 (Shelton/Port Angeles). Continue on US-101 N for almost 107 mi (110 mi to Port Angeles). Turn right on Deer Park Loop for 0.5 mi and follow as above (145 mi, more than 3 hours from Seattle; 240 mi, 4½ hours from Portland).

ROUTE: From Deer Park TH, take Obstruction Point Trail (toward Obstruction Point, also called Obstruction Peak) WSW down 350 ft gradually for more than 0.5 mi through the woods (views ahead) and over an unassuming tree-covered flat saddle. Hike steeper SW for more than 0.25 mi up S-turns on or near the ridgeline (old burn, lupine, paintbrush) before traversing more easily S of a ridge bump and Green Mountain as trees thin (more than 1.25 mi from TH). The trail undulates WNW up a brief steep pitch, then moves more easily to the ridge again (just W of Green Mountain) then down a bit on the N side, rolling through meadows (smaller pines, grasses, wildflowers) and through a large opening. Climb steeply W through even larger meadows (on ridgeline, no views outward, rockier) toward a lower summit of Maiden Peak, breaking out of the trees up the scenic meadow (rutted Obstruction Point Trail, almost 3 mi from TH).

Traverse left (S then W) of the lower summit for 0.75 mi to a saddle between summit bumps. You cross a rocky cliff line with ease, going WSW across a very steep hillside undulating down a bit (few trees) to a vague spur just S of the saddle W of Maiden Peak. It's possible to make a beeline for Maiden Peak from this first saddle by

Steep meadows approaching Maiden Peak's lowest summit reveal a taste of things to come with views soon expanding toward Mount Olympus!

hiking quite steeply W up the barely discernible bushwhack route judiciously (looser rocks) briefly, keeping left (S) of the cliffs without trouble. Continue W for the main saddle (easier) instead as you leave Obstruction Point Trail (6280 ft) just SE of the saddle for the faint climber's trail right (NW then NE) for 0.25 mi steeper and much rockier but not difficult (keep right/S of cliffy areas) to Maiden Peak. See deeper into the Olympics, including Mount Deception and N to the Canadian Rockies, Eldorado Peak in North Cascades, and SE to Mount Rainier! From the wide saddle W of Maiden Peak, find your way easily down to Obstruction Point Trail, turning right (SW) toward Elk Mountain.

Traverse SW down across a short rockier section past Maiden Peak West Peak to the ridgeline again. Hike S down 0.75 mi (see Elk Mountain) as Obstruction Point Trail steepens briefly (loose rock, few short trees) to the partially tree-covered pleasing saddle known as Roaring Winds Camp (6000 ft, 4.25 mi directly from TH). It's around 1 mi to the intersection with Elk Mountain Trail near the summit of the long but not protrusive mountain for the Olympics. Work through a tiny boulder field easily at Roaring Winds Camp, then traverse SW more steeply to the left (S) of the ridgeline (around cliffy area) through a weakness before climbing very steeply WNW across broken shale then through a small grove of trees. Move super-steeply N straight up open terrain (6 tight switchbacks) to the ridge (with 2 more switchbacks) out of the trees, then leave the crest left (S) briefly again (smaller rocky weakness), hiking steeply up loose scree to regain the high ridge (no more trees, unfolding views) with an easier stroll WSW to the signed intersection (6620 ft, Elk Mountain Trail left to Badger/ Grand Valleys, more than 5.25 mi directly from TH).

Look W to see most of the elusive Mount Olympus. Approaching the intersection, you'll see S to Lillian Ridge, Moose Peak, Grandview Peak, and the entirety of Grand Valley. From the signage, begin the partial bushwhack right (NW) steeply for 0.25 mi up to the highest of a few of Elk Mountain's summits. Hike 100 yards (scree, scant grass) to the high ridge, turning left (W) on the climber's trail over the wide rocky ridge with some blacker rock close to the top (old USGS benchmark). Views finally include Obstruction Point as well as the Bailey Range beyond Long Ridge to the W and all of Badger Valley with several colorful small tarns under Lillian Ridge!

For less traveled West Elk Mountain (or Obstruction Point TH 2 mi away), walk W from the intersection just SE of Elk Mountain on Obstruction Point Trail for 0.5 mi, easily descending a few feet as you round the corner and see the goal (a rocky red buttress) past a lingering snowfield. Walk NW up briefly around 75 ft past the black lichen-covered rocky mound (right of trail) for the best angle to approach West Elk Mountain (around 6 mi from TH). Obstruction Point is more in your face than ever as the remainder of Obstruction Point Trail (1.25 mi) moves W then cuts S across the rocky E face of the prominent landmark (easier) to a large saddle at Obstruction Point TH. For the bushwhack (no sign, 6525 ft) to West Elk Mountain, leave the main trail right (N, left of scree-filled, steeper slope) straight through grasses around 100 yards to a rockier area near a small saddle just W of the tiny peak. Enjoy the visual surprises from the saddle, finding the climber's trail NE up the steeper, boulder-covered small summit block slightly right then along the narrow loose ridge (wildflowers, drop-offs) to the top.

For Elk Mountain from Obstruction Point TH, hike 0.25 mi NNE on Obstruction Point Trail (crampons and ice axe required with snow into mid-August), easily passing the sign (right, Badger Valley) under Obstruction Point. Work 0.25 mi straight (N) to a small saddle, then traverse steeper NE and E for 0.75 mi to the unsigned turnoff for West Elk Mountain (before the black rock). Continue 0.75 mi E fairly easily to the signed intersection for Elk Mountain Trail where you bushwhack left (NW) for 0.25 mi to the rounded summit. Continue along Grand Ridge to Maiden Peak for around 2 mi one way (steep ups/downs). See Moose Peak to Grand/Badger Valleys Loop on page 104 for clues, including a loop down Elk Mountain Trail to Badger Valley then back up to Observation Point TH.

32 | BLUE MOUNTAIN

ELEVATION: 6007 ft; vertical gain of only 175 ft from the official TH (plus 450 ft or more from the CG)

DISTANCE: 0.5 mi round-trip loop (plus 1.5 mi round-trip from the CG)

DURATION: ½–1 hour round-trip

DIFFICULTY: Mix of easy (rocky, wide, drop-offs near top, popular) and moderate from the CG (slightly steeper, dusty, gravel, traffic)

TRIP REPORT: Blue Mountain and Obstruction Point are both barren bookends on Grand Ridge, with Green Mountain, Maiden Peak, and Elk Mountain between them in the mostly treeless range. Blue Mountain lies within Mount Olympus's rain shadow, receiving only 50 inches of rain per year. This briefest of walks just inside Olympic National Park (outside fee zone) is best near sunset July to September for wondrous vistas. See N to Port Angeles, Vancouver Island, Mount Baker, and Glacier Peak, then SE to nearby Tyler Peak, Baldy, Grey Wolf Ridge, Mount Walkinshaw, and Mount Clark! No fee or restroom.

TRAILHEAD: Blue Mountain TH. See Grand Ridge to Elk Mountain on page 98 for directions from Deer Park Rd for 16.5 mi to Deer Park CG. Continue left (N, AWD preferred) for 0.75 mi from the kiosk/pay station at the beginning of the CG, steeply up a rocky switchback on one-lane Deer Park Rd to the end at a small lot (145 mi, more than 3 hours from Seattle; 240 mi, 4½ hours from Portland).

From Blue Mountain to Baldy, Greywolf, and Mounts Walkinshaw, Clark, and Deception!

ROUTE: From Deer Park Campground, head right (N) from the fork up Deer Park Rd, winding steeply (wide, dirt, gradual) 0.75 mi to the small lot at the official TH. For Blue Mountain viewpoint, as a bonus, walk left (N) from the lot 100 ft on the spur trail through a few trees to a clearing on a rocky ridge section with an outstanding overlook.

For the counterclockwise summit loop, head right (S) promptly from the fork up Rain Shadow Loop Trail (self-guided interpretive tour, brochure, nine points of interest) as views persist curving left (N) steadily up the wildflower-splashed open slope over the wide trail to the highest ridge. Turn right around 15 ft to the actual top near some reddish rock. You'll enjoy a gorgeous panorama for minimal effort from the usually windy top! Finish the brief loop N down the ridgeline (somewhat steeper) past the Trail sign (bordering drop-offs, viewpoints) through a few trees, finishing with a painless walk W out of the thin woods to the parking lot.

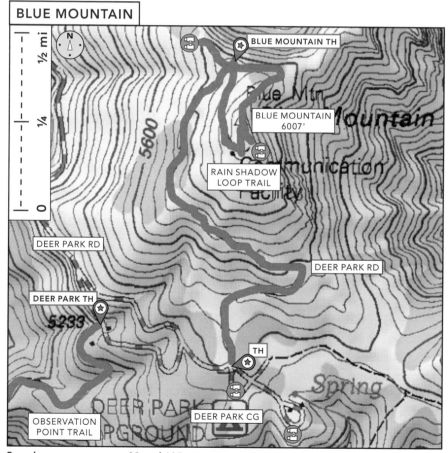

BLUE MOUNTAIN

See also maps on pages 99 and 105.

33 | MOOSE PEAK TO GRAND/BADGER VALLEYS LOOP

ELEVATION: 6753 ft on Moose Peak, 5400 ft at Gladys Lake; vertical gains of around 1400 ft one way directly to Moose Peak, at least 3600 ft for Moose Peak to Badger Valley loop (3100 ft for Moose Peak to Grand Valley loop), at least 3000 ft for valleys loop (no summit) including the lakes, and 2600 ft for the lakes via Grand Pass Trail one way

DISTANCE: 6 mi round-trip for Moose Peak, 11.5 mi round-trip for Moose Peak to Badger Valley loop (10.5 mi round-trip Moose Peak to Grand Valley loop), 12 mi round-trip for valleys loop (no summit) including the lakes, around 10.5 mi round-trip for the lakes via Grand Pass Trail

DURATION: 2 hours to Moose Peak, 7–9 hours round-trip including the valleys loop; 2½ hours one way to Gladys Lake via Grand Pass Trail, 5–7 hours round-trip

DIFFICULTY: Mix of strenuous for options without Moose Peak (ups/downs, family-friendly, well traveled, bugs through August, steeper at times) and very challenging for Moose Peak, including loops (scree, steep to super-steep, ups/downs, route-finding, drop-offs briefly, proper gear required through steep snowfields under Moose Peak and Obstruction Point until August, very long with loop, GPS device helpful)

TRIP REPORT: One of the most sought-after hiking objectives within Olympic National Park is the Grand and Badger Valleys loop! This is one of the oddest treks, however, in that it begins at a higher elevation along Lillian Ridge before descending 1500 ft into spectacular (partially forested) wildflower-covered valleys. Some stay on Lillian Ridge up to Moose Peak for riveting vistas then continue with a loop down to Grand Valley near Gladys Lake before moving down past Moose and Grand Lakes, finishing either up Grand Pass Trail or through Badger Valley! Many purchase a Wilderness Camping Permit online to camp, but several day hike options are also at your fingertips! Wildlife sightings may include hawks, eagles, marmots, deer, elk, and black bear.

Lillian, Hurricane, and Grand Ridges all converge at Obstruction Point with Elk Mountain and Maiden Peak attainable on Grand Ridge from Obstruction Point TH via Obstruction Point Trail (see Grand Ridge to Elk Mountain on page 98). National Park fee required (yourpassnow.com), and an outhouse is present.

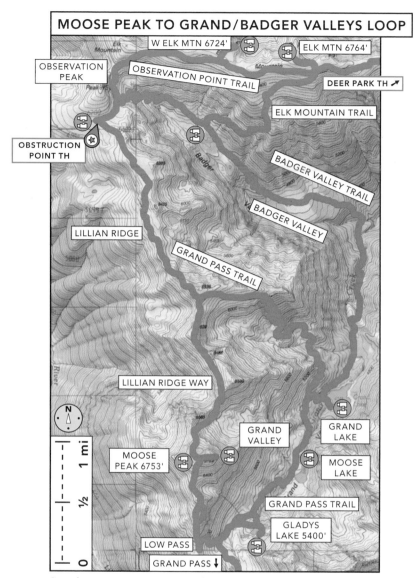

MOOSE PEAK TO GRAND/BADGER VALLEYS LOOP

W ELK MTN 6724'

ELK MTN 6764'

OBSERVATION PEAK

OBSERVATION POINT TRAIL

DEER PARK TH ↗

ELK MOUNTAIN TRAIL

OBSTRUCTION POINT TH

BADGER VALLEY TRAIL

BADGER VALLEY

LILLIAN RIDGE

GRAND PASS TRAIL

LILLIAN RIDGE WAY

GRAND VALLEY

GRAND LAKE

MOOSE PEAK 6753'

MOOSE LAKE

GRAND PASS TRAIL

GLADYS LAKE 5400'

LOW PASS

GRAND PASS ↓

1 mi

½

0

N

See also maps on pages 99 and 103.

TRAILHEAD: Obstruction Point TH. See Grand Ridge to Elk Mountain on page 98 for directions to Port Angeles. Keep right (into a one-way) on E Front Street 1 mi, turn left on N Race St (signal) for 0.75 mi and onto Mount Angeles Rd for less than 0.5 mi, and fork right onto Hurricane Ridge Rd (paved, narrowing, closed in winter—check ahead) for 17.5 mi to Hurricane Ridge Visitor Center (5.25 mi to Heart O' the Hills Ranger/Entrance Station). Turn sharply left from the start of the long parking lot on Hurricane Ridge for signed Obstruction Point Rd. Carefully drive 7.5 mi (gravel, one-lane, surprisingly smooth for the first 3.5 mi then slightly rougher and steeper,

Blue-green Moose Lake in the center of Grand Valley up to Grandview (Grand Pass) Peak.

2 switchbacks, drop-offs, no guard rails, 2WD okay, AWD preferred, views) to the end in the flats (165 mi, almost 4 hours from Seattle; 255 mi, 5 hours from Portland).

ROUTE: Begin the (counterclockwise) loops, direct route to Grand Valley, and the route to Moose Peak right of signed Obstruction Point Trail (to Grand Ridge and return spur from Badger Valley) on narrower Grand Pass Trail heading SSE with wide-open terrain (patches of snow) for less than 0.5 mi up the more defining Lillian Ridge. Rounded Moose Peak is spotted SE from the TH as well as nearby Elk Mountain NE, and to the W and SW is the Bailey Range to Mount Olympus! Walk easier SSE along the wide ridge for another 0.25 mi before descending right (SW) steeply for 8 switchbacks and tight turns (rock steps). Traverse left (S) down a bit more, then hike up (SE) easily back to the ridge crest (less than 1.25 mi from TH). Continue SE up Lillian Ridge (easy, colorful tarns in meadows left) a bit steeper before traversing right (W) around a sizable ridge bump (easier) to the signed juncture (pointing left down Grand Pass Trail, 6440 ft, more than 1.5 mi from TH).

Hike down Grand Pass Trail to Grand Valley as most do, or continue following Lillian Ridge to Moose Peak. To go directly to Grand Valley (Grand, Moose, and Gladys Lakes), continue straight (E), traversing down less than 0.5 mi before moving steeply SSE for 1 mi down around 20 switchbacks and turns (few trees, then small meadows, views). Finish across a side creek, easing less than 0.5 mi S to a major intersection in Grand Valley (4955 ft). For Grand Lake and/or Badger Valley, take the signed trail left (E, Grand Lake Trail), and for Gladys Lake head right (SSW) up Grand Pass Trail

1.25 mi (passing Moose Lake, see ahead for clues).

For Moose Peak from the juncture on Lillian Ridge, hike right (S) past the sign onto Lillian Ridge Way (not officially maintained) up the rocky thin fin of a ridgeline (steeper, brush), then cruise more easily down to a saddle (2 mi from TH). See all of Moose Peak's N face ahead with its lingering snowfield and the sawtooth ridge you will follow briefly. Traverse right (W) of two sizable ridge mounds, walking SE then S across steep scree fields to the start of the jagged ridge. Work your way SW (steeper, looser) and go right (W) around or over small gendarmes a few feet to an obvious notch where you descend left (S) of the spiky ridgeline (2.5 mi from TH). Descend the rocky path very steeply ESE 75 ft over the open slope, then traverse SE briefly (wildflowers) before ascending super-steeply up 4 tight switchbacks (passing below the ridge gendarmes). Trudge even steeper (loose scree, some prefer snow travel here before August) WNW directly to the ridge for better tread. Continue S up Lillian Ridge Way steeper just right (W) of the crest with easier walking, approaching the nearby widening top of Moose Peak.

From the half rock circle, see SE down to smallish Gladys Lake up to Grand Pass and Grandview Peak (6701 ft). Beyond to the SE and S are Mount Walkinshaw, Mount Deception, the Cameron Glaciers, and Sentinel Peak, with the Mount Olympus Massif past the Lillian River valley to the WSW (spot Lake Lillian). For the very best overlook of the day, however, continue E down the rocks semi-steeply for 100 yards (off-trail, simple) until you see Grand, Moose, and Gladys Lakes all in one awe-inspiring vista!

Return to the TH or continue the valley loop left (SW) from the broken shale on Moose Peak down Lillian Ridge Way very steeply (loose pebbles, steep slope), then walk over a mini saddle that undulates SSE a few feet easily (wider scenic ridgeline) to a notch with a large rocky bump on each side of the ridge (almost 0.5 mi from Moose Peak). From the S side of the notch, a boulder garden confuses some hikers on the main route, as some are pulled left (SE) down a bushwhack route that parallels just below the ridgeline (somewhat rougher) a couple hundred yards to the crest again. The preferred Lillian Ridge Way moves a few feet up right (SW) from the rock garden to the pronounced trail just right (W) or on the ridgeline itself (heading S). Both routes meet briefly, continuing steeply S down to a decent saddle (Low Pass, 5950 ft), where you leave the ridge (more than 0.25 mi from boulder garden). Move left (E) down Lillian Ridge Way from the switchback then, taking 2 more steep switchbacks (vegetation, wildflowers, see cool rock formations up left) before the trail becomes narrower and enters Grand Valley to the unsigned juncture with Grand Pass Trail at a tiny creek (5555 ft, more than 0.25 mi from Low Pass, almost 4.5 mi on counterclockwise loop over Moose Peak).

See and hear cascades to the right as you meander left (NE) on Grand Pass Trail easily for less than 0.5 mi (small tarns) through a larger meadow to the unsigned junctures for Gladys Lake (best of all area lakes) before and also just into the trees (1.5 mi and 1 hour from Moose Peak on the loop). Turn right (SSE) on Gladys Lake Camp

Spur through the meadow (watch for wildlife), keeping left (N) of the glassy shallower lake extension past a few trees and a post in a clearing. Walk right down a few feet to the water's edge near the outlet creek. The deeper, main colorful lake meets at the outlet with the best viewpoint 75 ft farther SW across the boulder field (no trail, E of Gladys Lake) to capture perfect reflections of Moose Peak on Lillian Ridge!

Turn right (NE) on Grand Pass Trail from the Gladys Lake spurs (past campsites), moving down Grand Valley (wildflower-lined meadows, few trees) over the rocky route steadily but not steep. Continue down rock steps then steeper steps and 4 switchbacks NE to Moose Lake (0.5 mi from Gladys Lake spurs), easing nearest the water. Head N on the W side past a crossroads across a creek (short log) then another juncture, keeping right past yet another juncture (privy at left). Keep straight (NNE, avoiding other spurs) to the N end of Moose Lake (6 mi on counterclockwise loop), where walking 40 ft down the spur right takes you to a nice view past the logjam of the long lake up to the majestic ridge extending NE from Grand Pass and Grandview Peak. Continue for less than 0.5 mi N, as the path undulates down more easily across creeks (meadow, trees) to a major intersection in a large meadow. For the direct route to the TH, fork left up Grand Pass Trail (see first paragraphs, reversing the description almost 2 mi steeply NW to the juncture with Lillian Ridge Way, and beyond).

For Grand Lake and Badger Valley, fork right on Grand Lake Trail for almost 0.25 mi E down 3 steeper switchbacks to a signed juncture on the W side of Grand Lake at what would be switchback 4 near a scenic inlet creek. Follow Grand Lake Trail right (ESE) for 0.25 mi, including over Grand Creek and others to the S end of the rather big lake for another fascinating perspective! Then walk right (NNE) from the switchback and log over the creek onto Badger Valley Trail, passing the tree-choked lake on its W side; the easy trail narrows as you pass a spur (roots, high brush). Cross Grand Creek over a log footbridge (almost 0.5 mi from Grand Lake Trail), hiking N up then down 9 switchbacks into trees (rockier, across tiny creeks) before the trail undulates crossing Grand Creek again (log bridge with wire handrail). Enjoy the friendlier grade (endless huckleberries, others in September) winding N down with 2 switchbacks (mossy forest) to a log bridge (questionable handrail) over picturesque Badger Creek (4050 ft, more than 1.5 mi from Grand Lake Trail, 3 mi more to TH).

Ascend Badger Valley Trail NW through the largest Douglas firs of the hike! Moss covers everything near the creek as you steadily climb (roots) up 8 increasingly steeper switchbacks and turns, easing W near the ninth turn (almost 0.5 mi from creek crossing). Walk W through long, narrow open meadows, even moving down a tad (see Obstruction Peak ahead with Grand and Lillian Ridges on each side of the valley) before hiking NW along the edge of another meadow back into the woods between hemlocks steadily uphill. Cross a small creek and climb 7 steep switchbacks (NW) into trees up a slight rise. Hop a minute creek (5050 ft) flowing from Elk Mountain, then hike steeper NW up S-turns breaking out of the trees for good. Badger Valley Trail eases then winds a bit steeper up slightly overgrown lush meadows before leveling to the signed intersection with Elk Mountain Trail (5350 ft, almost 2 mi from creek crossing at bottom of Badger Valley). That route moves steeply around 1.5 mi right (NE) up to Obstruction Point Trail near Elk Mountain.

Continue straight (NW, watching for Olympic marmot) traversing the high steep meadows (wildflowers, bordering trees) easily W to the base of the final turns under Obstruction Point. Hike steadily up 16 tight switchbacks W (semi-loose, smooth scree, western pasqueflower) to the juncture with Obstruction Point Trail. Walk left (SSW) on wider flatter Obstruction Point Trail for 0.25 mi to the TH.

34 | LAKE ANGELES

ELEVATION: 4300 ft at the lake, 4760 ft at jagged rocky overlook; vertical gains of 2450 ft and 2900 ft, respectively

DISTANCE: 3.75 mi to the end of the trail W of Lake Angeles or the overlook, 7–7.5 mi round-trip (8–8.5 mi for both)

DURATION: 1½ hours up (½ hour more to overlook), 3–4 hours round-trip total

DIFFICULTY: Mix of strenuous for the lake (steady steep, tree roots okay, family-friendly, popular on weekends) and very challenging for the overlook (route-finding, scrambling, very steep, drop-offs, brief exposure)

TRIP REPORT: On the northern edge of Olympic National Park (just outside fee zone) is this local's romp to a remarkable subalpine lake with an option to hike above it onto large boulders covering a rugged shoulder with perches and views from the colorful lake to nearby Port Angeles, the Strait of Juan de Fuca, and Vancouver Island! Wildlife sightings may include birds of prey, mountain goats, and black bear. Possible year-round with proper gear, but usually snow-free July to October. No fee or restroom.

TRAILHEAD: Heart O' the Hills TH. See Grand Ridge to Elk Mountain on page 98 for directions to Port Angeles. Keep right (into a one-way) on E Front Street for 1 mi, turn left on N Race St (signal) for 0.75 mi and onto Mount Angeles Rd for less than 0.5 mi, fork right onto Hurricane Ridge Rd (paved, narrowing, closed in winter—check ahead) for 5 mi, and turn right just before Heart O' the Hills Ranger/Entrance Station on the driveway signed Trailheads-Heather Park/Lake Angeles 500 Yards to the end (90 mi, 2½ hours from Seattle; 235 mi, 4–4½ hours from Portland).

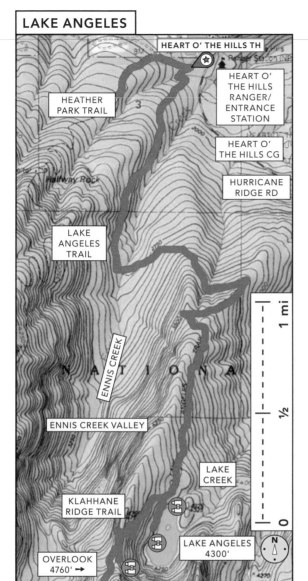

LAKE ANGELES

HEART O' THE HILLS TH

HEART O'
THE HILLS
RANGER/
ENTRANCE
STATION

HEATHER
PARK TRAIL

HEART O'
THE HILLS CG

HURRICANE
RIDGE RD

LAKE
ANGELES
TRAIL

1 mi

½

ENNIS CREEK

0

N A T I O N A

ENNIS CREEK VALLEY

LAKE
CREEK

KLAHHANE
RIDGE TRAIL

LAKE ANGELES
4300'

N

OVERLOOK
4760' →

ROUTE: Begin right of the kiosk SW on Lake Angeles Trail turning over Ennis Creek W Fork (easily) before walking up 2 sweeping turns (ferns, mossy flora, larger trees). Ascend 2 quick switchbacks (0.5 mi from TH), hiking 0.5 mi or more S, and cross an old footbridge and then a short log bridge over mossy Ennis Creek. Continue ENE up a slightly overgrown clearing with a switchback as you cross a knoll (felled trees lining woods, less brush). Enjoy breaks in the pitch SE up the traverse (roots, ample shade), passing large boulders, then ascend 2 quick switchbacks heading SW (steeper, rockier) up a rise with S-turns before easing (2 mi from TH). Hike 0.25 mi (passing No Open Fires sign) to a switchback, then climb SE and S steeper another mile with a switchback then an easier turn as the route levels S to an unsigned juncture in the woods (almost 4300 ft, overlook right, less than 3.5 mi from TH).

Lake Angeles Trail continues straight (S) easily for less than 0.25 mi to the first spurs for the lake, the briefest one is near huge boulders along the glassy blue-green water. You should also work right (SSW) on the lake's W side over the narrower trail for another 0.25 mi to its official end for the closest angle of the island before deciding whether or not to swim out to it!

For the overlook after visiting the lake, head up Klahhane Ridge Trail, turning sharply left (SW) steadily steep then very steep, as the path narrows (looser gravel).

Continue SW up 5 tight switchbacks to the thin shoulder, then 2 more quick switchbacks to a higher locale on the shoulder (almost 0.5 mi from lake juncture). Leave Klahhane Ridge Trail before it continues down on the W side of the rugged shoulder from a tiny saddle (or follow it quite steeply to more overlooks or the high ridge). You could practice your scrambling skills right (N) a few yards off-trail, bouldering to Point 4795, but the unobstructed overlook for this jaunt is left (S) from the main trail only around 150 ft away. Steeply ascend the faint spur (small trees, brush) carefully over thin boulders on the crest just above the trees. Then either walk the knife's edge on top of the crest for 30 ft (exposed), or follow a somewhat safer natural line just right (W) below the rocky crest the same distance to better ground near a few choice picnic spots with a clear shot down to the lake (and island), out to Puget Sound, and straight up the shoulder to precipitous Klahhane Ridge and aptly named Rocky Peak. It's very calming with no sounds coming from the Lake Angeles basin and a distant waterfall heard from nearby Ennis Creek valley. An absolute gem!

Sumptuous Lake Angeles (with island) reflects statuesque mountains up to Klahhane Ridge as you inspect lakeside viewpoints.

ELEVATION: 920 ft at Marymere Falls, 2050 ft at first viewpoint on Mount Storm King Trail, 2700 ft at primary viewpoint, 3130 ft atop ridge bump; vertical gains of 250 ft, 1450 ft, 2100 ft, and 2550 ft, respectively

DISTANCE: 2 mi round-trip for falls alone, 4 mi round-trip for first viewpoint, 5.5 mi round-trip for primary viewpoint, 6.5 mi round-trip for ridge bump (plus less than 1 mi round-trip for falls)

DURATION: 1 hour round-trip for falls alone; ¾ hour directly up to the first viewpoint; 1 hour or more up to the primary viewpoint; 2 hours up to the ridge bump, 3 hours round-trip (plus ½ hour round-trip with falls)

DIFFICULTY: Mix of moderate for falls (brief, steeper near falls, possible year-round), strenuous for first viewpoint (family-friendly, steep, switchbacks, drop-offs), and very challenging (extremely steep, very narrow ridge at times, not possible when wet, loose rock, avid hikers only, drop-offs, scrambling, some exposure past End of Maintained Trail sign, Class 3/4 to ridge bump, bugs including wasps July through late August)

TRIP REPORT: Marymere Falls Nature Trail holds an adorable little mossy loop around the falls while the rest is super easy. There's nothing easy about Mount Storm King Trail! The route is ultra-steep with set ropes in several sections to aid hikers up to staggering overlooks from the narrow ridge. Where most people stop and call the summit or fake summit is actually neither as there are many higher bumps and hills (not recommended) following the W ridge to Mount Storm King (4537 ft). No fee, and flush toilets are present.

TRAILHEAD: Mount Storm King TH (Storm King Ranger Station). See Grand Ridge to Elk Mountain on page 98 for directions to Port Angeles. Keep right (into a one-way) on E Front Street for 1.5 mi, and turn left (signal) on US-101 W/N Lincoln St for 1 mi. Curve right from the E Lauridsen Blvd intersection (signal) to stay on US-101 W for 19 mi, and turn right on Lake Crescent Rd (milepost 228) then right again from the crossroads into the large parking circle, or drive straight from the crossroads briefly to the end into a backup lot at Mount Storm King Pier (160 mi, 3 hours from Seattle; 250 mi, 4½ hours from Portland).

ROUTE: For both routes, walk past the kiosk and sign moving behind Storm King

Ranger Station (usually closed) over the sidewalk onto Marymere Falls Nature Trail. Head through trees E 100 yards, then walk S through a narrow tunnel under US-101. Stroll SW easily (ferns, mossy trees, large Douglas fir and others) to a signed juncture at almost 0.5 mi from the TH (0.5 mi right to Lake Crescent Lodge). Keep left (SE) on Marymere Falls Nature Trail briefly (hear Barnes Creek) to the signed intersection for Mount Storm King Trail at a huge boulder (more impressive old-growth fir and cedar). See next page for falls.

Hike left of a large mossy boulder E very steeply up Mount Storm King Trail through the woods as stout trees are replaced by Pacific madrones and manzanitas up 15 true switchbacks for almost 1.5 mi on or just S of the narrowing ridge to the first small overlook from a rocky point (see across Lake Crescent to Pyramid Peak). Return easily.

Climb steeper carefully E for less than 0.5 mi up two distinct areas with ropes (gloves help); don't depend on them but use as guides (more helpful on descent). Arrive past a few trees on the thin ridge (views, drop-offs) near the End of Maintained Trail sign. Stay on the bushwhack path for 0.25 mi E, being mindful up two more roped areas to the primary larger rocky viewpoint left off-trail. Nothing obstructs the bright blue lake far below, or Pyramid Peak, Mount Muller, or the Strait of Juan de Fuca!

Hike the narrow rocky ridge fin E, finding the path down to a small saddle before the ridge bump overlook, which is half tree-covered (left, N side) and half precipitous rocky cliff (right, S side). Grind up the steep loose rock along the obvious route on the hill then from the open overlook, gaze down to Pyramid Peak across the deep blue water! See the extreme ridge down to the parking lots at the Ranger Station, as well as up the ridge past several more tedious obstacles to the true summit! Return methodically for 2.75 mi down to the Marymere Falls Nature Trail.

Short-and-sweet family jaunt to Marymere Falls is not to be missed when visiting Lake Crescent within Olympic National Park!

For the falls, walk left (ESE) from Mount Storm King Trail with ease less than 0.25 mi to the next signed juncture, turning right (S, opposite Barnes Creek Trail) on Marymere Falls Nature Trail across Barnes Creek (solid bridge) at a beachy area. Head right (W) over Falls Creek (smaller bridge with tiny cascade), then climb stairs up 3 steeper switchbacks to the mini-loop trail. Proceed left (S, clockwise loop, this side prone to closure) for 0.25 mi narrowly with instant views of the minor but lovely waterfall (90 ft in two drops, slows to trickle by autumn) and small pool within a mossy grotto. Stairs with some fencing lead steeper to the end of the spur. Turn left up the primary trail for the immediate main overlook of the misty cascade, then descend the W side 0.25 mi somewhat steeper N (rocks, roots) before finishing easier to the TH.

36 | PYRAMID PEAK

ELEVATION: 3100 ft; vertical gain of 2500 ft

DISTANCE: More than 3.5 mi up, 7.25 mi round-trip

DURATION: 2–2½ hours up, 4–5 hours round-trip

DIFFICULTY: Strenuous (steady grade, defined trail, slightly monotonous, loose at times, switchbacks, trekking poles helpful, bugs May into July)

TRIP REPORT: Farthest N in Olympic National Park, the old lookout cabin on Pyramid Peak was built during World War II for its great vantage point and relative safety being surrounded by lake on three sides, but it was decommissioned a few years later when the war ended. Only a hollow shell without doors or windows remains, but views persist from Lake Crescent, Lake Sutherland, Mount Storm King, and the Strait of San Juan de Fuca to Vancouver Island. No fee, and an outhouse is present at North Shore Picnic Area.

TRAILHEAD: Pyramid Peak TH or North Shore Picnic Area. See Grand Ridge to Elk Mountain on page 98 and Marymere Falls & Mount Storm King Trail on page 112 for directions almost 26 mi past Port Angeles on US-101 W. Turn right beyond Lake Crescent (milepost 221) on Camp David Jr Rd (passing Fairholme CG, roughly paved, narrow) for 1.5 mi, then into smooth dirt/gravel for 1.5 mi more to find the TH at left with small pullouts on both sides (near large yellow pedestrian crossing signs) and North Shore Picnic Area 200 ft farther right (170 mi, more than 3 hours from Seattle; 260 mi, 5 hours from Portland).

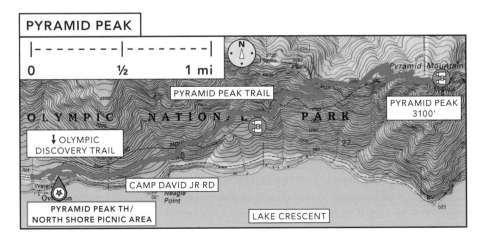

Lake Crescent showcasing Pyramid Peak and Mount Storm King from the pier at Fairholme Campground and picnic area.

ROUTE: From the picnic area (just above the lake), walk left of the outhouse up the spur WNW for 150 ft, crossing Camp David Jr Rd to Pyramid Peak TH. There is some cool rockwork to begin (signed Spruce RR/Pyramid Peak Trails) 100 ft up 2 easy paved switchbacks to a junction with Spruce Railroad Trail/Olympic Discover Trail (multi-use wide track runs almost 130 mi from Port Townsend to La Push). Cross to signed Pyramid Peak Trail, following the fairly easygoing traverse ENE up, passing some good-sized trees. After 1.25 mi up, cross a tiny creek then 0.25 mi farther a dry, steeper draw. Shortly after, cross a small creek cutting through the washed-out trail section, then move over two large (cut) logs just W of the infamous rockslide area at 1.75 mi up (1600 ft).

Carefully cross the long, steep old rockslide (regraded every few years) 150 ft SE down the narrower path with loose stones (great views) back into trees. Ascend 4 steeper switchbacks N, then duck under a set of huge fallen trees before traversing more easily ENE. At less than 2.5 mi up, steeply ascend 6 tight switchbacks 0.25 mi N to the high ridge (2400 ft), hiking E a bit easier (abundant flora). Walk slightly left (N) of the ridgeline then straight up it for 2 steep turns before moving left (NE) of the crest again (large Douglas fir and others). At 3 mi up, climb 6 quick switchbacks steeper SE to the ridgeline, easing somewhat ENE. Move just left again then (steeper) up 2 switchbacks onto the ridge in the trees. Work SE just left (N) of the thin ridge or on it (old-growth fir, Oregon grape, paintbrush, views) from Pyramid Peak Trail (above rocky outcrops), finishing ESE through trees a bit steeper for 100 ft or so to the dilapidated lookout. Walk past the building 30 ft or so S (nearest a cable tethered to a tree stump) for a grander viewpoint through fewer trees (drop-offs). Look SW and SE toward Mount Storm King, Mount Baldy, Lizard Head Peak, Aurora Peak, and Sourdough Mountain across the lake. Lake Crescent's deep-azure blue has never looked better!

37 | SOL DUC FALLS

ELEVATION: 2050 ft at the high point (1860 ft at falls); vertical gain of around 200 ft

DISTANCE: 2 mi round-trip

DURATION: ½–1 hour or so round-trip

DIFFICULTY: Easy (very brief ups/downs, wide, trendy, drop-offs near falls)

TRIP REPORT: Simple family walk to the most iconic waterfall in the Olympics! Pass through a giant ancient forest to the top-notch display off the Sol Duc River. National Park fee required (yourpassnow.com), and restrooms are present.

TRAILHEAD: Sol Duc TH. See Grand Ridge to Elk Mountain on page 98 and Marymere Falls & Mount Storm King Trail on page 112 for directions. Then 28 mi past Port Angeles on US-101 W, turn left on Sol Duc-Hot Springs Rd for almost 14 mi, winding to the end (passing an Entrance Station promptly, Eagle Ranger Station at 11.75 mi, Sol Duc Hot Springs and Resort at 12 mi, Sol Duc Campground at 12.5 mi, open late March into mid-October, same as the road). Find a long parking area and circle which fill quickly on summer weekends (180 mi, 3½ hours from Seattle; 275 mi, 5 hours from Portland).

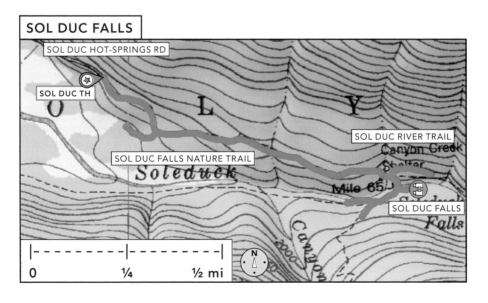

ROUTE: Follow Sol Duc Falls Nature Trail (kiosks, signage) SE down a few steeper stairs then very easily through tall old Douglas fir, western hemlock, and red cedar. Less than 0.25 mi from the TH, cross a tiny creek (passing campground spur right) and walk up 0.25 mi ESE (wide stairs), crossing a more scenic mossy stream (footbridge), then continue up easily across two smaller creeks before moving downward as the route levels ESE across two more minuscule creeks and passes a signed fork. Continue right (SE, mossy historic cabin/shelter left), walking down a few feet and across the larger bridge over Sol Duc River with the falls just upstream (48 ft in two drops split by boulders into three or four streams ripping forcefully down the rock as they meet again in a narrow gorge)! Walk left (E) from the juncture after the bridge to the viewing platform; the vantage point changes depending on the

Sol Duc River splits exquisitely into quintessential Sol Duc Falls!

spray and time of day. Be cautious beyond the wooden fencing with slippery tree roots closer to the water.

SNOQUALMIE REGION–ALPINE LAKES WILDERNESS

"It isn't enough to have just a few righteous people talking about preserving trails. We need a lot of them."

TRAIL

ELEVATION: 450 ft at Snoqualmie Falls Upper Observation Deck, 150 ft at Lower Falls Viewpoint; vertical gain of around 50 ft from either TH to each waterfall (plus 300 ft for Snoqualmie Falls Trail between viewpoints)

DISTANCE: 0.25–0.5 mi round-trip from either TH directly; 0.75 mi one way on Snoqualmie Falls Trail, more than 1.5 mi round-trip max

DURATION: 5 minutes from either TH to view the falls, ½–1 hour round-trip with lingering (plus 1 hour round-trip with Snoqualmie Falls Trail from either TH)

DIFFICULTY: Mix of easy (briefest walk from either TH, paved upper trails, stairs, drop-offs, upper and lower observation decks from primary TH are ADA accessible, boardwalk may be slippery to Lower Falls Viewpoint, spray) and moderate on Snoqualmie Falls Trail (fairly steep, gravel, wide)

TRIP REPORT: One of the Pacific Northwest's most distinguished waterfalls sees more than 1.5 million visitors per year as an easy roadside stop without any work! The falls are a powerful force in the spring under heavy runoff as well as on the occasional winter's day. Day-use parking fee ($5) required closest to the falls, free at all other areas, and restrooms are present at both THs.

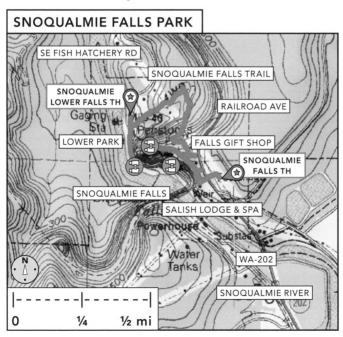

SNOQUALMIE FALLS PARK

SE FISH HATCHERY RD

SNOQUALMIE FALLS TRAIL

SNOQUALMIE LOWER FALLS TH

RAILROAD AVE

Gaging Sta

LOWER PARK

FALLS GIFT SHOP

SNOQUALMIE FALLS TH

SNOQUALMIE FALLS

SALISH LODGE & SPA

Powerhouse

Substa

Water Tanks

WA-202

N

SNOQUALMIE RIVER

0   ¼   ½ mi

Mist rises from Snoqualmie Falls with Salish Lodge under ominous skies.

TRAILHEAD: Snoqualmie Falls TH or Snoqualmie Lower Falls TH. From Seattle, take I-90 E to exit 25 (for WA-18 W), turn left onto WA-18 E (Snoqualmie Pkwy) for 3.75 mi, turn left on Railroad Ave (WA-202 W) for 0.5 mi, and turn right after the covered walkway (above) into the first of three large parking lots. For the closest (fee) lot, turn left after the covered walkway from Railroad Ave then quickly right into the small lot. For Snoqualmie Lower Falls TH from the primary TH, continue on Railroad Ave (WA-202 W) less than 1.5 mi, turn left on easy-to-miss 372nd Ave for 0.25 mi (narrowing), and fork left on SE Fish Hatchery Rd for less than 0.5 mi to the end at a long parking circle.

From Portland, take I-5 N to exit 142A (Auburn), merge onto WA-18 E for 27 mi to Snoqualmie Pkwy under the Interstate, and follow as above (28 mi, ½ hour from Seattle; 180 mi, 3 hours from Portland).

ROUTE: From the primary TH, walk WSW through the partially covered walkway 200 ft to the cliff-lined overlook trail (nearest Salish Lodge & Spa). Turn right (NW) on the wide paved sidewalk for 200 ft (down stairs) easily to the Upper Observation Deck. Other paved trails bypass stairs for those inclined (see signs that say No Drones or UAV Flying Permitted). It's another 100 ft down steeper stairs to the smaller Lower Observation Deck (spray-prone) while you gaze down to the majestic waterfall (268 ft high, 50–100 ft wide)!

Between observation decks Snoqualmie Falls Trail heads E a few feet then left

(N, signed Trail 0.5 Mile), passing a large kiosk describing the trail to Lower Falls Viewpoint. Cross the service road and walk N steeply down the wide gravel track, winding past interpretive markers noting local wildlife and flora including huckleberry, Oregon grape, thimbleberry, salmonberry, red elderberry, western sword fern hemlock, maple varieties, western red cedar, and Douglas fir. Move under power lines, finishing SW on an easier straightaway down to the junctures at Lower Falls TH in Lower Park.

From Lower Falls TH, walk past the Lower Park Plaza kiosk and juncture (left, less than 0.5 mi up steeply to Observation Decks/primary TH) onto Snoqualmie Falls Trail SSW for 100 ft along the river, passing the active Plant Two powerhouse. A railed boardwalk with fencing cuts through, taking you down steps through the forest S a few feet more to Lower Falls Viewpoint, albeit from farther away than the upper viewpoints. Danger signs and locked gates prevent people from moving any closer to the river, which is prone to flash flooding.

39 | MOUNT SI LOOP

ELEVATION: Almost 4000 ft at Haystack Basin, 4167 ft on Mount Si; vertical gains of 3300 ft and 3500 ft, respectively, and 3700 ft for the loop

DISTANCE: Almost 8 mi round-trip for Haystack Basin; 4.25 mi to Mount Si directly, 8.5 mi round-trip; 5.25 mi to Mount Si up Mount Teneriffe Trail, 9.5 mi round-trip loop

DURATION: 2 hours to Mount Si directly; 3 hours to Mount Si up Mount Teneriffe Trail, 3–6 hours round-trip

DIFFICULTY: Mix of strenuous for Haystack Basin or loop (crowded, switchbacks, steadily steep, traction required with snow December to March or through May on Mount Teneriffe Trail), and very challenging for the summit (Class 2/3 scramble, fairly solid rock, ultra-steep, drop-offs, touch of exposure, more difficult when wet)

TRIP REPORT: More than 100,000 people a year hike Mount Si, so it's highly recommended to begin early and avoid weekends if possible, or you will struggle to park. The mountain holds less snow than its neighbors as winter enthusiasts trek to boulder-filled Haystack Basin (Snoqualmie Valley Overlook) under the summit. Mount Si is known as the Haystack because of the sheer sloping rock leading to the imposing peak! Be respectful of others; uphill traffic always has the right of way (driving included) and dogs must be on leashes. Discover Pass required, and restrooms are present.

TRAILHEAD: Mount Si TH. From Seattle, take I-90 E to exit 32 (North Bend), turn left on 436th Ave SE for 0.5 mi, turn left on SE North Bend Way for 0.25 mi, turn right for 2.25 mi on SE Mount Si Rd/FR-9010, then turn left into the parking areas with the TH farthest N in the middle.

From Portland, take I-5 N to exit 142A (Auburn), merge onto WA-18 E for 27 mi, fork right onto I-90 E (Spokane) for 7 mi to exit 32, and follow as above (40 mi, less than 1 hour from Seattle; 190 mi, more than 3 hours from Portland).

ROUTE: For all routes, begin N (past Natural Resources Conservation Area sign, kiosk) on Mount Si Trail easily (skipping spurs left), then wind up tight turns and 9 switchbacks 0.75 mi NNW steeply (wide, rocky, good-sized firs) to a major intersection (1300 ft). Continue left (W, direct route, clockwise loop) on Mount Si Trail from the signed fork (opposite Roaring Creek Trail/Lower Teneriffe Connector/Talus Loop Trail) toward Snoqualmie Valley Overlook and the summit almost 0.5 mi steadily (tall forest, ferns), keeping sharply right (NE) from a faint juncture up 3 switchbacks for another 0.5 mi steeper to the Snag Flats juncture (2180 ft). The briefer Talus Loop Trail moves right (NE) for another loop option to shorten the hike (1450 ft vertical gain, almost 4 mi round-trip; look ahead and to the map for clues).

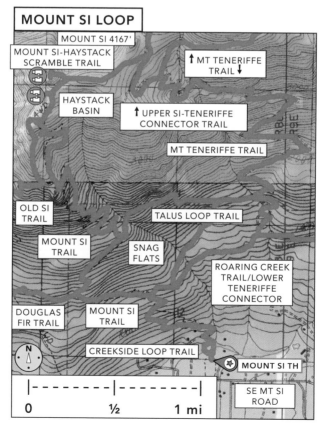

Middle Fork Snoqualmie River from the workout to Mount Si.

Walk left (W) on Mount Si Trail briefly past respectable old fir over interpretive boardwalks (one noting bark on burned side of Douglas fir compared to non-burned side). Head NW from Snag Flats up 20 moderately steep switchbacks steadily for 2 mi (younger forest) to the highest juncture with the unsigned and ridiculously steep Old Si Trail (left, 3720 ft). Continue right (NE) steeply up the defining ridge on Mount Si Trail for less than 0.25 mi with rock steps to the bottom of Haystack Basin. Work up the path over the rock field (out of trees, wildflowers, see summit) easily a few feet where a small sign points left (W) for Snoqualmie Valley Overlook. See Snoqualmie Valley to Mount Rainier, Middle Fork Snoqualmie River, Lake Sammamish, Lake Washington, Seattle, and the Olympic Peninsula!

For the summit (or loop), continue less than 100 yards NE up the narrower rocky main trail to the partially tree-covered saddle at an unsigned little intersection. Turn left (NW) for the top 0.25 mi away on Mount Si–Haystack Scramble Trail as you traverse right (NW) around 100 ft (under precipitous cliffs) to a super-steep rocky gully left (near tree roots clinging to boulders). Scramble W slowly one at a time over the most worn of a few possible routes up the rock slabs (watching for falling stones from others) with solid holds around 100 ft narrowing to the highest ridge. Then hike left (S) a bit easier for 100 ft narrowly (severe drop-offs, use caution) over the thin path, moving slightly right (W) then straight up the high ridge (nearly treeless) to the boulder-embedded summit. See countless lakes stretching to Vancouver Island and North Cascades, including Mount Baker, Mount Shuksan, and Glacier Peak! Mount Si North Peak is close NNW with a spur path few investigate.

For the clockwise loop to the TH from the unsigned saddle intersection above Haystack Basin, continue left (E) less than 0.5 mi along the high ridge easily on Upper Si–Teneriffe Connector Trail (into trees), over a small bump and then down from the ridge to an unsigned junction on a switchback. Keep right (S) down the main trail less than 0.5 mi with another switchback steadily to the next juncture. Head right (SE) onto Mount Teneriffe Trail down 2 steeper turns almost 0.5 mi then cross a small creek through the flats as the route steepens (views) near a rocky switchback under a small cliff band. Descend additional switchbacks S, passing an unsigned spur left (E, Teneriffe Falls Connector Trail), with 2 more turns to a more prominent signed juncture (1600 ft, 2.5 mi from high ridge junction) with Talus Loop Trail on a switchback.

You have two options to the TH. Talus Loop Trail is rocky and slightly more difficult but with better views (briefer). For this, turn right (W) on Spring Trail across a creek, moving up less than 100 yards before turning left (SW) from the fork (opposite route 0.75 mi to Mount Si Trail) onto Talus Loop Trail for 0.75 mi down steeply through a large scree field to Roaring Creek Trail/Lower Teneriffe Connector near the end of the primary loop. For the primary loop, keep left (S) from the juncture (for Talus Loop Trail) more than 0.25 mi down the steep Mount Teneriffe Trail with 4 turns (near water, dense brush) to the next juncture. On the final switchback is a creek (don't cross) where you turn right onto Roaring Creek Trail 0.75 mi WSW to the Mount Si Trail intersection. Undulate easily over a couple creeks, leveling on the traverse (mossy forest, ferns) past the end of the optional Talus Loop Trail for 100 yards SW to Mount Si Trail. Turn left (SSE) down 0.75 mi to the TH.

40 | MAILBOX PEAK

ELEVATION: 4841 ft; vertical gain of at least 4100 ft

DISTANCE: 5.5 mi up, almost 11 mi round-trip

DURATION: Around 3 hours up, 5–7 hours round-trip

DIFFICULTY: Strenuous (steady, switchbacks, scree, jammed on weekends, family-friendly for those in shape, traction required with snow and in winter, more difficult beyond summit)

TRIP REPORT: Close to North Bend and Seattle, this popular route was redesigned years ago to prevent further erosion on the offensively steep and semi-dangerous old trail that's still used by many for conditioning. The primary route is challenging but straightforward and quite enjoyable with lasting views of the valley once you're above the tree line! Discover Pass required, and a restroom is present.

TRAILHEAD: Mailbox Peak TH. From Seattle, take I-90 E to exit 34, turn left on 468th Ave for 0.5 mi, turn right on FR-56 (SE Middle Fork Rd) for almost 1 mi up, keep left at the fork for 1 mi, and turn left (FR-56) for 0.25 mi. Turn right up SE Lake Dorothy Rd (past gate that closes daily at 9 PM, 5 PM in winter) for less than 0.25 mi to reach the end at a large parking lot just past the signed TH. If time is an issue or the lot is full, park in the pullouts from the bottom of the driveway on the sides of FR-56.

From Portland, take I-5 N to exit 142A (Auburn), merge onto WA-18 E 27 mi, fork right onto I-90 E (Spokane) for 9 mi to exit 34, and follow as above (35 mi, 1 hour from Seattle; 190 mi, 3 hours from Portland).

ROUTE: Proceed S (kiosk, white gate) through trees 100 ft on Grouse Ridge Way to a juncture. Turn left (kiosk) on Mailbox Peak Trail for 4.5 mi to meet the old trail near the W ridge of Mailbox Peak at 3900 ft. You'll head NE easily (thin evergreens, maples, tiny creeks, a solid footbridge) before 28 switchbacks (plus 3 little turns) ESE to the juncture. Ascend the steeper slope through switchback 10 (taller fir, cedar, mossy flora, ferns) before traversing more easily NE; the path steepens after switchback 14 (rocky, brushy, clearings). You climb rocky steps and move S up a narrower shoulder or just right (W) with steeper switchbacks and tight turns easing to the unsigned Mailbox Peak Old Trail juncture (steeply right, overgrown).

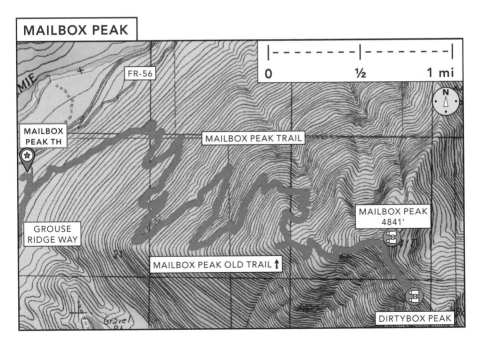

Mailbox Peak from the ridge spur bonus toward Dirtybox Peak.

Continue left/straight (ESE) up Mailbox Peak Trail (0.75 mi to summit) with 2 switchbacks E (leaving trees), then cross a sizable boulder field 100 yards SE over the wide flat rock (you'll be able to see the Olympics to Mount Rainier). Hike steeper tight turns (rocky steps) before moving briefly back across the rock field N (micro-break) with a switchback (see summit). Move up convenient stone steps much steeper (more difficult with snow and ice) with tight switchbacks and turns, laboring NE to the peak on a small rocky mound with a modified mailbox atop the marker. Across South Fork Snoqualmie River valley are Mount Washington, McClellan Butte, and Mount Rainier. Mount Si and others are NW with Mount Pilchuck and Glacier Peak to the N. See E to Kaleetan Peak and then follow SE along the ridge to Dirtybox Peak, Dirty Harry's Peak, and Web Mountain!

The route to Dirtybox Peak less than 0.5 mi away is an amusing bushwhack with decent scrambling for the first half, but then is overrun with trees and steeper bouldering from a lower saddle area. For more solitude, experienced hikers continue SE (Class 2/3) for 0.25 mi down, over, and around boulders (solid rock, sizable drop-offs) to enjoy outstanding viewpoints near the saddle!

41 | MOUNT WASHINGTON

ELEVATION: 4420 ft; vertical gain of 3200 ft

DISTANCE: 4.25 mi up, 8.5 mi round-trip

DURATION: 2½ hours up, 4–5 hours round-trip

DIFFICULTY: Strenuous (steeper in places, mostly family-friendly, rocky, okay signage, winter expertise and gear required with snow)

TRIP REPORT: A lot of people compare this day hike to Mount Si as they are both steep hikes around the same mileage and vertical gain, but they are almost completely different in feel and composition! Mount Si is much more popular and has more switchbacks, options, exposure, and larger old-growth firs. Mount Washington's route offers more solitude—almost no boom boxes blaring, very little trailside litter, and arguably superior views! Discover Pass required, and an outhouse is present.

TRAILHEAD: Mount Washington TH. From Seattle, take I-90 E to exit 38, turn right on SE Homestead Valley Rd for 100 yards, and turn right onto the gravel driveway (narrow, potholes) signed for Olallie State Park for less than 0.25 mi to reach the end with plenty of pull-in parking at left.

Mount Rainier with Chester Morse Lake and Masonry Pool as seen from Mount Washington Trail.

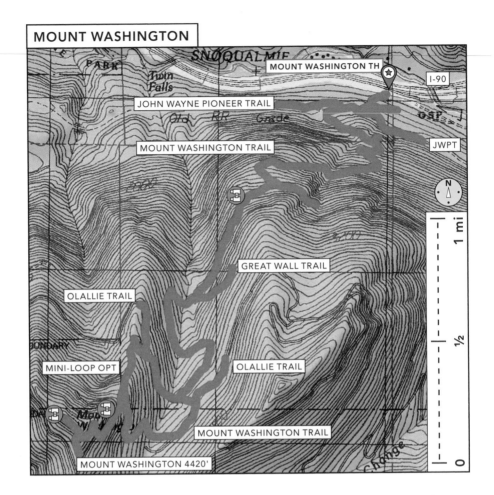

MOUNT WASHINGTON

(map labels)
SNOQUALMIE
PARK
Twin Falls
MOUNT WASHINGTON TH
I-90
JOHN WAYNE PIONEER TRAIL
Old RR Grade
GSP
MOUNT WASHINGTON TRAIL
JWPT
N
1 mi
GREAT WALL TRAIL
OLALLIE TRAIL
½
BOUNDARY
MINI-LOOP OPT
OLALLIE TRAIL
Mtn
MOUNT WASHINGTON TRAIL
MOUNT WASHINGTON 4420'
Change
0

From Portland, take I-5 N to exit 142A (Auburn), merge onto WA-18 E for 27 mi, fork right onto I-90 E (Spokane) for 12 mi to exit 38, and follow as on previous page (35 mi, less than 1 hour from Seattle; 200 mi, up to 3½ hours from Portland).

ROUTE: Begin (between boulders) past the small sign for John Wayne Pioneer/Twin Falls/Mount Washington Trails up the spur (steep, overgrown, narrow) for 200 yards W, turning right (W, same trails) easier up the gravel logging road for 100 yards to the next juncture on a little apex under power lines in the clearing (views). Keep straight (W) from the signed fork onto John Wayne Pioneer Trail (Palouse to Cascades State Park Trail) for 150 ft to the unsigned narrow Mount Washington Trail at left (small cairn, obvious). Take it S steeply for 0.25 mi or so up (rocky, spur left to skip) before easing to the first of 5 quicker turns (ferns, thick emerald forest, colorful rock walls, tiny creeks that dry up) with varying pitch S then W to a signed juncture (Mount Washington, 1.5 mi up). Traverse SW (Mount Washington Trail) with a small notable opening right opposite another rock wall (2750 ft). See across the South Fork

Snoqualmie River valley and left through a few trees toward the forested summit of Mount Washington! The route undulates SW easily through the tight forest, moving right (SW, opposite Great Wall Trail) across an actual (chilly) creek at 2.25 mi up. Stroll effortlessly then ascend switchback 6 where the route steepens for less than 0.25 mi S into the next flatter stretch, approaching a small meadow (scree field above, views outward). Move past brush, wildflowers, and tiny creeks back into trees (steeper, rockier) up near a wider turn (turn 7), then take switchback 8 shortly thereafter to a signed intersection (3500 ft). Mount Washington Trail shares a short stretch with Olallie Trail in both directions. The sharp right from the sign is a difficult mini-loop option that is best saved for the descent.

Continue left (E) a couple feet to another juncture (accurately signed Mt WA 1.2 mi) heading right (SW, cattle guard) on Mount Washington Trail, sauntering narrowly up a switchback into a boulder-filled meadow (bear grass, views). Ascend the next obvious rocky switchback, continuing N easily to the NE ridge of Mount Washington on another switchback (top of mini-loop option, 0.75 mi from bottom of loop). Walk left (SW) and slightly left (S) of the ridgeline steeply (thick stand of narrow pines) with 3 switchbacks onto the S ridge (fewer trees, see Mount Rainier). Look to the primary water source for the Puget Sound–Seattle region (Chester Morse Lake–Masonry Pool Reservoir Complex), which supplies drinking water to 1.5 million people! Skip the spur heading S as you finish easier N to the nearby top, moving just right of the radio antennae to the small boulder-embedded peak that pokes above most of the surrounding trees just enough to provide fabulous views! The obvious one is across the valley to Mount Si, Mount Teneriffe, Mailbox Peak, and others. There are also improved vistas of McClellan Butte plus more if you walk an easy 30 ft SE through a few trees.

Return down almost 0.5 mi, taking 3 switchbacks from summit area to the NE ridge mini-loop option. Spur thrill seekers can move left on the faint path over the ridgeline NNE (ultra-steep, challenging, narrow, minimal flagging) 0.25 mi, dropping over steep rock, between brush, and through thin trees before turning right (SE) off the ridge. The suddenly easier spur soon forks from a little orange blaze and continues right (SSE) on wider Olallie Trail (views) less than 0.25 mi to the end of the loop on a switchback past a log-filled tarn. Turn left (NNE) nearly 3 mi down to the TH.

42   DIRTY HARRY'S BALCONY & PEAK

ELEVATION: 2580 ft at Dirty Harry's Balcony, 4680 ft on Dirty Harry's Peak; vertical gains of around 1500 ft for balconies, 3500 ft for Dirty Harry's Peak (plus 200 ft for balconies)

DISTANCE: 2.25 mi one way to Dirty Harry's Balcony, around 4.5 mi round-trip; 4.25 mi to the summit, 9 mi round-trip total

DURATION: 1½–2 hours one way, 3–4 hours round-trip; 3 hours up, 6–7 hours round-trip

DIFFICULTY: Mix of moderate for balconies (steeper grade, fairly family-friendly, signed, very steep briefly at times, drop-offs, possible in winter with traction) and very challenging for the peak (super-steep, peaceful, drop-offs near high ridge, Class 1)

TRIP REPORT: Here's a popular warm-up through a brilliant emerald forest to several superb yet precarious overlooks that are ideal for summer sunsets or with a bit of snow when other hikes are still submerged! For a little more solitude and a lot more of a workout, the laborious route to the unofficial peak ends with three distinctly different viewpoints on the easily navigable summit plateau. Discover Pass required, and an outhouse is present.

TRAILHEAD: Dirty Harry's Balcony TH. From Seattle, take I-90 E to exit 38, turn right on SE Homestead Valley Rd for 1.75 mi, curve left (before onramp) under the Interstate for less than 0.25 mi, and find the signed TH left on a sharp curve (right) as it narrows into Grouse Ridge Rd with limited parking on both sides or roadside.

From Portland, take I-5 N to exit 142A (Auburn), merge onto WA-18 E for 27 mi, fork right onto I-90 E (Spokane) for 12 mi to exit 38, and follow as above (35 mi, less than 1 hour from Seattle; 200 mi, more than 3 hours from Portland).

ROUTE: Begin past the kiosk NE on Dirty Harry's Peak Trail (DHPT) through trees for 150 yards to Grouse Ridge Rd again. Follow it left for 100 ft (across bridge over South Fork Snoqualmie River), taking the signed trail right (E) a few feet to the first of several junctures. Keep right (E, opposite Neverland, past kiosk noting Far Side Climbing Area with signs and spurs) on DHPT, traversing along the wide path before ascending 2 switchbacks, crossing a tiny creek area, and hiking up 2 steeper switchbacks E (0.5 mi from TH) as you pass moss-covered boulders, ferns, and thin trees. Travel eases E (past climber's spur right) as you ascend a switchback left, make some quick turns, then hike up 10 rockier switchbacks NE to the first balcony (2050 ft, 1 mi from TH). Move right 25 ft (Caution Cliffs) through trees to the small perch as you see the nearby rock wall, ESE up the valley toward Snoqualmie Pass, and across to prominent McClellan Butte!

Walk 0.25 mi NE up 8 reasonable switchbacks and turns (well-maintained DHPT), ambling SE (pretty forest) past a climbing route (2325 ft, Lower Winter Block) on another switchback with semi-obscured views. Work NW up the friendly grade across a steeper slope (short cliff band above) through an open swath (wildflowers, views), then hike ESE up the rise (3 steeper turns, fewer trees, improved vistas), easing to the next balcony with the most expansive views (around 2500 ft, Upper Winter Block, 1.5 mi from TH). Take the spur right past large rocks (Caution Cliffs) 25–75 ft down sloped granite slabs (except when snow covered) cautiously for excellent views ESE to Bandera Mountain with Humpback Mountain and Silver Peak near Snoqualmie

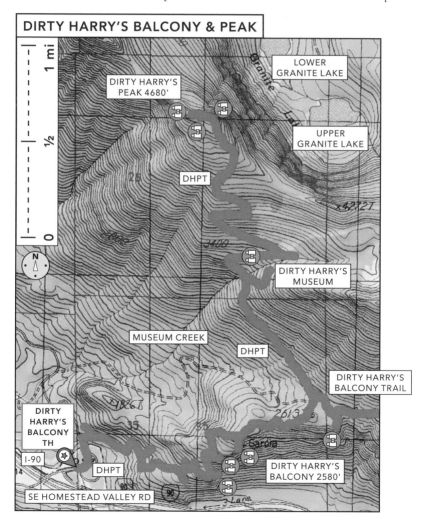

The view never gets old from the "balconies" to Snoqualmie Pass and McClellan Butte!

Pass. Be careful as you work your way a few feet down the boulders (wildflowers) to the cliff edge for an excellent view W down valley to Rattlesnake Mountain. Continue NE (DHPT) through trees down a bit then up steeper turns narrowing over the rise with another little vista on a switchback (2520 ft). Undulate painlessly to the intersection for Dirty Harry's Peak (left, 2 mi from TH).

For the primary balcony, walk right (SE) on Dirty Harry's Balcony Trail 100 ft to the next fork where heading left (ESE) for 0.25 mi on Ira Spring Connector Trail would take you to a bonus overlook (Little Balcony climbing area) with fewer trees impeding views W for sunset. Walk right (S) from the fork instead on Dirty Harry's Balcony Trail for 150 ft (narrows, quite steep final feet up) to the ledge just out of the woods (drop-offs). Look left up to Mount Defiance, across the valley to McClellan Butte, and ESE toward the pass.

For Dirty Harry's Peak from the nearby intersection in the woods, hike NW on DHPT for 0.75 mi traversing (across wide rock field, views); the path gets steadily steeper as you approach rocky Museum Creek. For those interested, just before and S of the little creek crossing is an unsigned bushwhack path right winding NE up steeply for less than 0.25 mi to an old logging truck (Dirty Harry's Museum) on the closed timeworn road within the overgrown woods. Continue up the narrowing DHPT for 0.25 mi, then ascend a steep rocky switchback, hiking E through a nice opening (views, seats cut out of large log). Reach a switchback at the bottom of a huge rock field (3450 ft), keeping left (NNW) up the clear but steep route (tiny creeks). The trail becomes even steeper as you approach a turn (1.5 mi from balconies intersection). Soon after is another corner as the route narrows (super-steep, steady) through the forest (more sun overhead) for less than 0.25 mi to another steep turn (dense trees) grinding up NNW.

Hike DHPT over the wide crest (loose rock, slightly overgrown), easing the last 100 yards to the nondescript highest point on the suddenly narrow ridge. Take the spur right (N) 25 ft up to the rock-embedded summit/cliff area (2.25 mi from balconies intersection) with quite a few trees around and terrific views near the edge. See Lower Granite Lake far below then across the valley N to Revolution Peak with Russian Butte behind (slice of Glacier Peak)! Continue W along the exquisite high ridge (DHPT) easily over the crest between tight trees 100 ft or so, passing a rock field with a stunning full shot of Mount Rainier behind McClellan Butte and Mount Kent. Walk W less than 100 ft narrowly to the end of the trail at a cliff-surrounded tiny overlook (major drop-offs) out of the woods where there's a great view NW across the saddle to the rocky S face of Dirtybox Peak with Seattle and Puget Sound in the background.

43 | McCLELLAN BUTTE

ELEVATION: 5162 ft; vertical gain of around 3700 ft

DISTANCE: More than 5.25 mi to the summit, 10.75 mi round-trip

DURATION: 3 hours up, 5–7 hours round-trip

DIFFICULTY: Very challenging (long, well traveled, ups/downs, drop-offs, minimal exposure; when wet or snow covered, more difficult and winter expertise and gear are required)

TRIP REPORT: McClellan Butte is a distinguished landmark appearing as a sharp triangular peak on the S side of the I-90 corridor. Under dry conditions, the route is a walkup suitable for devout hikers of all ages (fairly snow free July to October). Wildlife sightings may include eagles, pikas, mountain goats, cougar, and black bear. Northwest Forest Pass required, and an outhouse is present (BYOTP).

TRAILHEAD: McClellan Butte TH. From Seattle, take I-90 E to exit 42, turn right on Tinkham Rd (FR-55, into gravel, closed in winter) for 0.25 mi, and turn right for less than 0.25 mi up the narrow driveway (FR-55-101, signed McClellan Butte TH) to reach the end in a small parking circle.

From Portland, take I-5 N to exit 142A (Auburn), merge onto WA-18 E for 27 mi, fork right onto I-90 E (Spokane) for 16 mi to exit 42, and follow as on previous page (40 mi, 1 hour from Seattle; 200 mi, 3–3½ hours from Portland).

ROUTE: Walk past the small outhouse and sign for McClellan Butte Trail 1015, heading S (lush forest, ferns) into a brief clearing with buzzing power lines and foxglove. Continue S into mossy woods (plenty of felled trees off-trail), easy up to a signed four-way junction (less than 0.5 mi up). Proceed sharply right (N) on Trail 1015 (flatter, wider) for 0.25 mi, then move NW under more power lines (views) before you walk into trees, passing Alice Creek (at a big pipe, small pretty pools below). Head up through mossy boulders and a switchback to a signed juncture (more than 1 mi up). Turn sharply right on the wide old road (John Wayne Trail/Palouse to Cascades State Park Trail) only 30 ft before hiking left on Trail 1015 up 4 switchbacks SW (few larger trees, steady, easy) to the next juncture (FR-9020, more than 1.75 mi up). Walk across FR-9020 (closed to vehicles most times) to stay on Trail 1015 steeper (with varying pitch) up 21 switchbacks W over the next 1.5 mi. You ascend a switchback with the trail narrowing into a couple S-turns near the bottom to better tread past bear grass and an old bridge, followed by 3 switchbacks. You cross a scree field easily (views S across to Mount Kent) with some larger cedar and fir appearing around switchback 12. Then the route will steepen (stone steps), approaching switchback 17 and becoming even steeper before easing to switchback 21 (3500 ft).

The route eases before you hike fairly steeply (rockier) SW less than 0.25 mi, passing the first snow-filled gully with a melting snow bridge (to be avoided as it

Alpine Lakes Wilderness across Snoqualmie Valley with I-90 from McClellan Butte.

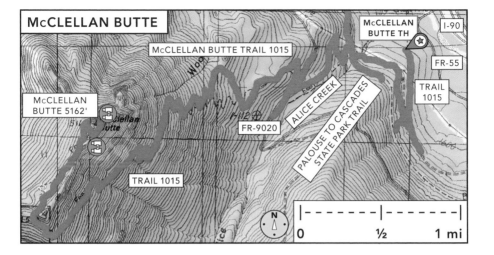

McCLELLAN BUTTE

McCLELLAN BUTTE TRAIL 1015

McCLELLAN BUTTE TH

I-90

FR-55

TRAIL 1015

McCLELLAN BUTTE 5162'

FR-9020

ALICE CREEK

PALOUSE TO CASCADES STATE PARK TRAIL

TRAIL 1015

N

0   ½   1 mi

collapses sometime in July). Take the very steep and narrow rocky trail left (below snow bridge) around 25 ft, crossing the creek (3800 ft), then ascend to the wider trail. Climb 4 switchbacks WSW to the next gully with even more snow (3.75 mi up) as you follow the spur left down 30 ft (steep) and across the creek bed (4000 ft). Look for a helpful short rope 12–15 ft up the opposite steep embankment (challenging for some) with the solid path moving very steeply 40 ft (few trees) up to the main trail. Continue steadily SW (Trail 1015), hiking up 2 switchbacks before moving more easily across thin avalanche chutes. The traverse becomes much steeper SW and across the SE shoulder off the long SW ridge of McClellan Butte (No Trespassing signs in woods for Cedar River Watershed). Look SSE down to Alice Lakes (under Mount Kent) before climbing 2 narrow switchbacks painlessly up the shoulder NW (slightly overgrown, few big blowdowns).

Walk around the corner of the high ridge, heading NE down a tad (across lingering snow patches, see McClellan Butte and more). Then the route undulates painlessly through tiny meadows before ascending 4 steeper switchbacks, heading SE (more stone steps) to the high ridge (5.25 mi up). Some skip the summit block for the outstanding views across the valley to Mounts Teneriffe, Si, and others, SSE to Mount Kent, ESE to Humpback Mountain and Silver Peak, and NE to Bandera and Granite Mountains!

Hike super-steeply N up the rock fin (cautiously) 100 ft, following the obvious route just right (E) of the crest (solid rock, great holds, slight exposure), finishing a few feet more easily over wider slabs to the boulder with a cairn at the apex. Wander 75 ft N over the broad butte (drop-offs, limited flat spots for safe picnics) near the rocky ledges for preeminent vistas across the valley to nearby Mount Defiance and Bandera Mountain, with Preacher Mountain, Kaleetan Peak, and Chair Peak behind. Look E up Snoqualmie Valley to Alta Mountain and Box Ridge and relish your commanding roost!

ELEVATION: 5584 ft on Mount Defiance, 5157 ft on Little Bandera Mountain; vertical gains of 3575 ft and 3000 ft, respectively, and around 4425 ft for both summits

DISTANCE: 11 mi round-trip for Mount Defiance, 7.5 mi round-trip for Little Bandera Mountain, 12.75 mi round-trip for both summits

DURATION: Almost 3 hours up to either summit, 4–6 hours round-trip; 7–8 hours round-trip for both summits

DIFFICULTY: Mix of strenuous for each summit (mostly signed, super-steep to finish both, rocky, narrow tops, bugs swarm July to September) and very challenging for both summits combined (arduous, long day)

TRIP REPORT: Wildly popular TH on nice weekends, but during the week it's much more tranquil and many people break off from the abnormally steep summit paths and stick to the many lakes in this part of Snoqualmie National Forest on the edge of Alpine Lakes Wilderness. Northwest Forest Pass required, and an outhouse is present.

Mount Defiance and Mason Lake from the boulders near Little Bandera Mountain.

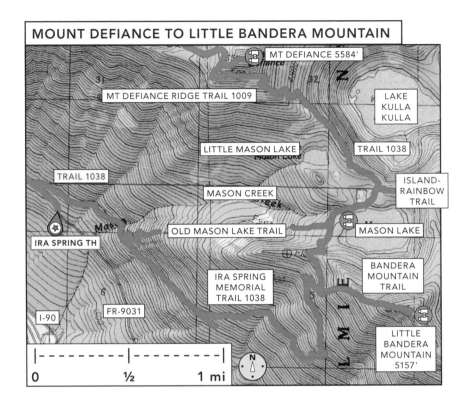

MOUNT DEFIANCE TO LITTLE BANDERA MOUNTAIN

MT DEFIANCE 5584'

MT DEFIANCE RIDGE TRAIL 1009

LAKE KULLA KULLA

LITTLE MASON LAKE

TRAIL 1038

TRAIL 1038

ISLAND-RAINBOW TRAIL

MASON CREEK

OLD MASON LAKE TRAIL

MASON LAKE

IRA SPRING TH

IRA SPRING MEMORIAL TRAIL 1038

BANDERA MOUNTAIN TRAIL

I-90

FR-9031

LITTLE BANDERA MOUNTAIN 5157'

0   ½   1 mi

TRAILHEAD: Ira Spring (Mason Lake) TH. From Seattle, take I-90 E to exit 45 (USFS Rd 9030), and turn left under the Interstate for 0.5 mi into gravel for another 0.5 mi to a juncture. Continue straight on FR-9031 (Mason Lake Rd, narrowing, rutted) for 3 mi to the end at a long parking area, which fills quickly as most park haphazardly along the road.

From Portland, take I-5 N to exit 142A (Auburn), merge onto WA-18 E for 27 mi, fork right onto I-90 E (Spokane) for 20 mi to exit 45, and follow as above (45 mi, 1 hour from Seattle; 200 mi, 3 hours from Portland).

ROUTE: Begin on Ira Spring Memorial Trail 1038 easily (free self-issue Wilderness Permit) NW through fir and maple along the old logging road, turning right (ESE) from the nearby juncture up the switchback (opposite routes to Putrid Pete's Peak, Web Mountain, and Dirty Harry's Peak) on Trail 1038. Soon cross picturesque Mason Creek (log bridge, almost 1 mi up) then pass Old Mason Creek Trail (left) 0.5 mi to the next juncture. Leave the old roadbed left (E, 2900 ft) to climb Trail 1038 much steeper (Douglas, silver, and noble firs, vine maples and salal) before you see the sharp McClellan Butte across South Fork Snoqualmie valley (Mounts Kent and Gardner left). After 3 switchbacks E cross large boulder fields heading N (wildflowers, stone steps) up steeply with 1 more switchback to the Little Bandera Mountain junction on another switchback (less than 3 mi up).

For Mason Lake (and others) and Mount Defiance first, continue left (N) from the junction 0.25 mi up (easier, rockier, see Mount Defiance), passing a boulder-laden notch in the saddle (4300 ft), then descend gradually 0.5 mi N (woods) with 3 switchbacks to Mason Lake (3.5 mi and around 2 hours from the TH). Follow the Main Trail signs left (W) of the scenic lake (over outlet creek, past privy) through a marshy area that holds snow (and mud) late into spring as do the surrounding hillsides above the lake.

It's 0.25 mi from Mason Lake NE to the next crossroads where you hike left (NW, opposite Island-Rainbow Trail) on Mount Defiance Ridge Trail 1009 somewhat steeply up 9 switchbacks near the ridgeline. You'll see Kaleetan Peak through trees as you ascend 2 more turns, traversing more easily W across a rock field and steep open meadow (many wildflowers) to a little ridge juncture for the summit trail (right, no sign). Clamber up the absolutely steep track a long 0.25 mi NE (turns, switchbacks), then from the rocky peak see Chair Peak, Kendall Peak, Granite Mountain, Little Bandera Mountain down to Mason Lake, Little Mason Lake, the larger Lake Kulla Kulla directly below, and Little Kulla Lake!

From the Little Bandera Mountain junction 0.25 mi down S of the boulder-laden notch in the saddle (above Mason Lake), follow the signage up Bandera Mountain Trail (ultra-steep, wide, rock-strewn) crawling NE (wildflower-covered open slope) to the ridge proper. Then hike ESE (micro-break) as the route becomes pretty steep again, finishing up the narrowing rocky top. There is a tiny landing with an overlook past a smattering of short pines and low flora residing on the (lower Bandera) summit. See across Mason Lake to Mount Defiance with Tusk O'Granite behind Bandera Mountain and so much more. Worth every agonizing step!

Wildflowers including Broadleaf lupine compliment the landscape to the top of Mount Defiance.

45   MELAKWA LAKE TO KALEETAN PEAK

ELEVATION: 4500 ft at Melakwa Lake, 6259 ft on Kaleetan Peak; vertical gains of around 2500 ft and 4450 ft, respectively

DISTANCE: 4.5 mi to the lake, 10 mi round-trip with Upper Melakwa Lake; 6.25 mi to the summit, 12.5 mi round-trip

DURATION: 2 hours to the lakes; 4–5 hours to the summit, 8–9 hours round-trip

DIFFICULTY: Mix of strenuous to the lakes (switchbacks, steep, rocky, popular) and very challenging to the summit (long, super-steep, narrow, route-finding, ups/downs, Class 3 gullies, bushwhack summit loop option)

TRIP REPORT: Denny Creek holds several quality cascades with the lower ones only a mile or so up the trail flowing over a flat sloping rock (known as Denny Creek Water Slide) between smaller falls into excellent swimming and splashing pools for families who have no desire to travel any farther. Muddy trails in spring and fall will make travel more difficult. For the goods at the lakes or the unparalleled views from the summit, hikers press on! Northwest Forest Pass required, and an outhouse is present.

TRAILHEAD: Franklin Falls TH. From Seattle, take I-90 E to exit 47 (Denny Creek/Asahel Curtis) and turn left on FR-55 over the Interstate to a stop sign. Turn right on FR-9034 for less than 0.5 mi, turn left for 2.25 mi on FR-5800 (signed for Denny Creek Rd/Trail 1014/TH/CG, closed in winter 2 mi before TH). Turn left past the CG for the TH on FR-5830 with ADA parking only before the locked yellow gate; otherwise, park where legal along FR-5800 or 0.25 mi farther in the long lot at right (spur path to FR-5830).

From Portland, take I-5 N to exit 142A (Auburn), merge onto WA-18 E for 27 mi, fork right onto I-90 E (Spokane) for 22 mi to exit 47, and follow as above (50 mi, 1 hour from Seattle; 195 mi, 3–3½ hours from Portland).

ROUTE: Take FR-5830 W (free self-issue Wilderness Permit) past the gate before the bridge (South Fork Snoqualmie River), turning N to meet the old Denny Creek TH 0.25 mi from Franklin Falls TH. Continue on wide Denny Creek Trail 1014 across a few footbridges easily (through the bog), including one over Denny Creek as you wind up N under a section of Interstate high above the forest floor. Pass a small cascade (steep spurs down) at 1.25 mi from Franklin Falls TH with less than 0.25 mi to the official creek crossing at Denny Creek Water Slide (warning signs—Impassable During

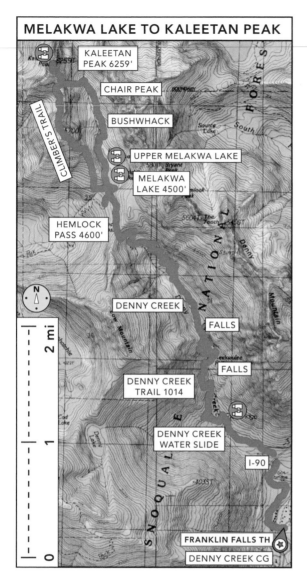

MELAKWA LAKE TO KALEETAN PEAK

KALEETAN PEAK 6259'

CHAIR PEAK

BUSHWHACK

CLIMBER'S TRAIL

UPPER MELAKWA LAKE

MELAKWA LAKE 4500'

HEMLOCK PASS 4600'

N

2 mi

1

0

DENNY CREEK

FALLS

FALLS

DENNY CREEK TRAIL 1014

DENNY CREEK WATER SLIDE

I-90

FRANKLIN FALLS TH

DENNY CREEK CG

High Water—until mid-June). Most times there are convenient rock steps to walk or hop across part of the 50-ft-wide section (signed Main Trail on W side).

Continue up rocky Trail 1014 (thinning forest), heading N after a turn as the brush on the sides remains thick (masses of wildflowers or huckleberries). Begin to see good-looking Keekwulee Falls after 3 switchbacks as it drops a couple times off the granite jutting out from the woods (125 ft high, 2.25 mi from TH). Snowshoe Falls (150 ft high) is 0.5 mi farther up the trail, but it is difficult to see any part of the three tiers even though you may hear them. When the water is low enough you can conceivably walk up the creek bed from Keekwulee Falls to view them better. Hike steeply for the first time (from Keekwulee Falls), traveling around 0.5 mi and 16 switchbacks NNW up the rock field (through trees) as the trail (rocks, roots) moves past Snowshoe Falls before moving NE easier back across Denny Creek to the right (E) side again. Continue 0.5 mi NNW steadily up the sunnier valley (wildflowers) then up 10 steeper rocky switchbacks NW before you cross a narrow creek bed (easier). Then traverse a scree field 100 yards and soon ascend 5 steep switchbacks through the forest NW, finishing the traverse to a saddle (Hemlock Pass, 4600 ft, almost 4.25 mi from TH). Contour N through the saddle and nearly 0.5 mi down a pinch (past Melakwa Lake Trail left) to Melakwa Lake. See Chair Peak N of the bright blue water, and work your way right (E) before the outlet less than 100 yards to catch sight of Kaleetan Peak. Across the outlet left (Pratt River, easily over logs) is the

Chair, Bryant, and Hemlock Peaks with The Tooth reflected perfectly into vibrant Melakwa Lake!

summit route juncture on the lake's W side with narrow rocky Trail 1014 heading 0.5 mi fairly simply around adjoining Upper Melakwa Lake (see last paragraph).

For Kaleetan Peak, move left (W, Toilet sign) from the juncture past a campsite up the hill 100 ft or so, then hike right (NW) from the privy fork up the clear but incredibly steep climber's trail 0.5 mi (woods) before breaking out into a large scree-filled slope (cairns, 5100 ft). Look toward the opposite ridge SE to Chair, Bryant, and Hemlock Peaks with The Tooth! Follow the treeless ridge crest (see summit and imposing gully route) steeply NW, passing a large cairn a few feet S of rocky Point 5700, then soon descend left (W) from the rougher, cruddy, craggy ridgeline almost 400 ft (ultra-steep, not possible if wet, muddy, or frozen without proper gear) for 0.5 mi on the traverse path. You'll work your way N (easier) momentarily then climb super-steeply up the cairned climber's trail more or less between boulder fields to the high ridge again near a small saddle S of the summit block (start of lollipop loop, 5600 ft).

Only 0.5 mi of steep mountain separates you from the apex as you follow cairns N up the ridgeline (scant trees) then steeper NW to the base of the main gully. Climb the 30-ft-wide gully (loose rock, a few choices, be mindful, some hikers wear helmets) ultra-steeply 100 ft or so N (and almost 250 ft vertical), narrowing to the peak. Your reward is one of the finest overlooks within Alpine Lakes Wilderness! Enjoy the panorama from the relatively safe top, being careful of the surrounding exposure. Kaleetan is Chinook for "arrow," which makes perfect sense!

From the small saddle S of the summit block, return by the same route or try the clockwise loop, which after the first 100 yards will essentially be easier to Melakwa Lake than by going down the ridge. The immediate couloir heading left (E) has two sides, a long straight chute right (S) and the preferred route that begins down the left (N) side of the couloir. Go one at a time down the steep sloping rock with loose gravel (no trail, Class 3) only a few feet toward a short choke, then follow it right, finding the main long gully with improved scrambling down the left side (more solid rock) quite steeply E to the center of the rocky basin (around 5000 ft, just S of Melakwa Pass).

Mostly boulder-hop SSE down the peaceful valley (only a few small cairns lower). You'll hear water under the rocks before you reach a small lush meadow and beautiful creek at tree line! Follow the creek bed judiciously S down to Upper Melakwa Lake with its great reflections, where you can see both lakes at once and the distant peaks above. Work through rock fields, passing the lake on either side (left, E side easier) to the S side of Upper Melakwa Lake, walking Trail 1014 from the outlet briefly S around larger, alluring Melakwa Lake (from its W side) to the end of the loop.

46 TUSK O'GRANITE TO GRANITE MOUNTAIN

ELEVATION: 5566 ft on Tusk O'Granite, 5629 ft on Granite Mountain; vertical gains of around 3750 ft for either summit; 4200 ft for the loop (including both summits)

DISTANCE: 5.5 mi directly to Tusk O'Granite, around 11 mi round-trip loop; 4.5 mi directly to Granite Mountain, more than 9 mi round-trip

DURATION: 3½ hours to Tusk O'Granite, 6–8 hours round-trip loop; 2½–3 hours to Granite Mountain, 5–6 hours round-trip

DIFFICULTY: Mix of very challenging for Tusk O'Granite or the loop (long, super-steep at times, bushwhacking, Class 2, ups/downs, route-finding, scrambling, GPS device helpful, semi-loose rock, traction with snow coverage) and strenuous for Granite Mountain (steady fairly steep, narrow at times, switchbacks, very popular, scree, avalanche prone in winter)

TRIP REPORT: The Granite Mountain Lookout (closed to public) is a superb goal for those training to tackle big Cascade volcanoes and for avid day hikers! You get some impressive vertical and stirring views without the worry of skirting razor-thin ridges

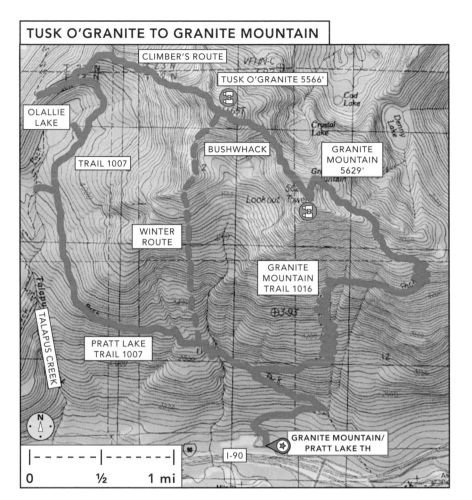

TUSK O'GRANITE TO GRANITE MOUNTAIN

CLIMBER'S ROUTE

TUSK O'GRANITE 5566'

OLALLIE LAKE

TRAIL 1007

BUSHWHACK

GRANITE MOUNTAIN 5629'

WINTER ROUTE

GRANITE MOUNTAIN TRAIL 1016

PRATT LAKE TRAIL 1007

TALAPUS CREEK

GRANITE MOUNTAIN/ PRATT LAKE TH

I-90

0   ½   1 mi

and cliffs for the payoff. Because of avalanche danger in winter, the route to Tusk O'Granite (West Granite Mountain) changes to its S ridge only (popular with snowshoers and others) and the route to Granite Mountain also crosses questionable terrain where you should use caution. The sweet ridge connects for an aspiring loop or side trip. Try July to October for more rocks and wildflowers with less snow. Northwest Forest Pass required, and a restroom is present.

TRAILHEAD: Granite Mountain/Pratt Lake TH. From Seattle, take I-90 E to exit 47 (Denny Creek/Asahel Curtis), turn left on FR-55 over the Interstate to a stop sign, and turn left on FR-9034 for less than 0.5 mi to reach the end (TH right) at a large, busy parking area and overflow roadside parking without blocking others.

From Portland, take I-5 N to exit 142A (Auburn), merge onto WA-18 E for 27 mi, fork right onto I-90 E (Spokane) for 22 mi to exit 47, and follow as above (45 mi, less than 1 hour from Seattle; 200 mi, more than 3 hours from Portland).

Tuscohatchie and Denny Lakes with Kaleetan and Chair Peaks in the clouds behind.

ROUTE: Begin N on Pratt Lake Trail 1007 (free self-issue Wilderness Permit) over a boardwalk then up stairs and 2 switchbacks easily through the lively forest for almost 1.25 mi to the intersection for Granite Mountain Trail 1016 (see next page for direct route to Tusk O'Granite, clockwise loop option). For Granite Mountain proceed right (NE) on Trail 1016 (narrow, rocky, steep) through trees almost 0.5 mi, then clamber N up more than 20 tight switchbacks and turns (beside mossy boulders and rocks close to seasonal creek) for 1.25 mi, crisscrossing an avalanche chute. You cross the creek, ending by going steeply up the final switchbacks (first set, last fir and big trees) to around 4000 ft. Head E, traversing easier (bear grass, huckleberries August into October) with 2 tight switchbacks (see Mount Rainier), then begin to march up 9 switchbacks N steeply again. Climb NW briefly (easier) over a grassy shoulder past a faint summit juncture, keeping right (NNW) very steeply up Trail 1016. The going gets easier after you reach a nearby notch (4 mi up).

Head into a larger, pretty meadow from the notch E of Granite Mountain's summit block (bear grass in July, fiery hillside in autumn) with a view to the lookout and more! The rocky trail lives up to its namesake for the remainder and beyond but is pretty recognizable even when partially snow covered. Hike a handful of switchbacks

NW very briefly gaining the NE shoulder of Granite Mountain before scrambling the scree trail left (SSW) very steeply (few trees) to the lookout tower's decks. See Mount Stuart, Kaleetan and Chair Peaks, Crystal Lake (directly below), and Tuscohatchie Lake! There's room to spread out safely along the boulder-covered high ridge. Return the same way or bushwhack NW for 0.75 mi to Tusk O'Granite (more than 400 ft drop to ridge saddle, continue reading for clues).

For Tusk O'Granite from the first intersection, remain on wide Pratt Lake Trail 1007 following the sign left (NW) for Olallie and Talapus Lakes. Traverse easily with only 4 or so switchbacks (several little streams with cascades), crossing narrow avalanche chutes that winter enthusiasts ascend right (when safe) to the nearby S ridge of Tusk O'Granite. Continue contouring (vine maple, mixed flora) to the N, into the basins, passing a juncture for Talapus Lake/TH (left, 3725 ft, around 2.5 mi from intersection below). Keep N on Trail 1007 for more than 0.5 mi easily (passing the juncture for Olallie Lake) to the N side of the basin near a saddle crossroads (NW of Olallie Lake). For Tusk O'Granite, leave the main trail just before you reach the saddle (4.25 mi from TH) for the climber's route (no solid trails) heading N directly a few feet to the somewhat tree-covered shoulder facing S. Then scramble large boulders and rocks toward the summit as you follow the shoulder very briefly, approaching Tusk O'Granite's NW ridge. With no snow or a good snowpack, the remainder is ideal, but with only a blanket of snow or when wet the going will be slippery and tougher, as you navigate large boulders (with hidden gaps). Hike ESE just right (S) of the NW ridge up the super-steep slope (gloves help), dipping right (S) again when the trees become too thick on the ridgeline, then from the wide-enough crest work very steeply SE (see Olallie Lake below with Pratt Lake under Pratt Mountain). The route finally eases SSE, crossing over little bumps to the true summit at an obvious little high point within the boulders. Vistas may even be better than from Granite Mountain as you spot the lookout on the higher peak an hour away SE!

For Granite Mountain from Tusk O'Granite, follow the widening high ridge SE (just right around a few trees), then head more to the left (N) of the crest, navigating easily but steeply down rocks to the tree-covered saddle between summits. Past a bump the going becomes quite steep again SE, up the rock nearest the ridgeline, as you judiciously select your route up the enjoyable section with the last bit being much easier and wider (scree, boulders) over the nearby summit plateau to the lookout.

ELEVATION: 4016 ft at Snow Lake, 4857 ft at Gem Lake; vertical gains of 1700 ft and 2750 ft, respectively

DISTANCE: 3 mi one way, 6 mi round-trip; 5 mi to Gem Lake, 10 mi round-trip

DURATION: 1½ hours to Snow Lake; 2½ hours to Gem Lake, 4–6 hours round-trip

DIFFICULTY: Mix of strenuous to Snow Lake (ups/downs, steady, roots, rocks, switchbacks, busy, bugs through August) and very challenging beyond (well traveled, steeper, long)

TRIP REPORT: Here's an entertaining day hike that's only super popular as far as Snow Lake. Seasoned hikers press on to Gem Lake or even Wright Mountain. Mid-July through October is preferable as spring snow lingers on the N side of the headwall into the Snow Lake basin. Northwest Forest Pass required, and outhouses are present (BYOTP).

TRAILHEAD: Snow Lake TH/Alpental Parking Lot. From Seattle, take I-90 E to exit 52 (West Summit), turn left on WA-906/FR-9041 under the Interstate, and take the second right on Erste Strasse for 1.25 mi to the end (gated beyond) into large gravel lots at left (which fill quickly on summer weekends) with the signed TH at right (a few feet into forest).

From Portland, take I-5 N to exit 142A (Auburn), merge onto WA-18 E for 27 mi, fork right onto I-90 E (Spokane) for 26 mi to exit 52, and follow as above (50 mi, 1 hour from Seattle; 200 mi, 3½ hours from Portland).

ROUTE: Begin N (kiosk/signage) on Snow Lake Trail 1013 a few feet up steps into steep turns and 1 switchback heading NW (see Alpental Ski Area under Denny Mountain) into trees (tiny creeks) before crossing a boulder field well below Snoqualmie Mountain (1 mi from TH). See Chair, Bryant, and Hemlock Peaks across South Fork Snoqualmie River valley. The route becomes rockier and steeper as you pass a signed junction on a switchback (Source Lake left, 1.75 mi from TH). Hike right (ENE, Trail 1013) briefly, then NW up 8 steeper switchbacks, keeping right of the Alpine Lakes Wilderness sign to the nearby small saddle and headwall above Snow Lake (4400 ft, more than 2.25 mi and 1 hour from the TH). There are faint spurs between the wilderness sign and the saddle moving left (W) 75 ft up to a rocky overlook of Snow Lake below and Mount Price across Middle Fork Snoqualmie River valley (some snowshoe to overlook in winter).

Hint of autumn from Gem Lake with the local peaks in Alpine Lakes Wilderness.

From the saddle switchback, descend 3 more moderate switchbacks N for 0.5 mi to Snow Lake (past Toilet spur). Reach a signed juncture at a picturesque little inlet creek area with a Lake Access spur moving left (W) past a tiny tarn 100 ft down to a rock-covered shoreline where many swim in the deep blue lake. From the juncture,

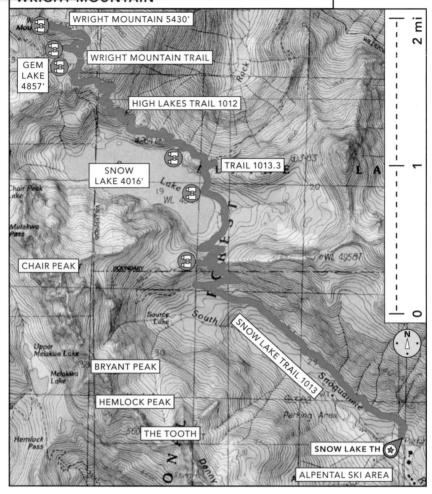

WRIGHT MOUNTAIN 5430'

WRIGHT MOUNTAIN TRAIL

GEM LAKE 4857'

HIGH LAKES TRAIL 1012

SNOW LAKE 4016'

TRAIL 1013.3

CHAIR PEAK

BRYANT PEAK

HEMLOCK PEAK

THE TOOTH

SNOW LAKE TRAIL 1013

SNOW LAKE TH

ALPENTAL SKI AREA

2 mi

head right (N, Trail 1013) over the boulder-laden creek (with small cascade into a little pool), then move easily over boardwalks on the E side of the sizable subalpine lake to another overlook area in a clearing at a Trail sign near other spurs. Sunrise hours would be optimal for viewing Snow Lake's glassy waters reflecting Chair Peak's top and Mount Roosevelt, but any time will do!

Return to the TH or continue past the Trail sign down a few feet closest to the lake (N), passing yet another great overlook before climbing N (steep steps) past a camping sign then over a small saddle to the end of Trail 1013 at a signed juncture (0.25 mi from last overlooks). Proceed left (NW) for Gem Lake and Wright Mountain (opposite Rock Creek Trail) on High Lakes Trail 1012 down 3 steep turns to cross the outlet at Rock Creek (log bridge). Momentarily, move N away from the water then NW up 4 switchbacks and turns. Ascend steps and 3 steep turns, passing a brief level area (few trees), then walk down 2 turns past a dirty tarn and head up 1 turn, passing more small meadows (boulder-embedded flat trail) as you move away from Snow Lake to a switchback (more than 4 mi from TH). Hike NW up 7 more moderate turns to easier terrain (shallow tarns, views). Ascend rock steps and walk 100 yards across a boulder field, then move up 2 quick rocky turns briefly (see Gem Lake).

Spot the route up to Wright Mountain above the stunning smaller blue lake as you walk N easily (past privy spur) to a signed juncture on the right (E) side close to the water (5 mi from TH). The narrower Wright Mountain Trail moves right (N) either past the Campsites sign or a few feet farther (spur) from Trail 1012 around 100 yards before the scree field. It's worth it to stay on the main trail past Wright Mountain Trail a few feet into the scree field (N side of Gem Lake) for sweet views of Chair Peak! You could also continue 0.5 mi on Trail 1012 and spurs (ups/downs) around the noteworthy lake before departing.

48 | WRIGHT MOUNTAIN

ELEVATION: 5430 ft; vertical gain of 3300 ft (including Snow and Gem Lakes)

DISTANCE: Almost 5.5 mi to summit, 11 mi round-trip

DURATION: 3½ hours to summit, 6–8 hours round-trip if lingering

DIFFICULTY: Very challenging (barely scrambling to summit, Class 1/2, drop-offs, long, steeper at times, ups/downs, solid but narrow rugged tracks, route-finding)

TRIP REPORT: Wright Mountain holds prevailing panoramas of the local pinnacles within Alpine Lakes Wilderness from a nondescript highpoint, and with more solitude than the lakes region. Northwest Forest Pass required, and outhouses are present (BYOTP).

TRAILHEAD: Snow Lake TH/Alpental Parking Lot. See Snow Lake to Gem Lake on page 148 for directions (50 mi, 1 hour from Seattle; 200 mi, 3½ hours from Portland).

ROUTE: See Snow Lake to Gem Lake on page 148 for the description to the E side of Gem Lake. Head right (N) from the junctures (leaving Trail 1012, Campsites sign) up the steep, rutted, overgrown spurs a few feet passing small tarns on a saddle (better tread) into Wright Mountain Trail (see Glacier Peak), continuing left (NW) steeply.

Snow and Gem Lakes under Chair Peak, Kaleetan Peak, and others from Wright Mountain!

Pass other tarns (look ENE to Mounts Hinman/Daniel, Overcoat Peak, Chimney Rock, Lemah Mountain, and Chikamin Peak), then climb steep tight turns (boulder field, cairns) and 4 switchbacks W.

The solid trail disappears over the steepening, wide-enough ridgeline as you scramble up the boulder field. There's a subtle cairned option traversing left of the sheer ridge (briefly back into trees, somewhat easier) as you go SW then W. The primary route takes you more or less very steeply straight up the rocky ridge (NW then W) with semi-loose stones as both routes meet momentarily nearest the summit (jaw-dropping views above most trees and scrub, drop-offs). See Mount Baker to the N, plus nearby Preacher Mountain NW beyond Lower Wildcat Lake! And of course the look over Gem and Snow Lakes to Kaleetan, Chair, Bryant, and Hemlock Peaks, and The Tooth with Denny Mountain is totally dope!

49 | KENDALL PEAK

ELEVATION: 5784 ft; vertical gain of at least 2800 ft

DISTANCE: Almost 5.5 mi up either lower route to summit (plus 0.5 mi taking Kendall Katwalk and N ridge option), 11.5 mi round-trip max

DURATION: 3–3½ hours up by most routes, 5–7 hours round-trip

DIFFICULTY: Mix of strenuous for the primary/direct routes (long, steeper at times, super-steep summit block, GPS device helpful) and very challenging for the N ridge route (drop-offs from Kendall Katwalk, bushwhacking, scrambling, very steep bouldering, mostly solid rock, Class 3/4, exposure, mountaineering skills and gear with snow or ice)

TRIP REPORT: Kendall Peak is tucked in far enough from Snoqualmie Pass to not seem like you are right on the I-90 corridor! Most people take the slightly longer, primary route on the PCT from the TH, but the less traveled Commonwealth Basin Trail offers a more rustic experience through the lush forest for the first couple miles or so (with a bonus waterfall), as both routes meet (lollipop loop sans summit, snowshoe in winter, 5 mi round-trip) continuing up the PCT. Past the direct summit route is a narrower, flat trail section (easy when dry) with huge slabs of steeply sloped rock along an ultra-steep area known as the Kendall Katwalk for less than 0.25 mi to a small saddle at the start of the N ridge route. The bouldering route up the N ridge is for experienced and aspiring mountain climbers only. Northwest Forest Pass required, and outhouses are present.

TRAILHEAD: Snoqualmie Pass/PCT TH or West Summit TH. From Seattle, take I-90 E to exit 52 (West Summit), turn left on WA-906/FR-9041 under the Interstate, and turn right on FR-9041 for less than 0.25 mi to reach the end at a long parking lot. There is a small stock parking circle (alternate upper lot, see the next page for Commonwealth Basin Trail shortcut) at left just before the main parking area. In winter or if the closest lots are full (summer weekend), turn right from exit 52 onto WA-906, turn right into the large (treeless) lot for West Summit (no fee), and walk carefully back along the road under the Interstate bridge, taking the first trail at right (PCT 2000) up briefly to the main TH near a picnic table in the woods.

From Portland, take I-5 N to exit 142A (Auburn), merge onto WA-18 E for 27 mi, fork right onto I-90 E (Spokane) for 26 mi to exit 52, and follow as above (50 mi, 1 hour from Seattle; 200 mi, 3½ hours from Portland).

ROUTE: Fill out a free self-issue Wilderness Permit from either of the main lots. For the route up the PCT from the upper lot, take the signed spur trail for PCT 2000 S for 100 ft, turning left near the main TH. From the main signed TH, walk 40 ft SE (woods) to a juncture (picnic table, right to West Summit TH), keeping left (SE) on PCT 2000 past the PCT spur (left from upper lot) for 100 ft to the intersection with the lollipop loop. Left (N) is the slightly overgrown Commonwealth Basin Trail 1033 (see the next page).

For the more traveled, simpler route, continue forward (SE, PCT) over tiny, clear creeks and a couple little bridges (nice grade), walking past a large felled tree (cut off the trail) into denser woods. Hike up (more than 0.5 mi from main TH) 3 switchbacks for 1 mi N (over pleasant tiny creeks, views), then it's almost 1 mi more NE, traversing to the intersection with Commonwealth Basin. You'll pass the sign

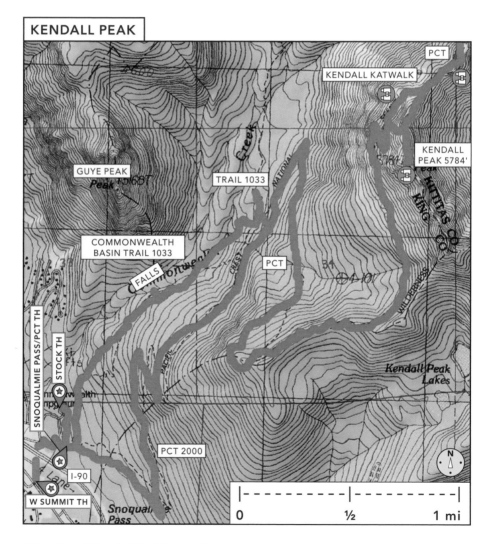

KENDALL PEAK

Lundin Peak, Red Mountain, and Mount Thomson left to right from Kendall Peak's N ridge route for scrambling enthusiasts!

entering Alpine Lakes Wilderness (see nearby Guye Peak with Red Mountain ahead) as you move up a sizable rock field (cliffs right) then down across the same boulder field approaching a cascade near/across the trail. Hop over another creek reaching the intersection (3800 ft, lollipop loop, almost 2.5 mi from TH).

For Commonwealth Basin Trail 1033 (Old Commonwealth Trail) to the same locale from the main TH, turn left (N, slightly overgrown) off the PCT, passing a faint path left, coming from the NE corner of the upper lot (unsigned 100-ft shortcut begins across road from outhouse in the circle just right of the picnic table between No Parking signs). Around 0.5 mi from the main TH, hike up steeper turns NE for 0.5 mi (rockier, thick forest), hopping over a tiny creek then becoming rockier and narrower for almost 0.25 mi more before easing (widening, tree roots, views) to a faint juncture. Take the spur left (N) 35 ft to a charming little double waterfall area worth checking during different seasons, the best viewpoint being from the big boulders in Commonwealth Creek. The top curtain is around 15 ft high with the lower falls a bit smaller as they cascade into clear blue-green pools!

Continue 0.25 mi NE easily along the creek (old footbridges, thinning pines, views) before crossing it over the double log bridge (if not washed out, otherwise this can be more difficult). Walk right (NE) from the fork on Trail 1033 another 0.25 mi through the sparse forest (muddy, easy) before crossing a tiny creek down in a holler, then Commonwealth Creek again (to E side) over rocks and logs, finding the rocky trail between trees. Hike NE across a small creek winding up the wet trail (4 turns, larger Silver fir, hemlock) to a juncture (more than 2 mi from TH). Turn sharp right (S, opposite Red Pass) for less than 100 yards (spur) to the PCT intersection (top of lollipop loop) where you turn sharply left to the summit.

From the small brown sign for Commonwealth Basin at the intersection, continue upward for more than 0.25 mi N (PCT) to a switchback. Traverse 0.5 mi S (thin evergreens, steep slope), including across a tiny mossy creek then a prettier cascade for 8 ft over rocks in the sheer creek to the visible trail. Move steeper up a rocky clearing for only 50 ft before turning sharply right (SSW, PCT) up into trees (steeper, rockier), ascending a switchback onto a ridge (1.25 mi from upper lollipop loop). Amble E up easily 0.5 mi (less flora), then climb 10 steeper switchbacks and turn ENE on or just left (N) of the ridge to a small notch. Leave the ridgeline on another long easy traverse N with nice tread (stunning panorama of Chair Peak's E face) around 1 mi for the direct summit route option (5330 ft). You'll cross a wide, lengthy rock field (wildflowers or berries) with a cliff band below the high ridge appearing up right, then climb 2 rockier switchbacks E to the faint super-steep climber's trail right (25 ft past an old stump on left, W side of PCT).

For the direct route to Kendall Peak, turn right (E) less than 100 ft before the Kendall Katwalk (overhyped but worth checking out) up the ultra-steep and loose summit path covering the open slope (around 35 switchbacks and tight turns) without cairns, finishing slightly right (SE) to the high ridge near the peak. Catch your breath walking the last few feet right (S) to the very top (serious drop-offs). See Keechelus Lake left of the ski areas near Snoqualmie Pass with Silver and Tinkham Peaks in front of Mount Rainier! The astute can make out Granite Mountain Lookout toward I-90, and ENE is nearby Alta Mountain (Mount Stuart in the distance).

For the N ridge route (clockwise summit loop), continue NE (PCT) around the corner, passing the narrower section (Kendall Katwalk, views, colors) for 0.25 mi easily to a small ridge saddle. Another option from the saddle is to keep left (NE) another 0.25 mi on the PCT (wildflowers, decent-sized trees) to a respectable overlook area of the local mountains and Silver Creek basin to the Gold Creek valley. The trail continues without problems for miles to Ridge Lake and others near Alaska Mountain. Turn hard right (S) instead from the saddle up the N ridge of Kendall Peak with the best views of the day behind you looking to the prominent Mount Thomson commanding respect right (NE) behind Red Mountain! Farther right are Chikamin Peak, Lemah Mountain, Chimney Rock, and Overcoat Peak. Bushwhack past several excellent perches, then scramble steeply sloped slabs and loose rock on or just left (E) of the ridge crest. The straightforward route (no cairns, less brush) narrows to the next problem, a large rocky gendarme (more bark than bite). Clamber steeply right (W) around the top, carefully returning to the high ridge again near the main crux. Now carefully cross the 3–8 ft wide catwalk (considerable exposure) for 25 ft, then continue on or off the ridgeline from the right (W, drop-offs). Hike S over the final ridge bumps with some easier scrambling (or from a bailout path a few feet farther right), passing the climber's direct route nearest the peak. For the summit loop, descend W very steeply for 0.25 mi easier to the PCT.

ELEVATION: 5395 ft on Tinkham Peak East Peak (more traveled summit most maps mistakenly call Tinkham Peak), 5605 ft on Silver Peak; vertical gains of at least 2000 ft for Tinkham Peak East Peak, 1800 ft for Silver Peak (directly), 3000 ft for all high points

DISTANCE: 5 mi round-trip for Tinkham Peak East Peak (with Mirror Lake), 6 mi round-trip for Silver Peak directly, 7.25 mi round-trip clockwise loop for Tinkham Peaks (with Mirror Lake), 9 mi round-trip longer loop including all high points

DURATION: 2–2½ hours up to either summit directly; 4 hours to summit both peaks clockwise, 5–7 hours round-trip

DIFFICULTY: Mix of strenuous for Silver Peak's more popular S ridge route alone (steep, scree, drop-offs) and very challenging for all other routes (long, ultra-steep, Class 2/3, scrambling, minimal exposure, loose, drop-offs, GPS device helpful, route-finding)

TRIP REPORT: Just S of the Snoqualmie Pass area is this quieter region with many exceptional day hiking options to challenge yourself or take a dip in the blue-green waters of Mirror Lake (7 mi round-trip, 1000 ft vertical gain, more moderate). Views from Tinkham and Silver Peaks outshine most that reside in the South Fork Snoqualmie River valley. No fee or restroom.

TRAILHEAD: Silver Peak/Windy Pass TH (or Mount Catherine TH). From Seattle, take I-90 E to exit 54 (Hyak/WA-906 W), turn right for 50 ft on WA-906, cross an unsigned intersection (with WA-906) straight onto Hyak Drive E (past ski areas) for 1 mi before passing a water treatment plant onto FR-9070 (small sign, gravel, closed in winter) for 4.5 mi to Windy Pass (AWD preferred for the last 0.25 mi past Mount Catherine TH where some park roadside at left, no signs, rough road ahead). From the pass, see a small sign in a clearing at right for Pacific Crest Trail 2000 N toward Snoqualmie Pass (your route left, S) with a smaller pullout on the right afterward.

From Portland, take I-5 N to exit 142A (Auburn), merge onto WA-18 E for 27 mi, fork right onto I-90 E (Spokane) for 28.5 mi to exit 54, and follow as above (60 mi, 1½ hours from Seattle; 210 mi, 3½ hours from Portland).

ROUTE: Begin S through Olallie Meadows (PCT) under the cliffy NE ridge of Silver Peak on an upward traverse that undulates (fir, cedar, roots, rocks) SSW for 1.25 mi.

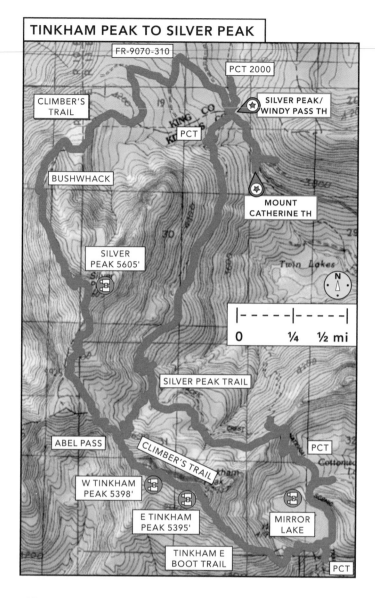

TINKHAM PEAK TO SILVER PEAK

FR-9070-310

PCT 2000

SILVER PEAK/ WINDY PASS TH

CLIMBER'S TRAIL

PCT

BUSHWHACK

MOUNT CATHERINE TH

SILVER PEAK 5605'

Twin Lakes

N

|- - - - -|- - - - -|
0   ¼   ½ mi

SILVER PEAK TRAIL

ABEL PASS

PCT

CLIMBER'S TRAIL

W TINKHAM PEAK 5398'

E TINKHAM PEAK 5395'

MIRROR LAKE

TINKHAM E BOOT TRAIL

PCT

Look to Tinkham Peak's impressive double summit (trees thin, wildflowers appear), walking 0.25 mi farther, then descend 4 quick switchbacks E. Work your way S up across a scree field before heading back into the woods, leveling to an unsigned intersection (cairns, 4325 ft, 1.75 mi from primary TH). Right (SW) is the direct route to Silver Peak sans Mirror Lake. For this, climb Silver Peak Trail quite steeply up turns and 4 switchbacks less than 0.5 mi to Abiel Pass (4747 ft) on the ridge saddle between Tinkham and Silver Peaks (see page 160).

Continue left (S) for Mirror Lake (clockwise loop/direct route for Tinkham Peak East Peak) on the PCT (N of towering Tinkham Peak) with a little tarn down left as the

Silver Peak Trail and the straightforward route up the steep S ridge of Silver Peak.

route flattens ESE (more tarns). Undulate up the traverse across a scree field into trees, then continue E up easily over a viewless saddle past a signed juncture (left, Cold Creek Trail, more than 2.5 mi from TH). Walk straight (SE) for 0.5 mi down 5 switchbacks to the lake with more junctures. Turn right (SW) on the PCT (opposite Mirror Lake Trail) for 12 ft to a fork where you keep left (S) on the main path or begin to explore the few spurs to the water. There are several campsites between trees near great reflections mirroring Tinkham Peak into the effervescent blue lake along its E side!

For the difficult ascent up Tinkham Peak East Peak's steep SE ridge to the summit, cross the logjam S of Mirror Lake without trouble, keeping right (left is the unending PCT) from the juncture (more than 0.25 mi from initial crossroads at lake) on unsigned Tinkham East Boot Trail. Move W (past campsites) over the most worn, narrow path as you leave the lake for more than 0.25 mi left (SW) super-steeply up a shoulder bypassing a few blowdowns before traversing a small rock field SW through a clearing easier. Continue S up the shoulder very steeply (briefly) gaining the SE ridge (No Trespassing signs left for Cedar River Watershed), then hike the steep route NW before Tinkham East Boot Trail eases somewhat. See the steep summit block ahead (less trees, minimal blazes, straightforward) as you break out into a rock field and work NW up the right (N) side of the ridge (cairns), passing some high meadows (see several lakes below). Finish quite steeply either on or just left (W) of the ridge's rocky fin (exposed, use extreme caution near lip of cliff band) to the top of Tinkham Peak East Peak. See Mirror, Cottonwood, and Lost Lakes, and larger Keechelus Lake, with two shallow bright blue-green ponds directly below the summit to the N! Then look over to Tinkham and Silver Peaks along the ridge, Kaleetan and Chair Peaks panning behind right, and the high tops NE to Mounts Hinman, Daniel, and Stuart!

For nearby Tinkham Peak (5398 ft, 0.25 mi away) and the loops, continue NW on the unofficial climber's trail left (S) of the ridge (right of the watershed boundary) down briefly to the small saddle between peaks. Then work up right (N) of a giant rock field nearest the ridgeline to the zenith (semi-exposed, be careful) as you break out above the trees. Enjoy comparable views plus a corner of Twin Lakes to the N and tiny Abiel Lake down W! Return or continue clockwise as the bushwhack route instantly changes to Class 2/3 (nearly impossible when wet, snowy, or icy). For Abiel Pass less than 0.5 mi away, climb NW down slowly just left (S) of the rotten rocky impasse on the ridgeline 40 ft or so, hanging onto branches and tree roots for help. Traverse the climber's trail briefly back to the ridge (touch of exposure), choosing more solid rock over slick rock as you continue NW very steeply (better tread) on or just left (S) of the ridge crest. The narrow path (slightly overgrown but tacky, fewer rocks) becomes simpler as you follow the watershed boundary to the saddle juncture; the loop makes perfect sense in this direction!

Abiel Pass (4747 ft, 5 mi from Windy Pass TH on clockwise loop) is a lackluster saddle with the juncture in a tiny clearing. Return right (NE, Silver Peak Trail) almost 0.5 mi steeply to the PCT or hike to Silver Peak, the highest point S of I-90 for miles around, as the going will be much less precipitous (Class 1) up the S ridge 1 mi to the summit. Hike straight (NW) up wider Silver Peak Trail super-steeply (rocky turns), heading right (E) of a sizable ridge bump (spur moves left to top of a high point) then down and over easily N to the next little ridge saddle. Walk up (open meadow, bear grass) past another faint fork (left, SW to Abiel Peak) as you break out above most of the trees hiking N (just W of rocky crest). Less than 0.5 mi from the Abiel Pass juncture, the scree trail defines itself to N (wildflowers, outstanding vistas) as you soon head right (E) of the ridgeline (see Annette Lake below), reaching a little saddle, then hike N steadily on or just left (W) of the crest to the wider rocky peak without difficulty (drop-offs). Most return to Abiel Pass en route to the TH.

For the bushwhack loop route to the TH (most difficult, 2 mi to TH) down part of the NNW ridge (not the cliffy NE ridge), continue NW from Silver Peak as the narrow climber's trail quickly becomes ultra-steep left (W) off the ridgeline. Then descend the most prominent path around 100 ft W (grass, gravel) before finding the rough traverse path NW and heading carefully back to the rocky ridgeline (cairns), following it NNW on and off the crest (short pines, less trouble, more fun). Leave the cliffy vertical ridge near its end (4600 ft), working your way steeply right (E) across the enormously long scree-filled gully (N of Silver Peak) briefly then down a narrower grassy area on the climber's trail. Follow it NE over a kinder shoulder (E of gully), then take the most worn of a few choices N (into trees) steadily before bending right (NE, leaving trees) across the rock field. Follow large cairns over the boulders, finding the more solid trail (slightly overgrown) a few feet to the gravel forest road (FR-9070-310, 1 mi from Silver Peak). Walk NE easily down the road a few turns, finishing right (FR-9070) to nearby Windy Pass TH.

51	RACHEL LAKE TO RAMPART LAKES

ELEVATION: 4650 ft at Rachel Lake, 5100 ft at Rampart Lakes; vertical gains of around 2000 ft and 2600 ft, respectively

DISTANCE: 4.5 mi to Rachel Lake, 10 mi round-trip; 5.5 mi to the first of Rampart Lakes, 12–13 mi round-trip total

DURATION: 2½ hours to Rachel Lake; almost 3½ hours to Rampart Lakes, 6–7 hours round-trip total

DIFFICULTY: Mix of strenuous for Rachel Lake (very steep, slightly overgrown, roots, boulders, trail-finding, not family- or dog-friendly unless they are badass, busy weekends, bugs into August) and very challenging for Rampart Lakes (steep switchbacks, GPS device helpful, overgrown, long, lingering snow into mid-July)

TRIP REPORT: This precious trek in the SW corner of Alpine Lakes Wilderness contains trails as rugged as any in Washington, but the rewards are plentiful, including the sizable picturesque (subalpine) Rachel Lake followed by the Rampart Lakes alpine basin, as spectacular as anywhere in the Pacific Northwest! People camp at these lakes lugging heavy packs up and down rough trails, but they're much more doable as day hikes. Northwest Forest Pass required, and restrooms are present.

TRAILHEAD: Rachel Lake TH. From Seattle, take I-90 E to exit 62, turn left on Kachess Lake Rd (FR-49) for 5.25 mi, and fork left on FR-4930 (signed, gravel, potholes, opposite Kachess Lake Campground) for 3.75 mi (passing more campsites) to reach the signed TH at right and two one-way parking areas at left.

From Portland, take I-5 N to exit 142A (Auburn), merge onto WA-18 E for 27 mi, fork right onto I-90 E (Spokane) for 37 mi to exit 62, and follow as above (70 mi, 1–1½ hours from Seattle; 225 mi, 3½–4 hours from Portland).

ROUTE: Hike steeply NE (Rachel Lake Trail 1313, free self-issue Wilderness Permit) less than 0.25 mi turning left up a faint switchback (some miss continuing narrowly up steep woods with signs indicating trail is 100 ft back on switchback). Walk NW a bit easier (roots, rocks) then steeper again before hopping over many small creeks entering Alpine Lakes Wilderness (less than 0.75 mi up). Cross more tiny streams following Box Canyon Creek NW over a slightly overgrown path (ferns, salal, huckleberries, Douglas fir, hemlock) that becomes rockier nearing a juncture (2.5 mi up, Hibox Mountain Climber's Trail right). Continue left (NW) back into trees on

Trail 1313 another 0.25 mi or so before the route steepens.

At 3.25 mi up, cross a creek whose bark is worse than its bite. See waterfalls up the creek bed before climbing steeply (roots) to another falls area near the first of 15 steep rocky switchbacks W. Atop the switchbacks, head SSW, crossing Box Canyon Creek (3.75 mi up, Trail 1313) from the bottom of a nice cascade, coming down the sheer rock slabs. Hike steeply (outstanding views, wildflowers) and move SW into trees, then very steeply NW up turns, following a small rocky creek bed (carefully). Trudge W up 7 more switchbacks (consistently steep) to the top of Box Canyon at Rachel Lake. There are many spurs with great perches left (E) of the water (campsites) for gazing across the colorful chilly lake to the cliffs under Rampart Ridge. Return to the TH, or continue for Rampart Lakes.

From the first juncture at Rachel Lake, two small signs appear trailside, one for a privy and one for Rampart Lakes Trail, which is marked with a Trail sign that you take right (N) of the lake for Rampart Lakes. Hike 100 yards or so, then ascend less than 0.50 mi up 17 tight, steep, rocky switchbacks and 3 quick S-turns W (wildflowers, views) to a nondescript intersection on Rampart Ridge (5150 ft, 4-ft-high narrow post with small rocks on top). Heading right (N) are the routes to Lila Lakes and Alta Mountain (see page 164), and left (S) is the leisurely route to Rampart Lakes basin.

Turn left (S); the trail undulates down the ridge (slightly overgrown, few trees) less than 0.5 mi on Rampart Lakes Trail to a large tarn (and others) out of the woods at the first juncture in Rampart Lakes basin. Continue right (SW) on Rampart Lakes Trail for a counterclockwise loop around the basin (1 mi or so) by moving over a tiny hill

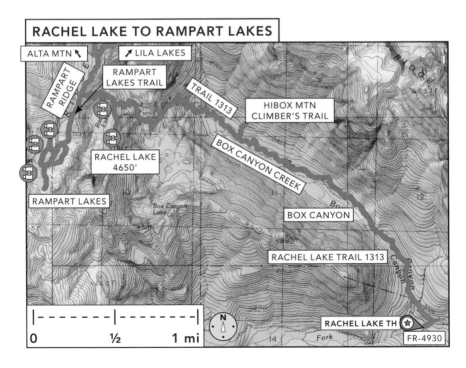

RACHEL LAKE TO RAMPART LAKES

ALTA MTN · LILA LAKES

RAMPART LAKES TRAIL

RAMPART RIDGE

TRAIL 1313

HIBOX MTN CLIMBER'S TRAIL

BOX CANYON CREEK

RACHEL LAKE 4650'

RAMPART LAKES

Box Canyon Lake

BOX CANYON

RACHEL LAKE TRAIL 1313

0   ½   1 mi

N

RACHEL LAKE TH ★

Fork

FR-4930

More than a half dozen lakes of interesting shapes fill the sublime Rampart Lakes basin.

and down to a creek following its left (E) side very briefly. Hop the creek near the outlet of the first of several marvelous lakes, climbing the opposite hillside a few feet SW over the rocky rise (wildflowers) past another juncture approaching another lake mid-basin (end of one possible loop, 5100 ft).

Keep right (NNW) instead of moving down left (S, toward picture-perfect campsite), passing tarns, additional spurs, and reflections near the main path as you round the mid-basin lake W to yet another juncture at the longest beautiful lake. Please explore right (N) from the spur 100 yards to an area near a lakeside tarn for more surprises! The water is clear blue-green with great reflections of the rocky (or snowy) ridge above the wide open (barely subalpine) secluded basin. Come back briefly from the spur and continue S along the left (E) side of the narrow lake past another nice surprise in a much smaller narrow lake just above the mid-basin lake you've passed. Quite striking! Keep walking S along the longer lake (faint Rampart Lakes Trail) to its outlet at the largest lake tucked into the back of the scenic basin farthest S. Saunter left (E) briefly, then pop over the creek with an option (right, along the E side of large lake on Rampart Lakes Backdoor Trail). Continue left (N, Rampart Lakes Trail) instead along the mid-basin lake. Go past the campsite up to the end of the little loop.

From the outlet of the first major lake you arrived to, you have another option to either head right (E) once over the little creek on another brief loop past a few tarns N to the juncture at the beginning of Rampart Lakes basin (near spur to Rachel Lake overlook), or to head left (N) along the creek a few feet then NE over the tiny hill, traversing to the same juncture. See Hibox and Alta Mountains from many vantage points along the lakes within the basin, and return up Rampart Ridge to the intersection (post) turning right almost 5 mi roughly down to the TH.

ELEVATION: 6151 ft; vertical gain of 3400 ft

DISTANCE: 6.5 mi up, 13 mi round-trip

DURATION: 4–5 hours up, 7–8 hours round-trip

DIFFICULTY: Very challenging (super-steep, long day hike, drop-offs, lingering snow until mid-July from high ridge requires mountaineering skills and traction)

TRIP REPORT: Hike past Rachel Lake and follow scenic Rampart Ridge to Alta Mountain with the option to visit Rampart Lakes basin (see page 161) before or after. The ridge up holds arresting vistas of Lila Lakes basin (another add-on option),

Lila Lakes under Box Ridge and Hibox Mountain from Alta Mountain Trail!

Box and Chikamin Ridges, and the surrounding statuesque mountaintops and valleys. Northwest Forest Pass required, and restrooms are present.

TRAILHEAD: Rachel Lake TH. See Rachel Lake to Rampart Lakes on page 161 for directions (70 mi, 1–1½ hours from Seattle; 225 mi, 3½–4 hours from Portland).

ROUTE: See Rachel Lake to Rampart Lakes on page 161 for the description and map on page 162 to the unsigned intersection on Rampart Ridge above Rachel Lake (5150 ft, around 5 mi and 3 hours from the TH). Continue right (NNE) on narrow brushy Lila Lakes Trail for less than 0.5 mi

ALTA MOUNTAIN

N

ALTA MOUNTAIN 6151'

BOX RIDGE

RAMPART RIDGE

LILA LAKES

ALTA MOUNTAIN TRAIL

LILA LAKES TRAIL

LILA LAKES

Lake

LILA LAKES TRAIL

RACHEL LAKE TH

0

¼

½ mi

T   I   O   N

See also map on page 162.

(thinning trees) to a cairned fork on the ridge crest. For Lila Lakes, keep right (NE) on Lila Lakes Trail for 0.75 mi (up brief then down 200 ft), winding past a smaller lake to the end of the established path in picturesque Lila Lakes basin (scant trees) between two pretty lakes. From the ridge fork, stay left onto Alta Mountain Trail (1.25 mi to summit), climbing the very steep, open slope N less than 0.5 mi to more moderate ridge hiking (5600 ft). Alaska Mountain NNW makes a great backdrop up the colorful route with Lila Lakes basin below to the E and Hibox Mountain and friends above on Box Ridge!

After a more level area (drop-offs, wildflowers), hike steeper up 2 quick switchbacks easing NNW, then climb very steeply (loose) NW as the eye candy increases from the next flat, narrower section (6000 ft). See Alta Mountain (trees flanking its SW side) with manageable obstacles along the high ridge as you walk 100 ft or so passing a few random evergreens, then continue 0.5 mi N to the summit over or around the rocky ridge bumps carefully. Scramble the last 100 ft steeply up the boulder pile (just right, E of trees) to the top (sizable cairn). The mesmerizing view from nearby Hibox Mountain SE panning counterclockwise includes Three Queens, Four Brothers, Glacier and Chikamin Peaks, Huckleberry and Alaska Mountains, Mount Thomson, Kendall Peak, and more!

CENTRAL CASCADES–
ENCHANTMENTS

53 | THORP MOUNTAIN LOOKOUT

ELEVATION: 5854 ft; vertical gain of 1700 ft

DISTANCE: 2.25 mi up, 4.5 mi round-trip

DURATION: 1½–2 hours up, 3 hours round-trip

DIFFICULTY: Strenuous (family-friendly but sometimes steeper, narrow, solid trail, overgrown in places, switchbacks)

TRIP REPORT: Here's a backdoor TH to an excellent summit in the Teanaway neighborhood N of Cle Elum. The shortened jaunt and drive, while avoiding the official Thorp Mountain TH much farther N, will have you patting yourself on the back while being rewarded with tremendous views of the region, including Kachess Lake. There's plenty of great camping off Salmon La Sac Rd. No fee or restroom.

TRAILHEAD: Knox Creek TH. From Seattle, take I-90 E to exit 80 (Salmon La Sac/ Roslyn), turn left on Bullfrog Rd for 2.75 mi, and take the second exit in the second consecutive traffic circle onto WA-903 N for 5.75 mi (including through Roslyn to Cle Elum Lake) then onto Salmon La Sac Rd for less than 7.5 mi. Turn left just past

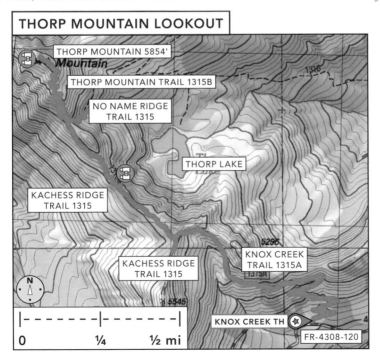

Kachess and Little Kachess Lakes as pondered from Thorp Mountain.

Cle Elum River Campground on FR-4308 (signed French Fork Creek, gravel) for 4.75 mi easily, then fork right on FR-4308-120 (Knox Creek Rd, one-lane, slightly overgrown, steeper switchbacks, AWD recommended) for exactly 2 mi up to the TH on the right (tiny old sign for Knox Creek Trail 1315.1 on a tree) with only a couple pullouts opposite and a few feet farther where possible without blocking the road.

From Portland, take I-84 E through the Columbia Gorge to exit 104 (Yakima/Bend), turn left on US-97 N (Goldendale/Yakima) for 60 mi onto WA-22 W (from a signal, toward I-82) for 3 mi, and turn right for I-82 W for 49 mi then onto I-90 W (from either lane) for 26 mi to exit 84 (Cle Elum). Turn right as it becomes Oakes Ave for 0.5 mi, turn left (second signal) on WA-903 N for 2.25 mi, take the first exit in the traffic circle to stay on WA-903 N for 5.75 mi onto Salmon La Sac Rd, and follow as on previous page (100 mi, 2 hours from Seattle; 265 mi, 4½ hours from Portland).

ROUTE: Hike Knox Creek Trail 1315A (.1) N narrowly for 0.5 mi with 5 steady switchbacks up the steep open wildflower-laced meadow (see French Cabin Peaks across Knox and French Cabin Creeks). Traverse W less than 0.5 mi then climb tight turns (steeper, rockier) NW toward the ridgeline as the route mellows W, then SW to a signed juncture (1.25 mi up). Head right (NW) onto Kachess Ridge Trail 1315 (down a tad) for 0.25 mi or so along the high tree-covered ridge, then step right (E, 5240 ft) 12 ft off-trail over a little log to see Thorp Lake directly below and Red Mountain across Thorp Creek valley. Trail 1315 soon leaves the crest left (NW) easily then steeper to a signed juncture back on the ridge under the summit block (2 mi up).

Take Thorp Mountain Trail 1315B left (NNW, opposite Cooper Pass) the final 0.25 mi up 21 tight (steep, rocky) switchbacks to the lookout. Trees become sparse (wildflowers) for views of sizable Little Kachess and Kachess Lakes below! The lookout will be locked and boarded most times, but the surrounding deck provides first-rate panoramas. See the local lakes then pan N to Summit Chief, Bears Breast Mountain, Mount Hinman, and Mount Daniel; NE to Ingalls Peaks and the Stuart Range; and E to Jolly Mountain. Wander 100 ft farther NW past the lookout on the boulder-laden high ridge, past small evergreens for more perspectives, before returning pleasantly to the TH.

54 | DAVIS PEAKS LOOP

ELEVATION: 6426 ft on Davis Peak (primary), 6450 ft on Davis Peak Central, 6490 ft on Davis Peak Southwest; vertical gains of 3950 ft, 4000 ft, and 4100 ft, respectively

DISTANCE: 4.75 mi to Davis Peak, 9.5 mi round-trip; 5.25 mi to Davis Peak Central; less than 5.5 mi to Davis Peak Southwest, 9.75 mi round-trip summits loop

DURATION: 3½ hours to Davis Peak (plus ½ hour for each summit), around 6–8 hours round-trip

DIFFICULTY: Mix of strenuous for Davis Peak (92 switchbacks, solid trail, steady steep, not crowded, Class 1, not much shade) and very challenging for the other summits and loop (minimal scrambling, drop-offs, slight exposure, Class 3, route-finding, bushwhacking)

TRIP REPORT: Here's another impassioned day trip in Alpine Lakes Wilderness past a surreal overlook shelf up to an old lookout site near the only rounded peak (July to October works best), with staggering vistas that only improve for those continuing to the more intimidating summits. Wildlife sightings may include hawks, eagles, deer, and bear. No fee or restroom.

TRAILHEAD: Davis Peak TH. See Tuck & Robin Lakes on page 172 for directions to the signed fork on Salmon La Sac Rd (Salmon La Sac CG left). Continue right on semi-rough gravel Cle Elum Valley Rd (FR-4330, toward Tucquala Lake, washboard, AWD preferred) for 1.5 mi, and turn left at the Wenatchee National Forest TH sign (Davis and Paris Creek Trails) on FR-134 (rougher) for more than 0.25 mi steeply down 2 turns, passing a small square bailout lot (right) steeper and rockier (one-lane) 100 yards to the signed TH right on a fork (not left down FR-134 toward private property). Find a few pullout spots just past the TH along the boulder-filled spur (100 mi, 2 hours from Seattle; 265 mi, 4½ hours from Portland).

ROUTE: Take signed Davis Peak Trail 1324 (free self-issue Wilderness Permit) down 200 yards N, crossing Cle Elum River (solid bridge). Fork right (E) on narrow Trail 1324 above the river easily (slightly overgrown) then steeper (rocky) before the first of at least 60 switchbacks plus S-turns (0.5 mi from TH) for 2.75 mi N steadily up Davis Peak's S ridge, or more precisely Goat Mountain's long ridge, of which Davis Peaks are on the southernmost point. Pass large old-growth trees (mossy flora) through switchback 15, then see Cle Elum Lake after switchback 32 (1 mi up, paintbrush) before the jungle thickens for 0.5 mi (narrow) into a recovering old burn at switchback 42 (less trees). Hike onto the ridgeline up the next switchback (wildflowers, views) before steepening up more switchbacks (overgrown with salal), then cross blowdowns easily, continuing up S-turns and the final switchbacks (first set, almost 5400 ft).

Traverse 0.25 mi NNW off the ridgeline through scree (easier, evolving landscape, see Chikamin Ridge NW), then work fairly steeply up 8 rocky switchbacks NE back to the ridge. Stroll effortlessly NW past a few old burnt trees (wildflowers, views) as you gain the shelf area (5800 ft, 3.75 mi from TH) and see the rocky summit cirque under Davis Peaks and Mount Rainier SW over Cle Elum Lake! Some return from the overlook shelf as the main ridge widens before turning to join the rougher S ridge of Davis Peak Southwest on the W side of the summit cirque.

For the summits, continue N, finding the narrow route (more difficult when snow covered into late June) on Trail 1324 down a bit (brushy) under the high ridge with a short cliffy area 100 yards before curving right through some trees (NE, past bushwhack end of counterclockwise summit loop left, 4 mi from TH). Ascend the main trail almost 25 quick switchbacks and turns NE over the wide slope (fewer trees, more wildflowers), steepening to the remains of the lookout site (reduced to a rock circle). Views become amplified, but for postcard

DAVIS PEAKS LOOP

DAVIS PEAK SOUTHWEST 6490'

DP CENTRAL 6450'

DAVIS PEAK 6426'

DAVIS PEAKS VIEWPOINT 5800'

DAVIS PEAK TRAIL 1324

CLE ELUM RIVER

Footbridge

DAVIS PEAK TH

From Davis Peak Lookout site to Hawkins Mountain and Mount Stuart.

shots proceed NW easily only 100 ft off-trail over grass to the mostly treeless top of Davis Peak. The Stuart Range remains enchanting as you pan to nearby Davis Peak North, then barely left of Mount Jerry Garcia is Bears Breast Mountain with The Cradle above much closer Opal Lake (tiny) straight ahead to the N.

For the other summits and loop (Class 3), continue NW on Trail 1324 more than 0.25 mi to the end of the established trail on the high ridge under Davis Peak Central. Follow the obvious narrow track (drop-offs, fewer trees), heading left (SW) from a notch below Davis Peak around an obstacle and up 2 switchbacks to the high ridge again. Work carefully NW (rocky) up 2 steeper switchbacks nearest the larger boulders on Davis Peak Central. For the best vista of the day, climb only a few feet past a gnarled dead tree to a precarious perch (airy, one at a time) over uneven boulders to the actual top. There are fantastic views to several more lakes, including Lake Terrance below and Waptus Lake NW under Bears Breast and Summit Chief Mountains. Also, look N to pointed Cathedral Rock just right of Mount Daniel and Mount Hinman.

Continue SW less than 0.25 mi to Davis Peak Southwest, following the bushwhack route just left (S) or right (N) of the first gendarme from the narrow high ridge, climbing straight over the next boulder or just right (N) a bit easier but slightly exposed. The route eases again to the right (N) of the next boulder as you follow the rocky ridgeline briefly, leaving the crest just right then just left of the next gendarme, approaching a small saddle E of the summit. Hike WSW up the climber's trail, then bushwhack (no trail) 75 ft to the minuscule lackluster top (few short trees). Peer W to Spectacle Lake under Chikamin Ridge with Lemah Mountain and Chimney Rock soaring NW!

For the somewhat easier and briefer counterclockwise loop from Davis Peak Southwest (0.75 mi to overlook plateau), continue S down the ridgeline to the next immediate obstacle. You can bail just left (E) before the ultra-steep ridge section, working 60 ft down steep rocks, or from the nose of the ridge you can work 60 ft down a nifty rock ramp angling left (E) steeply to easier ground near a few trees. Hike down scree, keeping left (E, easier) a few feet to the ridge crest where you follow the steep climber's trail S (grasses, wildflowers, views), which eases near the saddle before (N of) the last prominent rocky ridge bump (as seen from below, worth skipping). Bushwhack from the saddle with no trail super-steeply left (E, into forest) 100 yards as you might track left (NE) somewhat to begin with no blowdowns to cross, thankfully reaching Trail 1324 again. Turn right (S) 100 yards up across the scree field to the overlook shelf (Davis Peaks Viewpoint) before descending the switchbacks.

55 | TUCK & ROBIN LAKES

ELEVATION: 5300 ft near Tuck Lake, 6325 ft at the high point just above Robin Lakes; vertical gains of 2100 ft and around 3200 ft, respectively

DISTANCE: 5.25 mi to Tuck Lake; 6.25 mi to Robin Lakes, around 14 mi round-trip

DURATION: 2½ hours up; 3½–4 hours up, more than 8 hours round-trip

DIFFICULTY: Very challenging (long, demanding day hikes, ultra-steep at times, moderate scrambling, route-finding, GPS device helpful, mosquito swarms near lakes July to August)

TRIP REPORT: Although hauling heavy backpacks up extremely steep trails for overnighters is the norm, these treasures in Alpine Lakes Wilderness can be accomplished as day hikes too. The region is known as the Little Enchantments for good reason! Wildlife sightings may include mountain goats. Northwest Forest Pass required, and outhouses are present near the THs (BYOTP).

TRAILHEAD: Deception Pass TH or Tucquala Meadows TH. From Seattle, take I-90 E to exit 80 (Salmon La Sac/Roslyn), turn left on Bullfrog Rd for 2.75 mi, take the second exit in the second consecutive traffic circle onto WA-903 N for 5.75 mi (including through Roslyn to Cle Elum Lake) and onto Salmon La Sac Rd for 10.5 mi before the road narrows (slowing you down) into broken pavement to a signed fork (Salmon La Sac CG at left). Continue right on semi-rough gravel Cle Elum Valley Rd

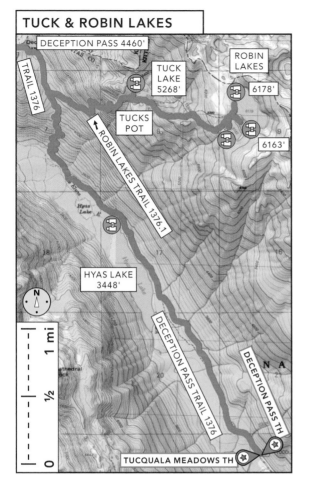

TUCK & ROBIN LAKES

DECEPTION PASS 4460'

TRAIL 1376

TUCK LAKE 5268'

ROBIN LAKES

6178'

TUCKS POT

ROBIN LAKES TRAIL 1376.1

6163'

HYAS LAKE 3448'

N

1 mi

½

0

DECEPTION PASS TRAIL 1376

DECEPTION PASS TH

N A

TUCQUALA MEADOWS TH

(FR-4330, toward Tucquala Lake, washboard, AWD preferred) for 9 mi to the Chatter Creek crossing (check ahead as high water could be difficult for some low 2WD before July), then drive 3 mi more roughly through meadows to reach the end (just past smaller Tucquala Meadows TH, FR-153, left) usually with ample parking between THs (110 mi, 2½ hours from Seattle; 275 mi, 4½–5 hours from Portland).

From Portland, take I-84 E through the Columbia Gorge to exit 104 (Yakima/ Bend), turn left on US-97 N (Goldendale/Yakima) for 60 mi onto WA-22 W (from a signal, toward I-82) for 3 mi, and turn right for I-82 W for 49 mi and onto I-90 W (from either lane) for 26 mi to exit 84 (Cle Elum). Turn right as it becomes Oakes Ave for 0.5 mi, turn left (second signal) on WA-903 N for 2.25 mi, take the first exit in the traffic circle to stay on WA-903 N for 5.75 mi then onto Salmon La Sac Rd for 10.5 mi, and follow as on previous page (110 mi, 2½ hours from Seattle; 275 mi, 4½–5 hours from Portland).

ROUTE: Begin easily on signed Deception Pass Trail 1376 (free self-issue Wilderness Permit) for 3.5 mi NW through the valley (minimal ups/downs) to the first switchback. You'll pass several campsites in the trees along Hyas Lake (great view from N end) and cross small creeks, old boardwalks, and bridges without difficulty, reaching the first of 20 steep switchbacks and turns (through forest) for another 0.5 mi N to the signed juncture for Tuck and Robin Lakes (below Deception Pass, 4225 ft, around 4 mi from TH).

Turn right (ENE) for 1 mi on Robin Lakes Trail 1376.1 to Tuck Lake. Head down (E) a bit, then slog up the terribly steep, narrow path (roots, loose rock) with

A family of mountain goats roam the boulders just above Robin Lakes across the valley from heavily glaciated Mount Daniel (7960 ft).

only 4 true switchbacks as you crawl NE more or less straight up the steep hillside (evergreens) only easing somewhat as you first see sizable Tuck Lake. Walk directly down to the lake left from a small opening for a decent shot or fork right (E) up the boulders, following a couple choices on the primary route up slightly then down to cross the outlet of Tuck Lake over a logjam to Robin Lakes Trail again. The handsome lake is completely enclosed within its own basin by steep-sloping granite as you cross hills over flatter slabs (views to surprisingly large glaciers under Mount Daniel). The much smaller Tuck's Pot (lake) is a few feet S. Explore the rocky rough landscape and return, or press on for the main course!

Continue following cairns steeper for 1 mi E to Robin Lakes as you descend a tiny notch S of Tuck Lake before scrambling ESE very steeply up the obvious path (Trail 1376.1) over boulders and rock (few pines, views). Leave the crest of the shoulder heading left (NE, 5820 ft, N of a little high point) while descending fairly steeply almost 100 ft before working your way E up abruptly to a little saddle on the widening slope. You'll find a couple of cairned routes up much larger steep granite slabs from the saddle. Hike steeply left a tad (NE, no trail; don't get pulled right, S near cliffs during whiteouts) before traversing right (SE) simpler up to a rounded flat corner on the slabs overlooking the Robin Lakes basin. The vista across Cle Elum River valley from Cathedral Rock to Mount Daniel is captivating, with long ribbons of water cascading down glaciers! The unfolding fairytale showcases two larger bright blue lakes and smaller ponds surrounded by rock and sheer granite walls to summits above. Melting snow and mountain goats (make noise and wave arms to deter) roaming the basin only add to the opulence! By September, the snow and goats are usually gone, but so are the bugs.

Head left down (N, 150 ft in elevation) Robin Lakes Trail a few feet (much easier) over to the larger lake, passing a little cascade between lakes from the small stream (trout jumping). Gaze deeply into the bright blue clear water from the rocky causeway or nearby. Also, walk S up a few feet to check out disgustingly beautiful views from the thin ridge between lakes (rises SE to Granite Mountain), where lucky campers claim the chillest sites within sporadic trees!

56 | PEGGY'S POND TO MOUNT DANIEL

ELEVATION: 5600 ft at Peggy's Pond, 7960 ft at Mount Daniel (7899 ft on Mount Daniel East Peak); vertical gains of 2500 ft for Peggy's Pond, around 5100 ft for Mount Daniel (plus 300 ft for East Peak) from the TH

DISTANCE: 5.25 mi to Peggy's Pond, 11 mi round-trip; 2.75 mi to Mount Daniel (including East Peak) from Peggy's Pond, 5 mi round-trip; 16 mi round-trip total from the TH

DURATION: 2–3 hours to Peggy's Pond, 4–6 hours round-trip; 3–4 hours up to the summits from Peggy's Pond, 6–8 hours round-trip (3–4 hours from Mount Daniel to TH)

DIFFICULTY: Mix of very challenging for Peggy's Pond (steep ups/downs, drop-offs, rocky, narrow, not for beginners, mosquito swarms July to August, GPS device recommended) and expert only for the summits (scrambling, ultra-steep, loose scree, narrow ridge at times, slight exposure, Class 3, route-finding, mountaineering skills and gear needed with snow, TH to TH rarely attempted)

TRIP REPORT: Travel to Peggy's Pond under the huge spire of Cathedral Rock, then climb the SE ridge of Mount Daniel to see several more remarkably colorful lakes en route to the glacier-surrounded summit massif comprising several named high points! Mount Daniel is without a doubt one of the most preeminent scrambles in Washington. Nearly all seeking a summit bid camp at Peggy's Pond or Squaw Lake. Northwest Forest Pass required, and outhouses are present, with outdoor privies at Squaw Lake and Peggy's Pond.

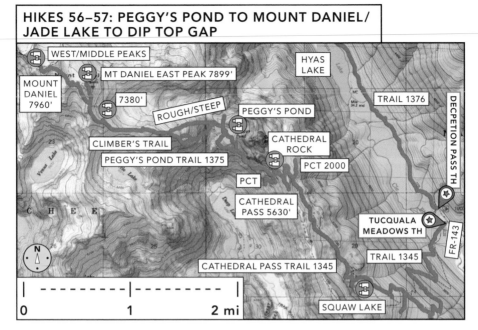

HIKES 56–57: PEGGY'S POND TO MOUNT DANIEL/ JADE LAKE TO DIP TOP GAP

WEST/MIDDLE PEAKS

MT DANIEL EAST PEAK 7899'

MOUNT DANIEL 7960'

7380'

ROUGH/STEEP

HYAS LAKE

PEGGY'S POND

TRAIL 1376

DECEPTION PASS TH

CLIMBER'S TRAIL

PEGGY'S POND TRAIL 1375

CATHEDRAL ROCK

PCT 2000

PCT

C H E E

CATHEDRAL PASS 5630'

TUCQUALA MEADOWS TH

FR-143

N

CATHEDRAL PASS TRAIL 1345

TRAIL 1345

0   1   2 mi

SQUAW LAKE

For hike 57, see also map on page 181.

TRAILHEAD: Tucquala Meadows (Cathedral Pass) TH. See Tuck & Robin Lakes on page 172 for directions (110 mi, 2½ hours from Seattle; 275 mi, 4½–5 hours from Portland).

ROUTE: Take Cathedral Pass Trail 1345 (free self-issue Wilderness Permit) across a tiny creek, then the Cle Elum River (solid bridge) before rising 2.5 mi SW (ancient forest) to Squaw Lake. Around 0.5 mi from the TH, hike up 11 switchbacks (first half steeper, wide, roots, rocks), moving right from a juncture (NW, opposite Trail Creek Trail, Squitch Lake) 0.5 mi farther fairly steeply up S-turns then varying in pitch to the decent-sized greenish pretty lake (near campsites, 4841 ft).

Head right (N) of Squaw Lake less than 1.5 mi NW to the signed PCT juncture near Cathedral Pass. You ascend 6 quick, steep switchbacks before mellowing, then move up steeper turns plus 6 more switchbacks. Hike steadily through tarn-dotted meadows (fewer trees, see Cathedral Rock, Mount Stuart) as the trail steepens to the juncture (end of Trail 1345), then fork left (NW) on the rockier PCT up a nearby switchback to tiny Cathedral Pass (5630 ft). Descend a few feet S without difficulty to the top of the Spinola Creek valley by moving right briefly (WNW, see teal-blue Deep Lake and Mount Daniel East Peak) to the junction with signed Peggy's Pond Trail 1375 on another switchback (1 hour from Squaw Lake, less than 1 hour to Peggy's Pond).

Take Trail 1375 right (NW) from the switchback for more than 0.75 mi to Peggy's Pond on a rather laborious traverse that drops a couple hundred feet before

Peggy's Pond under Cathedral Rock after coming down the steeps from Mount Daniel!

rising again as you must cross scree fields (thin brush, wildflowers) across an ultra-steep slope over the slick and slender path (be mindful). Move down 2 tight switchbacks then carefully slide steeply down 2 more very tight rocky switchbacks where the trail is obvious before traversing upward momentarily (somewhat improved), reaching a faint unsigned juncture (5400 ft) before entering the trees. Trail 1375 technically climbs right (NW) super-steeply up rocks directly to Peggy's Pond, but old Trail 1375 will be somewhat easier and longer (0.5 mi total), traversing left (W then N, brush) past a tarn before moving up NE steeper to trails splitting in the flats near Peggy's Pond.

There are a few paths near the shallow, clear blue lake directly under Cathedral Rock, but the area is easy to navigate. There are great campsites by the pond or close to a creek in the next basin N (with privy). For Mount Daniel, stay left (NW) near Peggy's Pond toward the tiny saddle/rise between basins, but take the faint mossy path (no sign, Mount Daniel Bootpath) 100 ft before (S of) the saddle from a faint crossroads toward large embedded boulders to eventually attain the SE ridge. Pass another tarn as the trail defines itself up very steeply left of the boulders through a few trees, then follow the rutted route W (last smaller trees) into a very steep little meadow to an unsigned juncture below a boulder field (5850 ft, 0.25 mi from Peggy's Pond).

The right-hand fork continues up extremely steeply WSW to the defined ridge; this route is a bit shorter, but the thin paths are slightly difficult to follow through the endless loose scree (or snow before August). The fork left from the meadow is more workable but very steep and semi-loose (more cairns), as both routes meet near large cairns (6700 ft, around 0.75 mi from Peggy's Pond). Turn sharply left (SW) for the primary route from the meadow, traversing without much difficulty before you hike straight uphill and the trail bends right (WSW, Mount Daniel Bootpath) very steeply (tight turns, loose rock), reaching a faint spur (6200 ft). Left from the spur heads S briefly past a few camps near the shoulder's edge before moving WSW up to meet the primary trail on a small rocky bench. Stay straight (SW) from the spur and head up boulders a couple hundred yards to the rock-filled bench, then climb more steeply NW closer to the developing ridgeline (see Deep Lake and a corner of Circle Lake). Stay on track (few large cairns) as the steeper route option from the rocky meadow below joins near a brief traverse W before climbing Mount Daniel Bootpath steeper a few feet to the narrower defined SE ridge (7000 ft, 1 mi and 1 hour from Peggy's Pond). Observe picturesque Circle Lake (not a circle), Mount Rainier, Mount Adams, Glacier Peak, Mount Daniel East Peak, the top of Hyas Creek Glacier in the desolate canyon just N (with milky turquoise tarns and an audible cascade), and part of the Stuart Range!

Continue W down (easier, scrub, short pines) to a small saddle before moving much steeper up the narrower ridgeline on the climber's trail (loose rock, pebbles). One very narrow ridge section (exposure) has a bailout path left (S) a few feet that works (see Spade Lake SW), arriving at a very large cairn in the center of the ridge (7380 ft, 1.5 mi from Peggy's Pond, 1 mi directly to Mount Daniel) before the route becomes more demanding to the summits. Hike NNW steeply (drop-offs, touch of exposure) as you cross a brief rock ramp (see down to sliver of Venus Lake, straight ahead NW to Mount Hinman then Mount Daniel between huge, dark gendarmes that seemingly block travel on ridge crest), then move left (W) of a short knife-edge ridge section down a bit into a loose, rocky gully. Traverse upward 100 ft WNW, then scramble one of a few possibilities carefully 100 ft N ultra-steeply (see caves left within nearby gendarmes) to the thin ridgeline atop the gully. Ascend looser steep rock NW, heading slightly right (E, cautiously) without difficulty around the gendarmes where the trail is pretty obvious as you make your way to another knife-edge ridge section with large boulders (see directly up S ridge to East Peak and traverse route to Mount Daniel). Move past the exposed ridge from either side, the left (W, watch points of contact) being somewhat more solid 40 ft to the path, slipping narrowly past the steeply sloped boulder. Cairns keep you left (W) of obstacles on the crest a moment to a small saddle at the summits intersection (cairn, 7600 ft, 1.75 mi from Peggy's Pond). A great landmark would be the large sharp spire on the ridge just above.

For East Peak (fun, ½-hour round-trip), scramble N super-steeply up the ridge right (E) of the large spire (sweet shot to Mount Rainier over Venus and Spade Lakes), then work between two huge gendarmes quite steeply up the climber's trail just right (E) of the ridge crest. Contour ultra-steeply a moment, easing to the rocky summit (drop-offs, but safe). Look over the topmost of Daniel Glacier to Middle Peak and Mount Daniel, and see directly down the canyon to Peggy's Pond under Cathedral Rock. Colorful Venus and Spade Lakes are tucked away in their own basins SSW, and a trained eye can spot Tuck and Robin Lakes within the rocky landscape to the NE. Pea Soup Lake is completely obscured, but the side trip is still tantalizing!

From the summits intersection, leave the high ridge, traversing the very narrow, loose Mount Daniel Bootpath (less than 0.75 mi to Mount Daniel) carefully NW over, down some, then up a bit (traction/ice axe required with considerable snow or ice) to the saddle between East Peak and the SE ridge of Middle Peak (be careful near Daniel/Lynch Glaciers). Work super-steeply W (200 ft up) over the widening scree-covered ridge before easing NW 150 ft or so, approaching the next traverse trail as the summit is finally within your grasp and, for once, closer than it appears! Traverse left (WNW) below Middle Peak without trouble on one of a couple choices over scree and snow to the tiny saddle E of Mount Daniel, keeping away from the Lynch Glacier (deep crevasses form over seasons). Hike steeply 100 ft WSW up to the naked mound just S of the rocky pillar (see Pea Soup Lake over glacier). Walk NW a few feet, then easily scramble from the base for only around 75 ft (steep, loose rock, boulders), winding clockwise to the airy summit (only room for a few at a time as vertigo sets in). Sensory overload! See over piercingly deep blue Pea Soup to the col (Dip Top Gap) between Dip Top and Lynch Peaks, then gaze N into Northern Cascades past the Monte Cristo Group from Mount Baker to Glacier Peak! Look W to nearby Mount Hinman with Mount Daniel's West Pyramid and Northwest Peak, a stone's throw away. There are also countless sub- and high-alpine lakes visible from this the highest point in both King and Kittitas Counties and the crown jewel of Alpine Lakes Wilderness.

Circle Lake with Mount Rainier, Three Queens, Lemah Mountain, Overcoat Peak, and others.

ELEVATION: 5442 ft at Jade Lake, 6660 ft at Dip Top Gap; vertical gain of around 3200 ft (plus 1300 ft for Dip Top Gap)

DISTANCE: 10.5 mi to Jade Lake (plus 1.5 mi to Dip Top Gap), at least 24 mi round-trip

DURATION: 6 hours to Jade Lake (plus 1½ hours to Dip Top Gap), 5 hours max Jade Lake to TH

DIFFICULTY: Mix of strenuous to Marmot Lake (very long day hike, significant ups/downs, mosquito swarms July to August) and very challenging above (route-finding, steep scree path, rock- and glacier-covered gully to Dip Top Gap, GPS device recommended, traction required)

TRIP REPORT: These Washington trophies lead to the spectacular basin belonging to bright turquoise Jade Lake in the Necklace Valley and the gap above with wicked views of Pea Soup Lake under Mount Daniel! These are not day hikes unless you're a serious trail runner, as most people camp at Marmot Lake and day hike to Jade Lake or Dip Top Gap with minimal camping areas physically available near Jade Lake. It's also more troublesome to carry a heavy pack to the intense upper lake, but if visiting midweek you might score the one and only flat spot. Wildlife sightings may include deer and mountain goats. Northwest Forest Pass required, and outhouses are present (BYOTP).

TRAILHEAD: Deception Pass TH. See Tuck & Robin Lakes on page 172 for directions (110 mi, 2½ hours from Seattle; 275 mi, 4½–5 hours from Portland).

ROUTE: See Tuck & Robin Lakes on page 172 for the description to the juncture below Deception Pass (Robin Lakes Trail right, around 4 mi from TH, 4225 ft). Trail 1376 mellows and widens near the juncture then becomes steeper again briefly, heading NW past the first Deception Pass crossroads (unsigned PCT sharply left, 4460 ft, 4.5 mi and 2 hours from the TH). Walk 50 ft farther (forested), turning left (NW) onto signed Marmot Lake Trail 1066 (opposite PCT fork right), nearly another mile easily (passing tarn, large scree field, more ponds) to the top of another little pass area (4760 ft, vistas improving).

Hike narrower Trail 1066 (W then NNW) for 1.25 mi steadily down 700 ft through lively Hozzbizz Basin before ascending again. You'll descend open meadows and cross West Fork Deception Creek into evergreens, moving down 4 quick

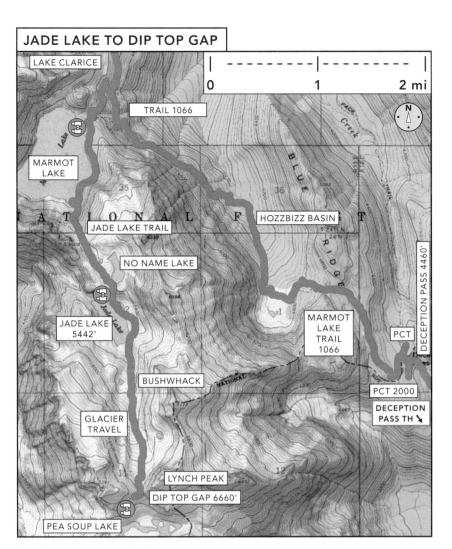

JADE LAKE TO DIP TOP GAP

LAKE CLARICE

0   1   2 mi

TRAIL 1066

MARMOT LAKE

HOZZBIZZ BASIN

JADE LAKE TRAIL

NO NAME LAKE

DECEPTION PASS 4460'

JADE LAKE 5442'

MARMOT LAKE TRAIL 1066

PCT

BUSHWHACK

PCT 2000

DECEPTION PASS TH ↘

GLACIER TRAVEL

LYNCH PEAK

DIP TOP GAP 6660'

PEA SOUP LAKE

See also map on page 176.

switchbacks (more lush meadows, wildflowers, tiny streams) before crossing the main creek again from the rocky trail to its low point in the valley. Then climb up 6 steep rocky switchbacks NW and cruise steadily over an improved track (easier, narrow, slightly overgrown, see Glacier Peak) before rising up 2 steeper switchbacks (past small waterfall), passing an unsigned junction. Fork left (SW, Trail 1066, opposite Lake Clarice Trail) for 0.5 mi narrower with 3 switchbacks up to the vibrant and largish Marmot Lake (4930 ft, 8.75 mi and around 4 hours from the TH).

Work your way left (E) of the water 0.75 mi S with some difficulty (past campsites) up and down annoying hills (steeply, narrowly, roots, felled trees) and multiple paths to navigate as they merge into Jade Lake Trail, continuing across a

Pea Soup Lake under Mount Daniel and the Lynch Glacier from Dip Top Gap. Breathtaking, and not because you just climbed another steep glacier to get this view!

boulder-filled avalanche chute (cairns) to the main inlet creek S of Marmot Lake. Then climb SSE much steeper (leaving the colorful lake) up a narrower stretch within a rocky gully until the route finally levels (views). Pass a drying tarn through the flatter meadow close to No Name Lake (10 mi from TH) and begin to see Jade Lake and the glacier up to Dip Top Gap. Descend quite steeply 200 ft in elevation S to the glowing (twilight) sea-green lake. Watch for mountain goats and walk left (SE) past a pond to midlake with camping possible from a small area in a clearing. Explore sweet spurs around both sides carefully (surrounded by steeply sloped granite).

For Dip Top Gap, move SE past the campsite (left, E of lake, views), steeply up Jade Lake Trail as it officially ends, but the bushwhack path continues (meadows, few trees) reaching a subtle fork above a steep short cliff band close to the lake (0.25 mi from campsite). Move right (SW), hugging the broken little cliff 100 ft very steeply down the narrow rocky path (slightly overgrown) to the lakeshore, approaching the inlet creek (just S of a brief sheer cliff band blocking travel along the shoreline).

You'll find limited cairns on the remainder of the fairly discernable route (snow-covered glacier, easier until June or so) 1 mi S to the gap/col as you start up the wide rocky gully left (E) of the creek bed or where permissible until the glacier begins. Crampons/ice axes are required until July or August (lingering cornice near steeper top), but from September into October micro-spikes and poles will suffice. During late summer and fall, climb the orange-colored slabs S up the center of the gully, finding thin routes up rocky rises (slightly right, W) that soon leave the rises to move left up the remaining snow and ice to Dip Top Gap. Too far left (E) lies a more difficult scramble, while moving up the left edge of the rock, stone, and boulder-blanketed ice is usually workable (see Monte Cristo Group, Sloan Peak, Mount Baker, and Glacier Peak). The trek steepens S briefly (larger boulders), reaching the left (E) or low side of the col (6660 ft) where you are suddenly greeted with in-your-face views of Mount Daniel and the imposing Lynch Glacier directly above the rather large and deep (dreamscapes) blue Pea Soup Lake!

Pea Soup used to be pea soupier in the early '90s when the retreating glaciers covered most of the lake, but it's still quite a sight! Straight up left (E) from the saddle is the rarely climbed Lynch Peak, and right (W) past a steep bump in the saddle is the more traveled route up slabs very steeply to Dip Top Peak. Move down briefly to the N side of the gap to see more of Mount Hinman and the rest of Pea Soup before returning to camp or the TH.

58 LONGS PASS

ELEVATION: 6400 ft just above Longs Pass (6250 ft); vertical gain of 2150 ft

DISTANCE: Up to 6 mi round-trip

DURATION: 3–5 hours round-trip

DIFFICULTY: Strenuous (steeper at beginning and end, switchbacks, rocky, wide)

TRIP REPORT: For dignified vistas of the ginormous chunk of granite (one of largest in the Lower 48) that is Mount Stuart, savor a simple hike with a flabbergasting payoff from the edge of Alpine Lakes Wilderness in the Wenatchee National Forest! Consider combining with part of Lake Ingalls to Fortune Peak on page 186. Wildlife sightings may include mountain goats. Northwest Forest Pass required, and an outhouse is present (BYOTP).

TRAILHEAD: Esmeralda TH. From Seattle, take I-90 E to exit 85 (Cle Elum/Leavenworth), turn left on WA-10 E/WA-970 E for 0.5 mi, turn right on WA-970 E (Wenatchee/Leavenworth) for 6 mi, turn left on Teanaway Rd (no signal) for 7 mi to a juncture, and continue straight onto Teanaway Rd N Fork for 5.5 mi, passing 29 Pines Campground to a fork. Drive slight right on signed FR-9737 (milepost 13, gravel,

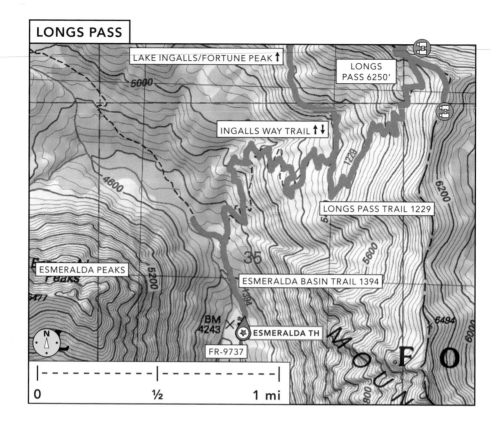

LAKE INGALLS/FORTUNE PEAK ↑

LONGS PASS 6250'

5000

INGALLS WAY TRAIL ↑↓

1229

4600

LONGS PASS TRAIL 1229

6200

4600

ESMERALDA PEAKS

5200

35

5600

ESMERALDA BASIN TRAIL 1394

1394

5477

6494

BM 4243 ×

ESMERALDA TH

6000

N

FR-9737

800

MOUN

0   ½   1 mi

washboard) for 4 mi, passing Beverly Campground (on left) for 3.5 mi more to DeRoux Campground (heads down fork left briefly from sign that says Entering Fee Site, Rec Pass Required). Continue right on FR-9737 (2WD okay, AWD preferred, see Esmeralda Peak) for 1.5 mi to reach the end into a small lot.

From Portland, take I-84 E through the Columbia Gorge to exit 104 (Yakima/ Bend), turn left on US-97 N (Goldendale/Yakima) for 60 mi onto WA-22 W (from a signal, toward I-82) for 3 mi, and turn right for I-82 W for 49 mi then onto I-90 W (from either lane) for 5 mi to exit 106 (for US-97 N/Wenatchee). Turn right on US-97 N for 0.25 mi, take the third exit in traffic circle to stay on US-97 N for 2.5 mi, turn right on US-97 N for 13 mi, turn left on WA-970 W (Cle Elum/Seattle) for 3.25 mi, turn right on Teanaway Rd (no signal) for 7 mi, and follow as on previous page (115 mi, 2½ hours from Seattle; 260 mi, 5 hours from Portland).

ROUTE: Take signed Esmeralda Basin Trail 1394 (free self-issue Wilderness Permit) along North Fork Teanaway River for more than 0.25 mi N up (wide, rocky, steep) to the first juncture. Turn right (NE) onto signed Ingalls Way Trail 1390 steadily for 1.75 mi up 16 switchbacks and turns to the next signed intersection out of the trees (almost 5400 ft).

For Longs Pass (opposite Ingalls Way Trail), turn sharply right (NE) 0.75 mi on Longs Pass Trail 1229 up 3 switchbacks then 14 switchbacks/turns steeper to the small saddle at the pass area. You'll spot most of the route through the subalpine environment (thinning small evergreens, see Mount Rainier behind Esmeralda Peak). Respect mountain goats that frequent the region while taking in the grandeur. For the bonus, work right (SE, less than 0.25 mi round-trip) from the pass up the unofficial track heading right (S) of a ridge bump to a rockier prominent section of ridge with a mini high point and picture-perfect angles of the entire ridgeline up to Not Hinkhouse Peak, the Ingalls Creek valley (to Mount Stuart and other Enchantment summits), and Ingalls Peaks!

Rusty moonscape up switchbacks to gallant views from Longs Pass.

59 | LAKE INGALLS TO FORTUNE PEAK

ELEVATION: 6463 ft at Lake Ingalls, 7382 ft on Fortune Peak; vertical gains of 2525 ft and 3150 ft (including the lake), respectively

DISTANCE: More than 4.5 mi to lake or summit, 9–9.5 mi round-trip (12 mi round-trip for both)

DURATION: Around 3 hours to lake or summit, 6–8 hours round-trip total

DIFFICULTY: Mix of strenuous for Lake Ingalls (steady steep, ups/downs, popular, boulders) and very challenging for Fortune Peak (long with lake, quiet, super-steep, Class 3, minimal exposure, loose scree, scrambling)

TRIP REPORT: Visit Lake Ingalls for incredible views from a hidden bright-green and clear high alpine lake with reflections showcasing Mount Stuart! And there's nearby Fortune Peak (SE ridge route) for more experienced hikers who'll enjoy a whole lot more from the top as countless summits in Northern Cascades unfold! Wildlife sightings may include mountain goats, cougar, and black bear. Northwest Forest Pass required, and an outhouse is present (BYOTP).

TRAILHEAD: Esmeralda TH. See Longs Pass on page 183 for directions (110 mi, 2½ hours from Seattle; 260 mi, 5 hours from Portland).

ROUTE: See Longs Pass on page 183 for the description 2 mi to the intersection out of the trees (almost 5400 ft). For Lake Ingalls and Fortune Peak, continue straight/left (N) on Ingalls Way Trail 1390 (opposite Longs Pass Trail), steadily steep up a long traverse 1.25 mi to Ingalls Pass (6500 ft), including 8 steeper rocky switchbacks (very little vegetation), as you finish easier to the scenic pass and juncture with options near a large cairn (3.25 mi and almost 2 hours from the TH, see the next page for Fortune Peak).

Continue straight from Ingalls Pass (NW, not left to summit, or sharp right from cairn onto primitive Ingalls Way Alt Trail 1390.2, loop return) for Lake Ingalls on Ingalls Way Trail 1390.1 (1.25 mi farther, clockwise loop), traversing the N side of the prominent SE ridge of Fortune Peak easily down scree into the grassy wildflower-covered meadow. Follow the thin path past campsites near a little creek in Headlight Basin (great overlooks), then navigate a boulder field N without dropping too far (cairns scattered semi-confusingly) to the solid path on the steep hillside. Walk more leisurely NE across tiny creeks (wildflowers), passing the return trail (1390.2, right).

Scramble left (N) on Trail 1390 very steeply for 0.25 mi to Lake Ingalls following

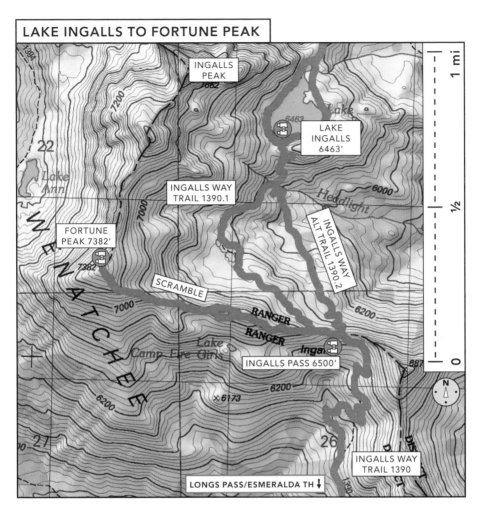

See also map on page 184.

several cairns up the boulder field (more than 200 ft) before walking down briefly and easily to the well-concealed, striking blue-green water within a rocky bowl! You arrive directly under Ingalls (highest), East Ingalls, and South Ingalls Peaks with a tremendous reflection of the titan Mount Stuart into the infinity pool! Work around the lake (W side, easier) and wildly rocky landscape as almost everyone does (carefully) and keep a safe distance from mountain goats (usually gone like snow by July).

To finish the loop, continue left (SE, Trail 1390.2) from the juncture 0.25 mi below the lake down several very steep tight turns (boulder field), then traverse SSE toward Ingalls Pass (narrow) over smaller creeks and a larger one (with nice cascade). The steep pitch varies with a few breaks including past a couple small tarns (reflections, wildflowers) before steepening up a dozen or so tight switchbacks SSE to the pass.

For Fortune Peak from Ingalls Pass (1.25 mi and around 1½ hours away), begin W up the most worn climber's trail easily along the widening ridgeline, moving just

Classic pic of Mount Stuart into glassy Lake Ingalls on a bluebird day!

left (S) when needed to a very steep point (changes to Class 3 abruptly). Down-climb slightly left (S) of the ridge bump with loose gravel between steep ramps and shelves 25–30 ft to the ridge proper again (better footing). Scramble WNW over the crest (few choices, cairns) then move barely right (N) a few feet (no trail) through a boulder field over the top of the next bump on the narrow ridgeline (semi-loose, large drop-offs, watch footing). Soon a bailout option appears to your left (S) 30 ft off the crest (from 6875 ft) down wide gravel-filled ramps to a low spot near a small saddle. Or just stay on the wafer-thin ridge section briefly until you get to the wider small saddle (notice bright blue-, white-, yellow-, green-, and orange-colored rocks locally) before scrambling the super-steep summit block (looser scree) NW up the climber's trail (wider ridge) to the broad peak. See tiny Lake Ann NW below then look N to the Monte Cristo Group, Mount Hinman and Mount Daniel, and Mount Baker past Sloan Peak!

60 EARL PEAK TO BEAN PEAK

ELEVATION: 7036 ft on Earl Peak, 6743 ft on Bean Peak; vertical gains of 3450 ft and 3150 ft, respectively; almost 4000 ft for both peaks (see Trip Report for Bean Creek Basin alone)

DISTANCE: Around 6.5 mi round-trip for either peak alone, less than 7.5 mi round-trip smaller loop for both peaks, returning down Bean Creek Basin; almost 10 mi round-trip longer loop for both peaks returning down Fourth Creek Basin and Beverly Creek

DURATION: At least 2 hours up to either peak, 6–8 hours round-trip for loops

DIFFICULTY: Mix of strenuous for Earl Peak alone (steady steep, solid trails, rocky) and very challenging for all other routes and loops (route-finding on high ridges, scrambling, narrow at times, minimal exposure, GPS device helpful, mountaineering skills and gear required with snow)

TRIP REPORT: Underrated and less traveled but mind-blowing is this spectacular expanse just S of the Stuart Range in the Enchantments! Families inclined to skip the summits enjoy cascades and wildflowers from Bean Creek Basin June to August (4.5 mi round-trip, 1100 ft vertical gain). Try late July to September to avoid snow. Northwest Forest Pass required, and there is no restroom.

TRAILHEAD: Beverly-Bean/Beverly Turnpike TH. See Longs Pass on page 183 for directions to 29 Pines Campground. Drive slight right from the fork on signed FR-9737 (milepost 13, gravel, washboard) for 3.5 mi, then turn right before the bridge over Beverly Creek onto FR-112 (signed, very narrow, overgrown, rough, okay for 2WD) for 1 mi to reach the end with parking on the sides (110 mi, 2 hours from Seattle; 255 mi, 4–5 hours from Portland).

ROUTE: Begin NNW on Beverly Turnpike Trail 1391 (free self-issue Wilderness Permit) over the footbridge then steadily up the old roadbed for less than 0.5 mi (abundant lupine) to a signed intersection. For Bean Creek Basin and the direct routes to the peaks (including primary counterclockwise loops), hike right (NE) from the fork up Bean Creek Trail 1391.1 (near Bean Creek, steeper) more than 0.25 mi (overgrown) before crossing the creek over rocks easily to the left (W) side. Walk NE through partly open steep meadows (lupine, red columbine, bear grass, daisies), crossing a little side creek within a long green gully (1 mi from TH), then move NE (somewhat easier) up 2 slender switchbacks and an S-turn before crossing a slightly rockier gully (views). Pop over Bean Creek again to a fork on the E side (5100 ft, 1.75 mi from TH, cairns, Earl Peak loops right).

For Bean Creek Basin (0.5 mi away) or Bean Peak directly, head left (NNW) following the rocky creek up Bean Creek Trail 1391.2 with some turns, mellowing past a nice camp into gorgeous wildflower-covered meadows reaching a chill cascade area! Return, or continue from the treeless basin much steeper more than 0.5 mi N (rougher, narrower, rocky turns) to the high ridge juncture right (SE) of Bean Peak (see the next page).

Walk right (ESE) from the fork over Bean Creek for Earl Peak first on Bean Peak Trail (steeper, thinning evergreens) briefly before hiking steeply E up 14 steady switchbacks to a saddle S of Earl Peak (exiting trees, see Mount Stuart and Sherpa Peak, more than 2.75 mi from TH). In the background left (NW) of the Stuart Range above reddish Bean Peak are Ingalls Peaks with Mount Daniel and Mount Hinman

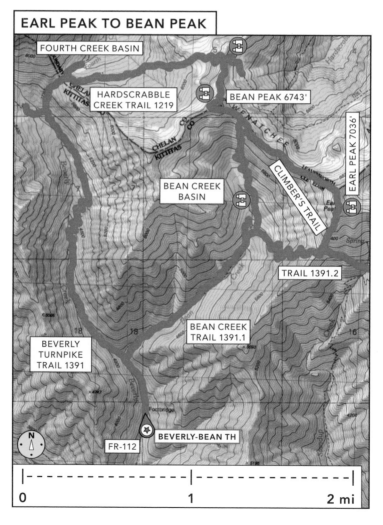

Reddish Bean Peak under Ingalls Peaks with Mount Stuart and Sherpa Peak standing immensely!

behind. Turn left (NNE) onto unsigned Earl Peak Trail from the saddle juncture (cairn) working up the steeper ridge almost 0.25 mi, then climb just left (W) of the crest a couple times, passing stunted old snags and wildflowers. Finish NE steeply past boulders over the wide-enough ridge to the inviting top!

For loops and Bean Peak, navigate the steep high ridge N down from the summit (unofficial trail) 100 yards easily before moving left (NW) onto the connecting ridge. Scramble steeply on and off the crest (fun scree-covered climber's trail) 200 yards, reaching the faint path near the bottom of the steeper section. Scramble boulders NW for 0.5 mi, hugging closely to the ridgeline (grippy rock but check holds), then for the next bump, work over larger boulders or traverse 30 ft left (S) below the ridge, finishing easier to the cairned juncture (6385 ft, 4.25 mi on counterclockwise loop with Earl Peak) for the briefer loop option left (S, down Bean Creek Basin, faint scree Trail 1391.2).

For Bean Peak and the loop into Fourth Creek Basin, continue NW along the steep climber's trail (reddish yellow rock), momentarily bouldering the remaining 150 yards to the summit (options, no trail). Traverse left (WNW) S of the peak across and up boulders (steeply sloped rock clinging on to summit block), reaching the highest part of the narrow SW ridge (connecting to Mary's and Judi's Peaks). Turn right (NE, cautiously, hint of exposure), climbing the final huge boulders to the top (at least 4.5 mi on longer loop option). Wow! Look down to the N, following the ridge to the nearby prominent rocky block known as Volcanic Neck, with Devil's Head just beyond. Towering above are Mount Stuart with Sherpa, Argonaut, Colchuck, Dragontail, Little Annapurna, and McClellan Peaks.

Find the simpler descent N from Bean Peak (loop) to a saddle junction under Volcanic Neck by hiking steeply between large boulders (at first) then somewhat more reasonably down on, or just left (W) of, the ridgeline (watching for snow cornices), finishing over smaller blue rocks to the defined crossroads. Take in the vistas from 5 mi into the longer trek and hear water from Hardscrabble Creek Basin on the right (E). Turn left (W) onto Hardscrabble Creek Trail 1219 steeply down scree with 6 switchbacks and turns into the top part of Fourth Creek Basin, then move somewhat left (WSW) near the tree line, finding the rocky, rutted trail down through a steep clearing (see tree-covered notch/saddle known as Fourth Creek Pass or Fourth Creek/ Beverly Creek Divide). Enjoy great views, semi-open wildflower-lined meadows, and almost ten micro-creeks to cross-traversing WSW (friendly grade, sparse pines) to Fourth Creek Pass with a signed juncture (less than 6.5 mi on longer loop) in the trees between Mary's and Bill's Peaks. Left (SW) and right (NE) is Fourth Creek Trail 1218.

Turn left (SW) more than 0.25 mi from the saddle on Trail 1218 (shared with Trail 1219) as the route turns down 1 switchback (rockier, steeper) then S-turns to another signed juncture (Fourth Creek Trail/Beverly Turnpike Trail). Turn left (SSE, Trail 1391) as the route eases down toward Beverly Creek (creeks merge), moving into smaller ponderosa pines, then cross a long scree field (7 mi on longer loop) working S across steep rocky meadows and more scree fields (lupine, paintbrush, others). Hike down 10 steeper switchbacks S toward the creek again (following E side), then the trail undulates easily (more flora). Cross Bean Creek where possible (interesting during high water), then hike up promptly to the intersection at the end of the loop where you continue straight (SSE) on Trail 1391 almost 0.5 mi down to the TH.

Volcanic Neck between Hardscrabble and Fourth Creek Basins.

61 | LAKE STUART TO HORSESHOE LAKE

ELEVATION: 5064 ft at Lake Stuart, 6400 ft max at Horseshoe Lake; vertical gains of 1665 ft and more than 3000 ft, respectively

DISTANCE: Almost 4.5 mi to Lake Stuart, 9–10 mi round-trip; 6.5 mi to Horseshoe Lake, 14 mi round-trip

DURATION: Less than 2½ hours up for Lake Stuart, 5–6 hours round-trip; 4 hours up for Horseshoe Lake, 8–10 hours round-trip if lollygagging

DIFFICULTY: Mix of strenuous (steady grade okay, larger rocks, family-friendly) and expert only for Horseshoe Lake as a day hike (long, trail-finding, ultra-steep, rougher when wet, traction with snow and ice, GPS device recommended); drone use prohibited in all Wilderness areas

TRIP REPORT: Here are two nuggets (more peaceful than neighboring Colchuck Lake) that reside just N of Mount Stuart, with Sherpa, Argonaut, Colchuck, and Dragontail Peaks all visible from some point! Conditioned trekkers pass Lake Stuart, negotiating several blowdowns through the Jack Creek Fire's (2017) charcoaled trees (very few felled trees to cross actually blackened), then climb the impossibly steep hillside leading to the immaculate Horseshoe Lake basin. Try late July through at least the second week in October when the larches (deciduous coniferous subalpine larches only grow between 5900–7900 ft) are glowing gold from the high lake basin with views and reflections rivaling the finest anywhere.

Because of underfunding, a general lack of respect, and overcrowding, a strict permit system is in place within all the Enchantment Zones for overnight adventures that must be applied for and acquired through a lottery system months in advance and printed ahead. Call Leavenworth Ranger Station or Wenatchee River Ranger Station (www.fs.usda.gov/recarea/okawen/recarea/?recid=59019) for more info and see the Trip Report for Colchuck Lake on page 197. Day hikers, however, can have at it! Parking locally is also a major concern, as at least half of Stuart Lake TH is allocated for those with an Overnight Permit, with the backup lot at Eightmile TH (adding more than 1 mi round-trip). Wildlife sightings may include mountain goats and black bear. Northwest Forest Pass required at both proximate THs including the roadway between, and a vault toilet is present at both THs with outdoor privies at Lake Stuart.

TRAILHEAD: Stuart Lake TH or Eightmile TH. From Seattle, take I-5 N to exit 171 onto WA-522 E (Bothell) for 24 mi, and exit right, merging onto US-2 E (Wenatchee) in Monroe for 85 mi. Turn right over the Wenatchee River (in Leavenworth) on Icicle

Horseshoe Lake to Jack Ridge with golden larch lighting up one of the most magical destinations in all of Washington!

Rd (roughly paved, potholes) for 8.25 mi, turn left on Eightmile Rd (FR-7600, dirt, signed for nearby Bridge Creek Campground) for a few feet, keeping right on FR-7601 (dirt, bad washboard, okay for 2WD, AWD high-clearance preferred) for less than 3 mi with Eightmile TH left (within trees). Continue around 0.5 mi to the end at a parking circle that fills early (parking along the W side of FR-7601 between THs okay).

From Portland, take I-84 E through the Columbia Gorge to exit 104 (Yakima/ Bend), and turn left on US-97 N (Goldendale/Yakima) 60 mi onto WA-22 W (from a signal, toward I-82) for 3 mi. Turn right for I-82 W for 49 mi onto I-90 W (from either lane) for 5 mi to exit 106 (for US-97 N/Wenatchee), turn right on US-97 N for 0.25 mi, take the third exit in traffic circle to stay on US-97 N for 2.5 mi, and turn right on US-97 N for 51 mi (several junctures). Turn left to merge onto US-2 W for 5 mi (through Leavenworth), turn left on Icicle Rd for 8.25 mi like above. For a quicker bypass option (skipping Leavenworth traffic) if driving from Portland and the S, merge onto US-2 W for only 3.5 mi, turn left on E Leavenworth Rd (no signal, just before river bridge) for 3.5 mi, turn left on Icicle Rd for 6.25 mi, and follow as on previous page (130 mi, 2½ hours from Seattle; 285 mi, 4½–5 hours from Portland).

ROUTE: Begin SSW on bustling Stuart Lake Trail 1599 (kiosk, free self-issue Wilderness Permit), which undulates upward gently S of Mountaineer Creek 1.5 mi before crossing it to the N. Navigate roots, rocks, and tiny creeks through thick woods with a couple turns approaching the solid bridge over the roaring creek. Then hike SW for 0.75 mi up tight S-turns and around 22 switchbacks (steeper, narrower, more boulders), easing to a signed intersection (4500 ft, Colchuck Lake Trail left) as you see the tops of Colchuck and Dragontail Peaks through a few trees.

Continue SW on Stuart Lake Trail easily for 1.25 mi, rolling up the valley (forest, meadows) with great shots to the majestic mountains above and ahead right of Mount Stuart (from Ingalls Peaks to Harding Mountain). Then head W more than 0.25 mi steeper up 8 rockier switchbacks. The route eases for the final 0.5 mi to the sizable lake from its N side, with plenty of older forest in the valley but also choice lakeside viewpoints, including one from a small rocky outcrop coming up as you head right (W, past spurs) around the water from the main trail. Granted, it's not the Colchuck Zone, but it's so much easier to attain and still riveting!

Walk 0.25 mi SW to the end of Trail 1599, passing campsites (and two signed privies) to the beginning of the unsigned Horseshoe Lake Trail. For the difficult route to Horseshoe Lake, amble 0.5 mi W narrowly (larger Douglas fir, ups/downs okay, overgrown) as you come down to a tiny creek at the start of the obstacle course 0.5 mi through the valley (without much elevation change). Cross the creek easily over logs then walk directly on one old blowdown, finding the path over more trees near the marshy meadow's edge (but never into it). Negotiate your way SW (semi-confusing at times, few cairns) over, under, and around decent-sized logs through the forest to a discernible landmark (horseshoe embedded in a thin tree) at the base of the climb to the lake. The horseshoe tree (5160 ft) has an arrow pointing right up the stupidly steep trail (easier to follow but over 1100 ft in 0.75 mi) WNW to Horseshoe Lake.

Ascend narrow Horseshoe Lake Trail straight up tight turns NW less than 0.25 mi through the burnt semi-open woods (improved views as a side effect) around large burned trees following the right (N) side of quaint but solid Horseshoe Creek (strangely not appearing on any maps). Go past big boulders before crossing the creek (first of five times total in less than 0.5 mi) to the left (S) side directly above a cool tiny cascade. Work your way steeply (cairns) as you cross the little creek back to the right on the trail then back to the left (S) promptly (6 mi from TH), hiking ultra-steeply WNW away from the babbling brook a few feet before crossing it again. Wishing you were a mountain goat, follow the increasingly painful pitch WNW past more granite slabs briefly before the route eases a tad from the final creek crossing (left, S side). Then grind steeply W up next to the creek (more obvious track) within a gully past slabs, vegetation, and boulders (see Lake Stuart far below) to the nearby glorious destination. With far fewer larger trees than Lake Stuart, views from the upper lake (with islands and alcoves) extend 360 degrees around the sculpted granite mini basin!

You could follow Horseshoe Lake Trail left (SSW) easily less than 0.25 mi, then take the spur left (S) from a fork 100 yards (becoming rockier) out to an overlook area on the flatter granite slabs (see sizable valley below to dwindling Stuart Glacier under Mount Stuart). Horseshoe Lake Trail continues WSW to outstanding vantage points (don't trample wildflowers or heather meadows) around and above the interestingly shaped lake as the main trail and spurs fade. Work right (W) from the outlet area as well a few easy feet up to 0.25 mi (partial bushwhack) on the N side of the lake to a huge boulder field with immense reflections of Mount Stuart across glassy blue-green water! Larches gleam like golden lace in early October, a fair trade instead of taking a dip in the slightly warmer water a couple months prior.

It's possible to loop counterclockwise (more difficult, 0.75 mi max) from the bottom of the boulder field, following the faint path W close to the lake. Ascend 20 ft up a grass- and dirt-filled ramp between large embedded boulders nearest the lake, then work your way over steeper slabs to the end of the lake. Continue SW roughly over boulders a few feet to a nearby saddle overseeing a more barren granite basin (holds Jack Lake, dry most times) up to impressive Jack Ridge. Work judiciously over boulders right (S) of Horseshoe Lake heading E to more visible spurs between trees. Pass interesting tarns near flatter ground on the most prominent path S of the lake becoming Horseshoe Lake Trail NE to the lake's outlet.

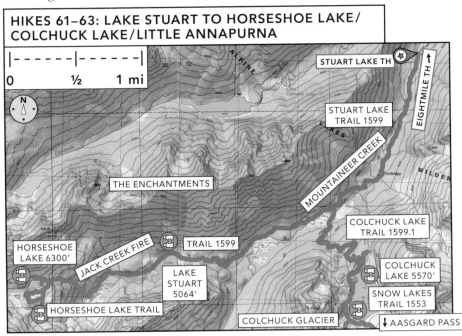

HIKES 61–63: LAKE STUART TO HORSESHOE LAKE/ COLCHUCK LAKE/LITTLE ANNAPURNA

|- - - - - -|- - - - -|
0   ½   1 mi

N

STUART LAKE TH

EIGHTMILE TH

STUART LAKE TRAIL 1599

MOUNTAINEER CREEK

THE ENCHANTMENTS

WILDER

COLCHUCK LAKE TRAIL 1599.1

HORSESHOE LAKE 6300'

JACK CREEK FIRE

TRAIL 1599

LAKE STUART 5064'

COLCHUCK LAKE 5570'

SNOW LAKES TRAIL 1553

HORSESHOE LAKE TRAIL

COLCHUCK GLACIER

↓ AASGARD PASS

For hikes 62 and 63, see also map on page 203.

ELEVATION: 5600 ft; vertical gain of at least 2300 ft

DISTANCE: 4 mi up, 9–10 mi round-trip

DURATION: Around 2 hours up, 4–5 hours round-trip

DIFFICULTY: Strenuous (uneven trails, tree roots, rocks, steep, too popular)

TRIP REPORT: See Trip Report for Lake Stuart to Horseshoe Lake on page 193. With more than 15,000 people a year signing up to camp within the Enchantments via a tricky lottery system where only a fraction of those will be permitted, it's understandable that many people get frustrated or give up, although it's still worth it (Enchantment Permit Area Zones and info: https://www.recreation.gov/permits/233273). A handful of trekkers arrange transportation and thru-hike the Enchantments one way (almost 20 mi total) with or without camping going from Snow Lakes TH (E side) to Stuart Lake TH (W side, preferred direction). Thankfully, day hikers can have at it without the difficult pass and fee sitch , unless that changes. Colchuck Lake might be snow-free by mid-June, but the lakes of the Core Enchantments usually hold snow and ice until August sometime. Wildlife sightings may include mountain goats. Northwest Forest Pass required at all THs, and vault toilets are present at all THs (outdoor privies at Colchuck Lake).

TRAILHEAD: Stuart Lake TH or Eightmile TH. See Lake Stuart to Horseshoe Lake on page 193 for directions (130 mi, 2½ hours from Seattle; 285 mi, 4½–5 hours from Portland).

ROUTE: See Lake Stuart to Horseshoe Lake on page 193 for the description to the first intersection 2.25 mi up (4500 ft). Take Colchuck Lake Trail 1599.1(A) left (S, opposite Stuart Lake Trail) a few hundred feet to cross the rushing Mountaineer Creek over a footbridge. Walk straight over the dry rock bed heading right (SW) through a large rock field briefly, then hike around a dozen steeper turns and switchbacks 1.5 mi (SW then SE) up to Colchuck Lake. You'll spot Dragontail Peak and others winding up (increasingly rockier, steeper, with brief downhill stretch) before the first glimpses of Colchuck Lake. Meander left momentarily to the N end of the lake for that picture-perfect glassy reflection unveiling Aasgard Pass, Dragontail Peak, and Colchuck Peak!

   The large, radiant turquoise lake comes to life in the sunlight and many are tempted to plunge into the chilly luminous waters on a hot day if for no other reason

Dragontail and Colchuck Peaks from Colchuck Lake in the Enchantments.

than to escape the mosquitoes or herds of mountain goats following you! Make noise if goats approach and explore right (S) around the spectacular lake if you'd like (1 mi to base of Aasgard Pass), passing campsites and campers. Follow Colchuck Lake Trail S 0.25 mi or so roughly (several ups/downs) as you move left (SSE, not right down spur to decent tarn), closer to the lake over rock slabs. Then amble a bit easier S more than 0.25 mi through tighter trees (another privy) before emptying down very steep turns into the massive rock field S of the lake under the peaks (approaching Colchuck Glacier). Follow decent cairns ESE, passing giant boulders, scree fields, thick flora, and small creeks (first major creek holds bushwhack route to Colchuck Glacier). You continue over, down, and up the narrow trail, ascending a rocky rise (out of trees) that is the beginning of the unforgivably steep ascent more than a mile to Aasgard Pass on Snow Lakes Trail 1553. Trail-finding to the pass will be much more difficult when the route becomes a technical climb with any snow or ice coverage. Return to the TH by the same route.

63 | LITTLE ANNAPURNA

ELEVATION: 7850 ft at Aasgard Pass, 8440 ft on Little Annapurna; vertical gains of around 4600 ft for Aasgard Pass, almost 5500 ft for Little Annapurna from the TH

DISTANCE: 6 mi to Aasgard Pass, 8 mi to Little Annapurna, 16 mi round-trip

DURATION: 4–5 hours to Aasgard Pass, 6–7 hours to Little Annapurna, 12–14 hours round-trip from the TH

DIFFICULTY: Mix of very challenging for Aasgard Pass (route-finding, bouldering, extremely steep, loose rock, dangerous with snow or ice when mountaineering skills and gear required) and expert only for Little Annapurna from the TH (very long, punishingly steep, GPS device helpful, slight exposure near summit, mosquito swarms until September)

TRIP REPORT: For acclimated hikers, the remarkable landscape within the Core Enchantments near Aasgard Pass and Little Annapurna can be reached and returned from in one grueling day! And for the rest, camping decisions must be made months in advance (see Lake Stuart to Horseshoe Lake on page 193 and Colchuck Lake on page 197, and for TH parking complications). Wildlife sightings may include mountain goats. Northwest Forest Pass required at both proximate THs, and a vault toilet is present at both THs with outdoor privies at Colchuck and Tranquil Lakes.

TRAILHEAD: Stuart Lake TH or Eightmile TH. See Lake Stuart to Horseshoe Lake on page 193 for directions (130 mi, 2½ hours from Seattle; 285 mi, 4½–5 hours from Portland).

ROUTE: See Colchuck Lake on page 197 for the description to the base of Aasgard Pass on a little rocky rise around 5 mi from the TH. From there it's only 1 mi but 2000 ft up to the pass area! Climb the disturbingly steep rocky track (Snow Lakes Trail 1553) SE up the center of the scree field (cairns), eventually moving left (E) of a visible mini-cliff band (black rock, larch oasis-Tree Island) more than one-third of the way up where accidents and fatalities occur from an alternate spur only recommended for experts if at all. Generally, stay far left (E) in the enormous gully but then move more center-right at the next little cliffy area, lumbering S straight up ultra-steeply (cairns). Look NNW to Colchuck Lake, Cashmere Mountain, Glacier Peak, Mount Baker, and others. The rocky sheer route will be vague at times but obvious bouldering SE straight up the wide terrain approaching Aasgard Pass

(7850 ft, also called Colchuck Pass) in the Core (Upper) Enchantments.

Above the pass is a tiny high point a few feet right (SW) with a small tarn pond seen below and jagged Dragontail Peak above (WSW). The lingering Snow Creek Glacier (stretches to Little Annapurna) borders the difficult traverse route to that peak as you pan left (S to SE) along the partially serrated ridge called Witches Tower to Little Annapurna, complimenting the colorful high alpine lakes including nearby Isolation Lake. Walk down left (SE) around the corner through the stunning otherworldly landscape, passing Tranquil Lake (with privy at left), the first of around two dozen lakes and tarns in the Core Enchantments, all with outstanding reflections of the esteemed local mountains and with only a smattering of larch trees (shimmering golden fiery tones late September), navigating between the lakes pleasurably, losing only 1000 ft over the span around 2.5 mi to Lake Viviane (Middle Enchantments)!

The standard route up Little Annapurna begins 1 mi down ESE from Aasgard Pass from Trail 1553 to around 7520 ft (330 ft to regain from Enchantment Basin). Move E past a few small tarns over the granite slabs then a side stream (that joins nearby Snow Creek). Stones line the flat trail past the stream over granite 30 ft, passing junctures (more difficult briefer summit spur options right, S) another 100 ft or so, turning right just before a wide saddle (above Inspiration, Perfection, and Crystal Lakes).

For Little Annapurna (1 mi away), hike S over faint spurs (unsigned) a couple minutes through the rock field, merging with Little Annapurna Summit Trail up the broad NE ridge and face (colorful tarn down right). The scramble SW steepens over sloped granite slabs (fairly safe cairned options) as the primary track center-right of the ridgeline is easy to follow. The cliff-lined route (drop-offs) closest to the ridge crest (just left, E) holds breathtaking views toward McClellan Peak's craggy SW ridge above Crystal Lake (directly below) and also just E of the summit toward some sharp spires!

Mesmerized by Crystal and Perfection Lakes, with shimmering larches between Prusik and McClellan Peaks from Little Annapurna!

Ascend grassy, rocky, narrow ramps (cautiously) steeply to meet the primary route (yielding to mountain goats). The climber's trail soon levels over the summit plateau SW, reaching another option with the faint right fork leading more directly to the actual apex. Either works briefly SW to the base of some large boulders between fascinating boulder clusters where you scramble a few feet to the peak without difficulty (drop-offs). Enjoy the panorama of nearly all the local mountains including Mount Stuart (W) behind Argonaut and Sherpa Peaks (left of Dragontail Peak). Enchantment Lakes are somewhat obscured from the very top but can be seen almost in their entirety just below.

64 | DRAGONTAIL PEAK LOOP

ELEVATION: 8842 ft; vertical gain of around 5600 ft

DISTANCE: Almost 7 mi up either route, around 14 mi round-trip

DURATION: 5–6 hours up either route, 10–13 hours round-trip from TH

DIFFICULTY: Expert only (decidedly long from TH, mountaineering, route-finding, Class 3/4, crampons/ice axe required on Colchuck Glacier, ultra-steep, bouldering, some exposure, GPS device required)

TRIP REPORT: From Colchuck Lake or the Upper Enchantments the Stuart Range's second tallest summit would be a worthwhile goal, but from the TH climbing Dragontail Peak is a daunting task! The counterclockwise loop is vastly more difficult but not mandatory for a summit bid. Wildlife sightings may include mountain goats. Northwest Forest Pass required at both proximate THs, and a vault toilet is present at both THs with outdoor privies at Colchuck and Tranquil Lakes.

TRAILHEAD: Stuart Lake TH or Eightmile TH. See Lake Stuart to Horseshoe Lake on page 193 for directions (130 mi, 2½ hours from Seattle; 285 mi, 4½–5 hours from Portland).

ROUTE: See Lake Stuart to Horseshoe Lake on page 193, Colchuck Lake on page 197, and Little Annapurna on page 199 for important TH info and the description to Aasgard Pass, and take either the primary route from Aasgard Pass (see page 203 for clues) or climb Colchuck Glacier for a more extreme outing. For the loop, leave Colchuck Lake Trail from the boulder field S of the lake at the first major creek crossing (4.75 mi from TH, no trail, steeper) as you bushwhack right (S) up part of the

One of the locals near Aasgard Pass with the primary route to Dragontail Peak over the cornice of Snow Creek Glacier near Witches Tower.

lower moraine past brush to the Colchuck Glacier (less snow cover late July into August, then becomes icier, forcing climbers up rocks right at times). There is a seasonal overhanging cornice at the top of Colchuck Glacier/Col that can be problematic before July. Also from the Colchuck Glacier side of the hike is a serious crux on the summit block from the N side of a notch known as Pandora's Box with a 20–30 ft long super-steep couloir that holds snow and ice until July.

Hike loose scree below Colchuck Glacier as far as you are comfortable before putting on your helmet and crampons and readying your ice axe for the very steep slope (35–40 degrees)! You should be experienced with how to self-arrest. Aim left (E) toward even more serious climbing options known as Backbone and Serpentine Ridges under Dragontail Peak as the glacier splits (follow the easternmost path) continuing S. Then climb more up the right (W) side of the narrowing glacier to avoid rockfall, ice, and potential crevasses later in the season. Views to Colchuck Peak (and Lake) improve with each step as the sheer granite closes in around you toward the top of the glacier (using extreme caution). The sustained steeps persist and even sharpen up the final boulders or snow S to the Colchuck Col (8100 ft) between Dragontail and Colchuck Peaks (1.25 mi from lake).

Right (W) from the saddle over 0.25 mi away is Colchuck Peak (8705 ft) for those interested. For Dragontail Peak, scramble sharp left (E) from the beginning of a small cirque (no signs, trails, or cairns) almost 0.25 mi up a very steep and rocky gully funneling narrowly to the very top. You'll see Argonaut Peak down the connecting ridge from Colchuck Peak, with Sherpa Peak and Mount Stuart just beyond! Pass nearby rocky spires that continue along the SW ridge toward the peak, which resembles the spiny tail of a dragon from a distance. Atop the gully, arrive to the notch/crux (Pandora's Box, 8700 ft), revealing the remainder of the route to the visible summit more than 0.25 mi away NE. Down-climb the slender N side of the notch

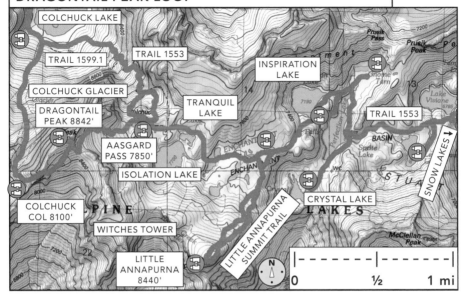

COLCHUCK LAKE

TRAIL 1599.1

TRAIL 1553

INSPIRATION LAKE

COLCHUCK GLACIER

DRAGONTAIL PEAK 8842'

TRANQUIL LAKE

TRAIL 1553

AASGARD PASS 7850'

BASIN

ISOLATION LAKE

CRYSTAL LAKE

COLCHUCK COL 8100'

WITCHES TOWER

LITTLE ANNAPURNA 8440'

LITTLE ANNAPURNA SUMMIT TRAIL

SNOW LAKES

0   ½   1 mi

For hikes 62 and 63, see also map on page 196.

(carefully if icy) 20 ft or so to the steeply sloped talus (or snow) slope. Either traverse NE a couple hundred yards (lingering snowfields not difficult) below (S of) the pillars on the high ridge then make a beeline N for the summit (or traverse farther NE briefly then head straight up the S ridge as in primary route from Aasgard Pass), or climb N (steeper) from the bottom of Pandora's Box to the nearby high ridge immediately and navigate NE around subsummits (more difficult, huge drop-offs). The final 30 ft or so to the peak is a steep scramble by all routes (some exposure) as Colchuck Lake comes into full view almost 3300 ft directly below (see corner of Lake Stuart). Stupefying!

To finish the loop, from the summit work down the steep wide S ridge (primary route, Dragontail Peak Summit Trail) less than 0.25 mi (loose rock, boulders) quite steeply to the small saddle (8500 ft) between Dragontail Peak and the Witches Tower (pinnacles some investigate). From the saddle see the route 0.75 mi NE to Aasgard Pass, with the first bit being the most difficult past the melting cornice at the top. Only those who are adept glissade 500–700 ft down the very steep Snow Creek Glacier (using an ice axe to control speed) under the best conditions (before mid-July) to Aasgard Pass in around two minutes. The preferred route from the saddle takes hikers far left (NNE) across the top of the glacier (directly under Dragontail Peak), carefully traversing past the cornice 100 yards (traction, packed trail apparent most times) before switchbacking NE very steeply down larger rocks adjacent the snowfield (N of, cairns) to the bottom. Move left (N) of a tarn over larger rocks more directly a few feet up to the top of Aasgard Pass before the long descent 6 mi to Stuart Lake TH.

ELEVATION: 5000 ft at Nada Lake, 5475 ft at Snow Lakes; vertical gains of 3700 ft, 4200 ft for both

DISTANCE: 5.5 mi up to Nada Lake, 11–12 mi round-trip; 6.75 mi up to Snow Lakes, 13.5–15 mi round-trip

DURATION: 2½ hours to Nada Lake; 3½–5 hours to Snow Lakes, 7–9 hours round-trip

DIFFICULTY: Mix of strenuous for Nada Lake (weekends popular, best for avid hikers, uneven, rocky, tree roots, mosquitoes and flies near water July to August, switchbacks) and very challenging beyond (very long, dusty, steep at times, optional dam crossing, water shoes and trekking poles recommended)

TRIP REPORT: Snow Lakes TH provides the easiest access to the Enchantments (Snow Zone), but for the convenience you'll have to endure many miles of deceivingly difficult trails before you get to the spoils at the lakes or Core Enchantment Zone (nearly 10 mi to Lake Viviane). Most day hikers are content with Nada Lake's interesting aspects or stop between Lower and Upper Snow Lakes from the dam crossing. Beyond the dam are surreal shots over the largest Enchantment lake to Prusik Peak and The Temple! See Lake Stuart to Horseshoe Lake on page 193, Colchuck Lake on page 197, Little Annapurna on page 199, and Dragontail Peak Loop on page 201 for more info. Wildlife sightings may include hawks, eagles, and others, deer, elk, mountain goats, and black bear. Northwest Forest Pass required, and

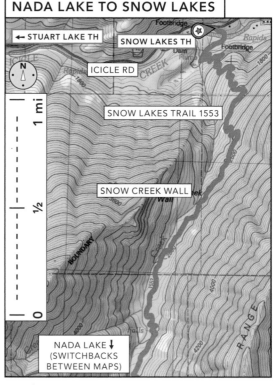

NADA LAKE TO SNOW LAKES

See also map on next page.

a vault toilet is present with privies at Upper Snow Lake.

TRAILHEAD: Snow Lakes TH. See Lake Stuart to Horseshoe Lake on page 193 for directions to Icicle Rd in Leavenworth for 4.25 mi (roughly paved, narrowing) to reach the small but active TH at left (signed, treeless). From Portland or eastern Washington, drive 2.25 mi left on Icicle Rd if taking the shortcut in Leavenworth (120 mi, 2 hours from Seattle; 280 mi, 4–4½ hours from Portland).

ROUTE: Begin S from the TH area (free self-issue Wilderness Permit) down Snow Lakes Trail 1553, crossing the usually raging Icicle Creek (footbridge). Keep right (SW) along the irrigation canal (past a faint crossroads) momentarily, then hike 24 moderate switchbacks SSE up the steep and mostly burned out hillside (views W up Icicle Gorge to Cashmere Mountain). Traverse SW a bit easier into the tight canyon opposite a large block of sheer granite known as Snow Creek Wall. Around 1.5 mi up, adorable mountain goats may appear on or near the trail. Remember, these are wild animals; every year a few people get too close to their horns and regret it instantly. Enter the dense forest SW along Snow Creek 0.5 mi, climbing 5 switchbacks (narrow) then another 6 switchbacks before rising above the creek S briefly, continuing S 0.75 mi up 16 more switchbacks (across large double rock field, views). Contour upward 0.5 mi SW (slightly overgrown toward Snow Creek), then move up 4 switchbacks S. There's a nice cascade before you cross the solid bridge to the W side of Snow Creek (4 mi from TH).

Continue 0.75 mi SW up 8 fairly easygoing switchbacks and turns (Trail 1553, trees), steepening 0.75 mi farther (4 more switchbacks) before arriving to the long, slender subalpine Nada Lake! Walk right (SW) around the N side over delightfully level ground and cross a creek feed coming from the W where the path fades. Pass lakeside viewpoints (and camps), then begin to ascend another large scree field in the clearing. Some people turn around after taking in the marvelous views of the slim canyon with the jagged Stuart Range above!

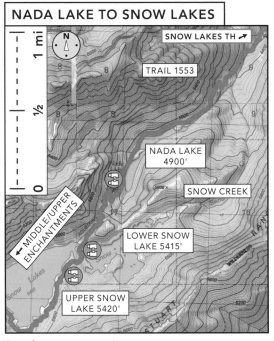

See also map on previous page.

Respectable McClellan Peak from the Enchantment's largest lake!

Continue more than 0.5 mi SW much steeper up the rocks and final 3 switchbacks (and turns), passing a small saddle before descending (easier) a tad to the old dam at Snow Lakes. Enjoy grand views across the logjam to Upper Snow Lake and McClellan Peak directly behind (WSW), with The Temple right (NW) and Prusik Peak between barely coming into view as you round the beautiful large clear lake beyond the dam. The water level at the dam between lakes is usually lower mid-July through September. Around a half foot of water (or less) flowing over the isthmus dam is perfect, but it could rise half a foot in one day with summer heat melting snow (keep in mind for day trips). Poles help as you proceed 100 ft S, enjoying the cool rush without being pulled down into Lower Snow Lake. The sights improve from the S side of Upper Snow Lake but the walking SW on Trail 1553 will be more tedious through endless tight trees over the bumpy thin route. Turn around from one of the few privies or small campsites (less than 0.5 mi from dam crossing) if not continuing somewhat agonizingly up to Lake Viviane in the Middle Enchantments.

ELEVATION: 4650 ft; vertical gain of 1800 ft from the upper TH (2100 ft from the lower TH)

DISTANCE: 3.5 mi up, 7 mi round-trip (8 mi or so round-trip from the lower TH)

DURATION: Around 1½ hours up, 3 hours round-trip

DIFFICULTY: Moderate (no signs, wide trail/old road, steady steep not bad, rocky, GPS device helpful, narrow paths to summits, snowshoe or cross-country ski in winter)

TRIP REPORT: Here's a day hike, also known as Twin Peaks, representing the highest points in the foothills just W of Wenatchee (sunrise or sunset for best lighting)! You won't see any horses or lakes but you will see the Wenatchee River valley, farther into Alpine Lakes Wilderness, the Stuart Range, and North Cascades from the tops! The area is also popular with mountain bikers (and those with ATVs) because of countless trails that shoot off the primary road/trail (near private property). Winter travel is possible, though a bit more difficult to the petite summits. No fee or restroom.

TRAILHEAD: Horse Lake Mountain Number 2 Canyon Rd TH. From Seattle, take I-90 E and other routes for 145 mi to Wenatchee, crossing over the Wenatchee River

Tronsen Ridge and the Stuart Range at sunset from Horse Lake Mountain.

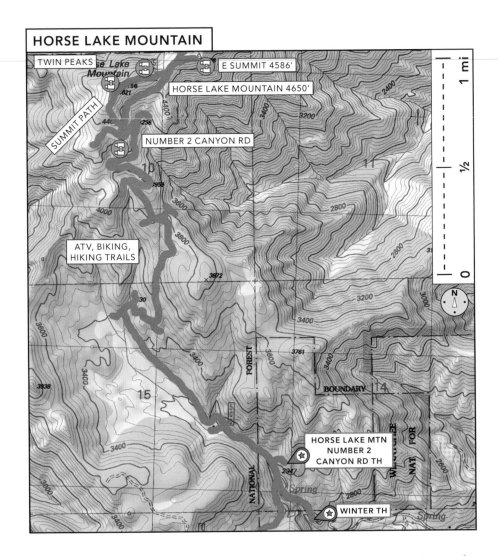

HORSE LAKE MOUNTAIN

TWIN PEAKS

E SUMMIT 4586'

HORSE LAKE MOUNTAIN 4650'

SUMMIT PATH

NUMBER 2 CANYON RD

ATV, BIKING, HIKING TRAILS

HORSE LAKE MTN NUMBER 2 CANYON RD TH

WINTER TH

Bridge onto WA-285 S (N Wenatchee Ave) for 1 mi. Turn right on Maiden Ln for 0.5 mi, continue left on N Western Ave for 2.75 mi, and turn right on Number 2 Canyon Rd for almost 4.5 mi into gravel/dirt. Park in the small pullout at left for the lower (winter) TH, or continue (rougher, rutted, AWD recommended) for around 0.5 mi for the upper TH, where there is a small pullout at right (before second gate).

From Portland, take I-84 E and others to Wenatchee and follow as on previous page (155 mi, 2½ hours from Seattle; 290 mi, 5 hours from Portland).

ROUTE: Begin NW up the continuation of Number 2 Canyon Rd from the lower TH for more than 0.5 mi past large ponderosa pines to the upper TH juncture (with FR-7101-510 heading left). Continue straight (NW) on narrower Number 2 Canyon Rd (FR-7101-500), passing meadows (balsamroot, others late May or so). Don't stray

The Columbia River within the Wenatchee Valley Area from the bustling local trail system.

onto bike paths as you ascend turns NNW for more than 3 mi, steadily winding up 4 sweeping switchbacks to an intersection near the summit trail. Views of the valley improve from overlooks, including one (left, S to Mission Peak) from a shoulder just before the faint intersection. Then walk right (NNE, opposite FR-7107) a couple feet spotting the thin summit trail left (NNW, clockwise summit loop) of Number 2 Canyon Rd. Take the narrower summit path much steeper 100 yards, gaining the mostly open high ridge with easier walking N past the nearby treeless twin summit (4621 ft, incorrectly listed as high point on some maps). The real vista unfolds 150 ft farther NE following the wide-enough ridge over the mini saddle to the true summit within a small cluster of trees. The forest opens past the top, allowing views W into Central Cascades, N to Mount Baker, closer to Mount Stuart and friends, plus much more!

Continue ENE down the solid summit path more than 100 yards to Number 2 Canyon Rd on another small saddle (crossroads). You could easily tack on the E summit (4586 ft) by taking the thin path up the steep open ridge 150 ft ENE to the bare top for splendid views! Descend Number 2 Canyon Rd (FR-7101-500) less than 0.5 mi SW from the saddle, looping easily to the faint three-way intersection just past the direct summit route option. Continue left (near the overlook) from the first switchback down Number 2 Canyon Rd SSE more than 3 mi to the upper TH.

67 | PALOUSE FALLS STATE PARK

ELEVATION: 900 ft at the TH; vertical gain of around 300 ft if you descend to various viewpoints on Palouse Falls Trail (otherwise minimal elevation change)

DISTANCE: 0.25–0.5 mi round-trip for the main viewpoint, including Fryxell Overlook; 1 mi round-trip for Upper Palouse Falls; 2 mi round-trip for the top of Palouse Falls one way and back, or from a clockwise loop along the cliff band (not recommended for most)

DURATION: ½–3 hours round-trip with several options, including dillydallying

DIFFICULTY: Mix of easy for the main viewpoint and Fryxell Overlook (very brief, popular on weekends, somewhat safe where fenced, very little shade) and moderate for Upper Palouse Falls, the top of Palouse Falls, and the loop (route-finding, loose rock, no fencing near Palouse River, easy but narrow paths flanking serious drop-offs, steeper options)

TRIP REPORT: Located in eastern Washington but worth bringing to the table is the official state waterfall (since 2014) in Palouse Falls State Park! The glacial canyon, formed by the Missoula Floods more than 13,000 years ago, sliced into the desert valley, giving birth to this spectacular waterfall a few miles upstream from the Snake River convergence. The falls vary greatly from a healthy spring average of 1700 cfs to 7000 cfs on a huge day, with record days raging at 27,000 cfs! (Check: https://waterdata.usgs.gov/nwis/uv?site_no=13351000) With great lighting near sunrise and sunset, the falls are best experienced on a multiday trip if coming from the Seattle or Portland regions, although accommodations near the state park are scarce outside of the tiny tent-only campground (11 walk-in sites, around $12/day). Avoid spring and summer weekends as the park is minuscule compared to the number of visitors it receives and you may have to wait several hours to access the TH road before a parking space becomes available with no other local options. Some trails and spurs are not officially maintained (leaving state park property) and you will be at your own risk for anything beyond a fence or barrier as ample signage warns there are inherent dangers in nature. Wildlife sightings may include hawks, rattlesnakes, and yellow-bellied marmots. Discover Pass required, and restrooms are present.

TRAILHEAD: Palouse Falls State Park TH. From Seattle, take I-90 E to exit 137 (Othello), merge onto WA-26 E for 83 mi, turn right (in Washtucna) on WA-260 W/WA-261 S (Kahlotus) for 6.5 mi, turn left on curvy WA-261 S for 8.5 mi, turn left on

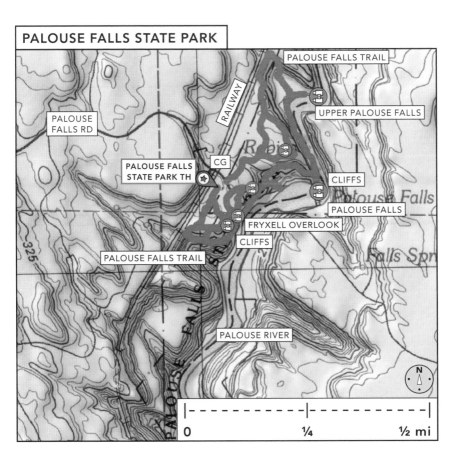

PALOUSE FALLS STATE PARK

PALOUSE FALLS TRAIL

PALOUSE FALLS RD

RAILWAY

UPPER PALOUSE FALLS

PALOUSE FALLS STATE PARK TH

CG

CLIFFS

PALOUSE FALLS

FRYXELL OVERLOOK

CLIFFS

PALOUSE FALLS TRAIL

PALOUSE RIVER

N

0   ¼   ½ mi

gravel Palouse Falls Rd (Palouse Falls State Park, rough gravel, narrow at times) for almost 2.5 mi with three separate small parking areas after the state park sign: the driveway at right for the upper/overflow parking (passing camp host), pull-in parking at left nearest the CG, and the nearby end for the primary parking closest to the falls and restrooms.

From Portland, take I-84 E to exit 179 (Hermiston) onto I-82 W (into Washington) for 30 mi to exit 113 (Kennewick), merge onto US-395 N for 7 mi, then exit for Spokane, merging onto I-182/US-12/US-395 for 1.5 mi to exit 14 (Spokane). Then exit 14B (US-395 N) for 31.5 mi, and exit right for WA-260 (Connell/Kahlotus). Turn right on WA-260 E for less than 24 mi, turn right (no signal) on winding WA-261 S for 8.5 mi, and turn left on Palouse Falls Rd for almost 2.5 mi as above (235 mi, 4 hours from Seattle; 280 mi, 4–5 hours from Portland).

ROUTE: From the primary parking lot, take the paved path just left of the grassy meadow E past the fence, picnic tables, and kiosk for 100 ft SSE down a few steps easily to the main viewpoint of the waterfall (186-198 ft high, 30 ft wide). You enter the dramatic emerald (April into June) river canyon with Palouse Falls roaring down

Palouse Falls rips through the colorful canyon leaving visitors in awe of the powerful state waterfall!

into a sizable amphitheater! Be cautious near fencing as the cliff drops quite abruptly down the columnar basalt. Walk easily in either direction for different angles to catch the rainbow effect! Move right (S) 100 yards or more to Fryxell Overlook (covered with picnic table) for a different angle of the falls and an improved look downriver toward Lyons Ferry. Halfway is the ADA interpretive viewpoint before the route steepens very briefly (unpaved) to Fryxell Overlook. There is also an ADA parking/ camping spot next to the restrooms. The ADA paved trail to the viewpoint begins from the kiosk heading right (SW) around 200 ft before curving left (SE) on the roughly paved trail less than 100 ft to the fenced corner viewpoint where the waterfall is showcased between the sheer basalt rock gorge and the Palouse River far below.

For Upper Palouse Falls, the top of Palouse Falls, and the clockwise loop around the narrow canyon, take Palouse Falls Trail (old jeep road, gravel) nearest the restrooms up and down some (sage, grasses) for 0.25 mi N to the end of the road. You'll pass a few spurs right (E, NE) without fencing that move less than 0.25 mi over the plateau at the top of the cliff band (fatalities not uncommon, not recommended for children, be mindful) above both local waterfalls for distinctive angles of the upper and lower valleys. Work your way to the E tip of the plateau for a view from above the thin rocky fin known as Castle Rock adjacent Palouse Falls.

Move left (NW) from the end of the wider Palouse Falls Trail (past cliff warning, park boundary signs), hiking quite steeply down the narrow rocky path 75 ft to the active railroad tracks at some tall steel fencing. Walk 150 ft NE along the fence easily to the continuation of Palouse Falls Trail before the rock wall from a switchback right. Hike S down semi-steep, loose gravel 150 ft, heading much easier SE through a meadow (high sage, grasses) for 100 yards to the riverbank near Upper Palouse Falls (20 ft high, 100 ft wide) opposite tall vertical rock walls known as the Mohawk (0.5 mi from TH). There is a spur path left (E) above the riverbank, but walk right (S) downriver on Palouse Falls Trail to the corner of a sharp twist in the canyon. Be cautious crossing over larger rocks (may be wet from spray) as you navigate 100 ft to the more solid trail near the cliff wall.

For the exciting and precarious viewpoints directly above Palouse Falls (and for canyon loop) 0.25 mi away, continue SSE, being careful near the swift river as the narrow rocky path moves up and down pleasantly out to the point. Pass a hazard sign just before the Castle Rock fin (1 mi from TH). Most people are content to feel the power and catch a glimpse of the plunge once past Castle Rock from the left (N) side while other brave souls venture 15–25 ft farther down loose gravel very carefully to the lip of the powerful waterfall for the best peek (no selfies zone).

Return to the TH or continue (loop, experienced hikers only) along the steep canyon as you move NW (cautiously) in front of Castle Rock (S side) under the cliff hugging the wall on slender Palouse Falls Trail (grasses, wildflowers). Curve SW (beneath the primary viewpoint), crossing a rougher section at 0.25 mi from Palouse Falls near an unsigned juncture with a super-steep spur path (more difficult, dangerous when wet), descending left (E) 100 yards to the bottom of the canyon near the base of the falls (no swimming due to deadly undercurrents, watch for spray).

Continue SW easier on faded Palouse Falls Trail (drop-offs, solitude) with fantastic vistas up and down the colorful canyon. Pass a narrow rocky gully (right, around 0.5 mi from Palouse Falls) as you walk past more yellow-bellied marmots, sage and wildflowers. Hike steeper around the corner, losing sight of the falls to a slightly wider gully up right (1.75 mi from TH on loop) with two options to the plateau near Fryxell Overlook: One is to scramble briefer right (N, no trail) 100 ft up the rocky steep gully, leaving the very top (right) somewhat easier to the flats near the overlook. You would walk left along the barricade a few feet to the opening near warning signs. Or follow Palouse Falls Trail easier W along the cliff wall beyond the gully 150 yards to a fence at the railroad tracks. Turn sharply right (E) 100 ft steeply up the trail to the flats then 150 ft N past sage to reach the upper parking lot (past barricade and No Safe River Access sign).

SKY VALLEY

ELEVATION: 800 ft at Lower Falls, 1150 ft at (Middle) Wallace Falls, 1500 ft at Upper Falls; vertical gains of around 500 ft, 1000 ft, and 1300 ft (plus 200 ft for bridge above Upper Falls), respectively

DISTANCE: 3.5 mi round-trip for Lower Falls (Picnic Shelter), 4–4.5 mi round-trip for Middle Falls Overlook (and Valley Overlook), 5.5 mi round-trip for Upper Falls (plus 0.5 mi round-trip for bridge above Upper Falls)

DURATION: 2–3 hours round-trip total

DIFFICULTY: Mix of moderate for Lower/Middle Falls (crowded, tree roots, minimal ups/downs, family-friendly, steps, sometimes steeper) and strenuous for Upper Falls or above (narrower, more difficult when muddy or icy)

TRIP REPORT: Wallace Falls State Park's easy access and large areas to explore entice Gold Bar locals and the hordes coming from Seattle alike! Parking will be difficult soon after the park opens on spring and summer weekends (open 6:30 a.m. till dusk April–September, 8 a.m. till dusk October–March). Several options lead mountain bikers and hikers 6–10 mi to Wallace and Jay Lakes, but for this outing we hike the shorter rustic trail along the Wallace River, passing several picturesque waterfalls with various vantage points! Discover Pass required (automated pay station), and flush toilets are present.

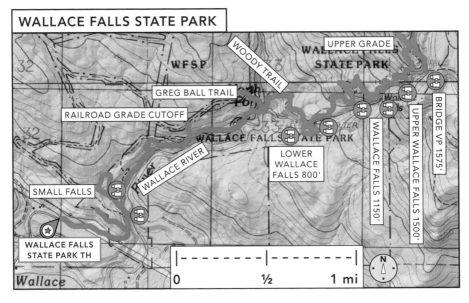

TRAILHEAD: Wallace Falls State Park TH. From Seattle, take I-5 N to exit 171 onto WA-522 E (Bothell) for 24 mi, then exit right merging onto US-2 E (Wenatchee) in Monroe for 11 mi. Turn left in Gold Bar on 1st St (milepost 28) for 0.5 mi, turn right on 1st Ave W/May Creek Rd for 0.5 mi then onto Ley Rd for 0.25 mi to a fork. Keep left on Ley Rd for 0.25 mi, and turn left onto the signed drive for Wallace Falls State Park for 0.25 mi, ending in the sizable lot. When the lot is full, roadside parking (where legal but not on Ley Rd) will add at least 0.5 mi of walking each way.

From Portland, take I-5 N to exit 154B (Renton) onto I-405 N for 21 mi to exit 23, onto WA-522 E (Woodinville) 14 mi, exit right merging onto US-2 E, and follow as above (45 mi, around 1 hour from Seattle; 220 mi, 3½–4 hours from Portland).

ROUTE: Begin SE past the kiosk and tiny gift shop on Woody Trail under huge buzzing power lines into the clearing (see Baring Mountain, Mounts Index/Pershing) before curving N briefly into trees (ancient hemlock, fir, cedar) to the first of several signed junctures (less than 0.5 mi from TH). Proceed right (N) 0.25 mi on Woody Trail (opposite Railroad Grade), parallel to the Wallace River (down steps), passing a small cascade before crossing a footbridge with Small Falls Interpretive Trail left after (NW, 75 ft over boardwalk to cute seasonal cascade, spur continues 0.25 mi for lollipop loop). Continue NNE on Woody Trail easily through the mossy forest (roots, rocks, ferns), then ascend 4 quick but steep switchbacks E. Traverse the easier path before hiking NE up past a spur (left, Railroad Grade Cutoff, 1 mi from TH), moving down and up as you wind past another signed juncture (left, Greg Ball Trail). Keep straight (E) down across the bridge over North Fork Wallace River then hike steeply up a couple turns (guardrails, steps) before easing SE (mossy ground cover) to the viewing area and open pavilion at lovely Lower Wallace Falls (212 ft, five tiers, mostly hidden). A couple of tiers are 40 ft down steep stairs along the railing where a smaller cascade drops eloquently into a turquoise pool (within lush grotto) that empties, cascading down the rocks.

Wallace Falls with snowy mountains above.

Continue NE steeply up Woody Trail less than 0.25 mi for the primary look to gorgeous Wallace Falls (three-tiered, 367 ft) from a multi-tiered switchback (Middle Falls Overlook, benches, 2 mi from TH). Press on 0.25 mi for more perspectives (or Upper Falls). The way is steadily steep up 7 tight switchbacks N then SE with a small unsigned spur down right 35 ft (railed viewpoint) near the top of Wallace Falls (sweet angle of long drop). Walk 40 ft farther for the juncture noting the Valley Overlook right down 2 steep switchbacks (steps) 75 ft to the platform at the very top (1200 ft) of Wallace Falls with small cascades above the main drop (mostly out of sight). Look outward toward Seattle, the Olympics, and the local mountains across the Skykomish River Valley, known as Sky River or Sky Valley!

For Upper Wallace Falls, climb steeper and narrower up Woody Trail NE with 2 switchbacks then around 8 more switchbacks (some with steps) through the emerald forest littered with ferns and mossy ground cover to another switchback that has a smaller, unsigned viewpoint to the elegant thin waterfall (five-tiered, only two tiers visible, 240 ft). For the (bonus) bridge above the Upper Falls, continue from the switchback past the mapped sign N up the rougher trail section easily (mossy forest, markers on trees) with turns and 2 switchbacks to the Upper Grade (signage), which meets other trails heading several miles up to the lakes or down to the TH (adding much more mileage and time, no views). Turn right (SE) on the wide, flat track instead 150 ft through the woods to the steel bridge for a narrow view out to the mountains and the clear river below plunging off the rocks to form Upper Wallace Falls. Return down Woody Trail less than 3 mi to the TH.

69 LAKE SERENE TO BRIDAL VEIL FALLS

ELEVATION: 2660 ft at the high point; vertical gain of 2100 ft (plus 300 ft with Bridal Veil Falls)

DISTANCE: Almost 4 mi to Lunch Rock at Lake Serene, 8 mi round-trip (plus 1 mi round-trip with Bridal Veil Falls)

DURATION: 2–2½ hours directly to lake first, 5–6 hours round-trip total

DIFFICULTY: Strenuous (steady up to falls juncture then fairly steep to either, switchbacks, rocky, very popular, trekking poles helpful, traction required with snow, easier to falls without lake)

TRIP REPORT: Directly below the formidable pillars of Mount Index in Snoqualmie National Forest is this striking, clear blue lake tucked in a hidden valley that reflects the nearly vertical mountain perfectly in the morning light! The crowds arrive early as the scene becomes somewhat less serene, between the breeze kicking in and people taking a chilly swim on a hot day. Try July to October midweek. The ancient tree, fern, and moss-lined steep hillside to the lake are home to the 1328-ft-long cascading Bridal Veil Falls, with two of the five tiers visible from the trails (more seen driving US-2 W from Baring). Some people skip the harder hike to Lake Serene for the falls (4.25 mi round-trip, 950 ft vertical gain) because they are dazzling in the spring. Northwest Forest Pass required, and vault toilets (BYOTP) are present with a privy at Lake Serene.

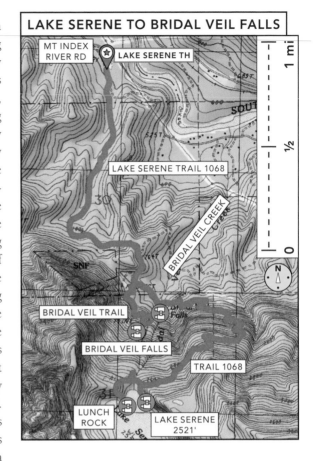

LAKE SERENE TO BRIDAL VEIL FALLS

MT INDEX RIVER RD — LAKE SERENE TH

LAKE SERENE TRAIL 1068

BRIDAL VEIL CREEK

BRIDAL VEIL TRAIL — Falls

BRIDAL VEIL FALLS

TRAIL 1068

LUNCH ROCK

LAKE SERENE 2521'

TRAILHEAD: Lake Serene TH. From Seattle, take I-5 N to exit 171 onto WA-522 E (Bothell) for 24 mi, and exit right merging onto US-2 E (Wenatchee) in Monroe for 20 mi. Fork right on Mount Index Rd (milepost 35) for 0.25 mi, then turn right on Mount Index River Rd for 200 ft along the gravel driveway to the parking area. Backups exist a few feet farther along Mount Index River Rd when the main TH fills quickly on weekends.

From Portland, take I-5 N to exit 154B (Renton) onto I-405 N for 21 mi to exit 23, onto WA-522 E (Woodinville) 14 mi, exit right merging onto US-2 E, and follow as above (55 mi, 1 hour from Seattle; 225 mi, 4 hours from Portland).

ROUTE: Begin S on Lake Serene Trail 1068 past the signage (self-register for Wilderness Permit) up the gated old gravel logging road easily for 0.25 mi passing the first of several small creeks (narrowing, rockier). Move S then SE (thick, mossy forest) as the pitch varies with bigleaf maples, alders, ferns, salmonberry, and huckleberry

Mist wafting upwards near a viewpoint at Bridal Veil Falls.

bushes (over your head in autumn), then the route levels rounding a minuscule saddle S (hear Bridal Veil Creek) less than 0.25 mi to the signed Bridal Veil Falls fork (around 1.5 mi from TH).

For the falls, follow rocky Bridal Veil Trail right (S then SE) quite steeply up 6 switchbacks (wooden steps, walkways, tree roots). Hear the cascade through the trees reaching a couple viewpoint paths that connect for a teensy loop. The first viewpoint spur heads left (E) over a boardwalk to a tough but manageable angle (clockwise loop, more spray). Be careful nearest the creek (especially with children) as you walk S up the stairs along Bridal Veil Creek to the nearby primary viewpoint of the sparkling waterfall! Finish the brief loop steeply down the opposite (W) side on Bridal Veil Trail.

For Lake Serene, continue SE on Trail 1068, descending the lovely forest across small arms of Bridal Veil Creek then a couple major ones. Climb a few feet, moving over another water crossing (footbridge, nearly 2 mi from TH), and see one of the lacy lower tiers up Bridal Veil Creek. Walk down another 100 ft (rocky, more steps), hopping over the creek under a much smaller (and closer) cascade with water dripping down the sheer rock. Hike much steeper (rock-embedded trail) 1.5 mi up 23 switchbacks total (E then SW, more rock- and wood-carved steps, giant trees). You'll traverse after switchback 8 momentarily (boulder path, meadows, fewer trees) with views improving (see Mount Index, nearby Ragged Ridge, Gothic and Del Campo Peaks, and rugged Gunn Peak) as you top the switchbacks becoming rockier for another 0.5 mi. Trail 1068 mellows somewhat W across a small creek (tiny cascade above) with a spur at left (outdoor privy).

The lake is only 100 ft WSW down steps and has fairly limited viewpoints to check out. From a brief spur left (SSE), the reflection shows the colossal ramparts that lead from the lake straight up the cliffs 3430 ft to the top of Mount Index. Melting snow from each year's avalanches gathers at the base near the water to complete the colorfest. To the right from the juncture, cross a bridge W over the outlet near the logjam, skipping the spur after (Bridal Veil Creek, 3.75 mi from TH), then continue up more steps quite steeply 100 ft SW now on Lunch Rock Trail. Walk down the same path heading left (S) a few feet easier to Lunch Rock, a great overlook just out of the trees at a large, steeply sloped boulder on the N end of the lake. Be careful not to slip in while eating your snack!

70 | ROCK LAKE TO TARN 5245

ELEVATION: 4546 ft at Rock Lake, almost 5300 ft at the high point overlook; vertical gains of around 2500 ft and more than 3000 ft, respectively

DISTANCE: 4.5–6 mi round-trip; more than 6 mi round-trip for Tarn 5245

DURATION: More than 2 hours to Rock Lake; 3–3½ hours to Tarn 5245, 6–7 hours round-trip

DIFFICULTY: Very challenging (sustained very steep ups/downs, deceiving mileage, rock fields, route-finding, not popular, scrambling, bushwhacking, traction with snow or ice until late July into August, GPS device required)

TRIP REPORT: Hiding along Maloney Ridge is a group of lakes within Alpine Lakes Wilderness that are a delight to visit for the few willing to put in the extra effort! The old fisherman's trail near Evans Lake is relentlessly steep up a narrow shoulder to a charming high point overlook that breaks out of forest enough to provide some of the best views of the day. People camp at the limited area around Rock Lake to expand their adventure to Tarn 5245 (unofficial, more of a small high alpine lake) or even Panorama or Purvis Lakes. No fee or restroom.

TRAILHEAD: Evans Lake TH. From Seattle, take I-5 N to exit 171 onto WA-522 E (Bothell) for 24 mi, exit right merging onto US-2 E (Wenatchee) in Monroe for 35.75 mi, and turn right on Foss River Rd NE (milepost 50, small sign, FR-68) for 3.5 mi (into gravel after 1.25 mi, minimal potholes) to an unsigned fork. Stay right on FR-68 (becoming rougher), then drive left from a sharp curve (juncture, 8 mi from US-2) onto FR-6840 (Maloney Ridge Rd, no sign) for 3 mi to reach the end at a sizable parking square just past a small tarn near Evans Lake (rougher, 2WD okay, slightly overgrown, narrow last mile).

From Portland, take I-5 N to exit 154B (Renton) onto I-405 N for 21 mi to exit 23, onto WA-522 E (Woodinville) 14 mi, exit right merging onto US-2 E, and follow as above (80 mi, 2 hours from Seattle; 250 mi, 4½–5 hours from Portland).

ROUTE: With little fanfare from the elevated parking area, walk 75 ft back down the road and find the solid route left (W) hiding within the overgrown brush (no sign). Climb the super-steep rocky and slender Rock Lake Trail SSW through overgrown sections (prickly bushes) 200 yards fairly roughly to the main shoulder. Continue SW up the shoulder narrowly more than 0.25 mi, then hike much steeper another 0.25 mi (great shot to Glacier Peak above a corner of Evans Lake). Move over a tiny hill (0.75 mi up), then steeply descend the rougher path S left (SE) of a decent pond. Find the clear trail across the outlet and continue super-steeply W up the tree-covered shoulder crest as it becomes ultra-steep (1 mi up). Soon after is a full view of Malachite Peak to your left (S), with snow-capped mountains behind. To the right (NW) over a nearby scree field is Baring Mountain with Gunn and Merchant Peaks.

Be cautious close to the top of the shoulder where the route meets Maloney Ridge at the high point (near the overlook)

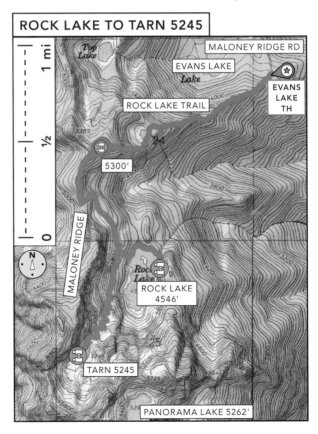

ROCK LAKE TO TARN 5245

MALONEY RIDGE RD

EVANS LAKE

Top Lake

Lake

ROCK LAKE TRAIL

EVANS LAKE TH

5389

5300'

MALONEY RIDGE

Rock Lake

ROCK LAKE 4546'

N

TARN 5245

PANORAMA LAKE 5262'

Pristine Tarn 5245 under Malachite Peak gets overlooked by most in Alpine Lakes Wilderness because of the extreme route, but these teenagers had no problem!

as the path narrows (rockier). The trail splits left and right 30 ft or so below the summit of the ridge bump overlook passing under the top. Take a moment to scramble the loose rock steeply to the very top where the best vistas reside from the thin flatter cap (5300 ft, few people at a time). Left of Malachite Peak and Rock Lake (SSE) are Summit Chief Mountain, Bears Breast Mountain, Mount Hinman and Mount Daniel, and Bald Eagle Peak (closer prominent pyramid), with several other mountaintops E. The few trees near the apex partially block views to another nearby ridge bump NW (Point 5389).

To proceed, move carefully around the rocky overlook from either side to the somewhat easier trail near the ridgeline, then walk S down Maloney Ridge (good-sized trees) and up again briefly (1.5 mi from TH) before the very steep descent to Rock Lake. Continue down the crest almost 200 yards more (easy over blowdowns), turning sharply left off the ridge. Walk NE (Rock Lake Trail, easier, narrower) as the landscape morphs into a rocky and grassy meadow (few mid-sized trees) with huge rock fields right under Maloney Ridge. Move steeper down (SE) through a second rock field to the beginning of a third, where the unsigned faint fork (less than 2 mi from TH, under 4800 ft) signals the start of the bushwhack route across the rock fields to Tarn 5245 versus heading straight down to Rock Lake.

For Rock Lake, fork left (ESE) into the woods down Rock Lake Trail, winding super-steeply briefly to the N side of the large blue-green lake in its own basin (scattered evergreens, cool cascades below lake's nearby outlet). Investigate, circumnavigate, and fish or swim before the steep climb back up Maloney Ridge. To continue directly to Tarn 5245, head S from the W side of the lake up the long, narrow rocky gully (inlet stream), scrambling steeply almost 1 mi WSW.

For Tarn 5245 from the faint fork above Rock Lake, continue right (S) off-trail, carefully traversing 100 yards across the open rock field (cairns), then work through a few trees and across the next boulder field (see gully ahead and Rock Lake below with attractive little island). Traverse another 100 yards S, passing more trees, then skirt some grass from the bottom of the next rock field a bit easier for 50 yards. Bushwhack S across larger boulders (few trees), carefully moving straight around 100 ft (up a tad), then climb up slightly right (SSW) somewhat easier over larger boulders (better footing), approaching the 35-ft-wide gully (2.25 mi from TH directly). Scramble up the gully SSW super-steeply from either side of the creek (loose rock), picking your own route (lingering snowfields to use or glissade down under good conditions) to the outlet of Tarn 5245 near a couple giant boulders that block the infinity pool view and enclose the narrow shallow lake into its own uniquely regal basin (3 mi from TH). Enjoy the peaceful setting (wildflowers, treeless) with rugged mountains just N of Malachite Peak dominating the rocky cirque far above the colorful clear water. To see Panorama Lake (frozen until late August), you would cross the outlet creek to the E side of the tarn (rougher a few feet) then head left (SE) 0.25 mi and 350 ft, bushwhacking up the somewhat grassier thin valley (wildflowers) to a rocky little pass above that lake.

71 | WEST FORK FOSS LAKES TO ATRIUM PEAK

ELEVATION: 4000 ft at Copper Lake, 4600 ft at Big Heart Lake, 5359 ft on Atrium Peak; vertical gains of 2500 ft, 3400 ft, and around 4400 ft, respectively

DISTANCE: 4.25 mi to Copper Lake; 7 mi to Big Heart Lake; 8 mi to Atrium Peak, 16–17 mi round-trip

DURATION: 2½–3 hours up; 4–5 hours up; 5–6 hours up, 9–11 hours round-trip

DIFFICULTY: Mix of strenuous for Copper Lake (rocky, uneven trails, steeper at times, switchbacks, busy), very challenging for Big Heart Lake (long as a day hike, ups/downs, rougher, mosquitoes July into September), and expert only for Atrium Peak (exceedingly long from TH, route-finding, drop-offs)

TRIP REPORT: The greatest concentration of sizable lakes within Alpine Lakes Wilderness can be explored over several days or just one. Most adventurists are satisfied stopping at Copper or Big Heart Lakes for the day hike (limited campsites at lakes), but those in prime shape can visit the steep hogback between Big Heart and

Angeline Lakes (Point 5359 called Atrium Peak) with electrifying overlooks! Northwest Forest Pass required, and an outhouse is present.

TRAILHEAD: West Fork Foss Lakes TH. See Rock Lake to Tarn 5245 on page 220 for directions 3.5 mi to an unsigned fork on Foss River Rd NE. Stay right 1 mi on FR-68, turn left on signed FR-6835 (notes defunct CG, other great sites en route) for 2 mi to the end at a decent parking area in the woods (75 mi, 1¾ hours from Seattle; 245 mi, 4½–5 hours from Portland).

ROUTE: Begin on signed West Fork Foss Lakes Trail 1064 (free self-issue Wilderness Permit) SSW up the valley parallel to the West Fork Foss River (thick mossy forest, see nearby towering mountains) before crossing the bridge over the boulder-laden riverbed (mostly dry or water running below) at almost 1 mi in. Continue S through large hemlock and at least one gigantic cedar (for a photo op just off-trail at right), then hike steeper turns before easing and descending a few feet to tree-enshrouded Trout Lake (1.75 mi from TH). Follow Trail 1064 S 0.5 mi up a couple quick turns (W of Trout Lake, dense flora, views), traversing a bit, then ascend 20 switchbacks W, hiking very steeply (ancient trees, rocky, boulders) while watching part of 600 ft long

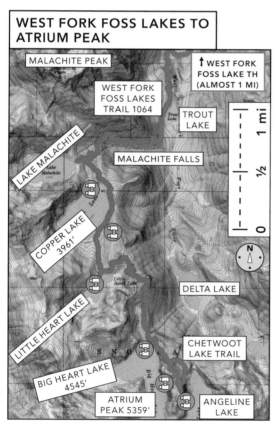

WEST FORK FOSS LAKES TO ATRIUM PEAK

Malachite Falls with at least four other named waterfalls in the cirque cascading down Copper Creek before it reaches West Fork Foss River! Climb a few log steps crossing Malachite Creek (footbridge, 3.5 mi up), then hike 2 quick switchbacks SW (easing) before moving up a turn and 3 more switchbacks (huckleberry, salmonberry) to a signed juncture for Lake Malachite at right (W, at 4 mi up, 0.25 mi steep spur). Hike SE instead up briefly (rocks, roots) to crest the top of the valley at the headwall below the lakes. Move down a hair then up log and rock steps (next to top of Malachite Falls) easier to Copper Lake.

Rock- or boulder-hop without trouble over the creek

Very blue Heart Lake from seldomly visited Atrium Peak in Alpine Lakes Wilderness!

below the logjam at Copper Lake and admire the views and reflections of Benkopp Peak, Peak 6010, and Malachite Peak into the bright blue-green water! Continue 0.75 mi S along the E side of the large lake as the trail undulates (constant views, picnic spots) and is choked with huckleberries (August–September). For Little Heart Lake (only 0.5 mi away, Trail 1064), move up 2 quick steep turns near the end of Copper Lake, bending S more leisurely away from the water becoming steeper (log/stone steps). Then take the spur right (SSW) from the outlet logjam a few feet for a better shot of the cyan-colored smaller lake within an admirable rocky bowl!

Trail 1064 quickly takes off (much steeper, rockier) above Little Heart Lake (more than 1.5 mi to Big Heart Lake). Climb 8 switchbacks N, easing right (NE, wider) around a little high point, then descend briefly SE (over mossy, old rock pile), moving right of a boulder-filled tarn. Hike S steeper up a little shoulder with a half-dozen or so tight switchbacks (look N to Glacier Peak between Silver Eagle and Malachite Peaks with Trout Lake below), then traverse SSE (steeper, large rock fields) before crossing a NE-facing broader shoulder easier. Walk up a tiny bit more S of the broad shoulder before descending more than 0.5 mi to Big Heart Lake (see Delta Lake left, and more). Move down 4 switchbacks S and across the bottom of a boulder field, then the trail undulates down as the magnificent lake appears to your right. The luminescent cobalt water first shows itself in a small rocky alcove leading to the grander lake near the outlet logjam. Cross over rocks or logs easy enough and check out a cascade below the outlet that is the topmost part of Big Heart Falls (1262 ft, mostly out of sight). Return after surveying the area, or dig deep for that something extra!

Hike around a mile to Atrium Peak or overlooks under the small summit between two insanely blue lakes! Pick up the narrowing Chetwoot Lake Trail (no sign, obvious) steeply SE up the little shoulder around 17 tight switchbacks and turns before easing again. Pass fewer trees over a flatter stint S before you descend slightly traversing left (E) across a boulder field (under cliff band as shoulder breaks up) below the more prominent jagged ridge (of Atrium Peak). Reach a faint juncture for the optional summit loop (around 0.5 mi from Big Heart Lake outlet) among the larger boulders (almost 5000 ft, small cairn right, S) before the official trail descends steeply around a notch on the ridge. Both routes end near an overlook area on the ridge S of Atrium Peak. Chetwoot Lake Trail (almost 0.75 mi) is a bit longer and more painful, having you descend very steeply and briefly, then climb just as sharply 500 ft up on an already exhaustive day (save for counterclockwise loop).

For the direct (preferred) route, leave Chetwoot Lake Trail from the summit juncture, scrambling S straight up large steep boulders briefly before moving slightly right to find the climber's trail right (W) of the rougher ridgeline over simpler terrain. Walk SE through wide lovely meadows (trail fades) just left (E) of the actual summit with its saw-toothed boulders. From around 75 ft below the very top you could bushwhack right directly through tight brush, scrambling S a few feet to the peak. You can also continue traversing around the summit briefly on more solid paths leading to the rocky S ridgeline, where you climb right (N) with minimal bouldering near the high ridge (use caution). Views from the summit along the high ridge down to the overlook are nothing less than amazing! From tiny Atrium Peak, all of the large and very blue Big Heart Lake can be seen, which is no simple feat. Boulder SE down the ridge from the summit, picking up the trail left (E) of the crest briefly as Angeline Lake appears. Join the official route (from the left, Chetwoot Lake Trail) 100 ft farther down the S ridge to the vague overlook on a small flatter area (5325 ft). Chetwoot Lake Trail continues down and up S almost 2 mi to Chetwoot Lake. See across striking Angeline Lake to Summit Chief Mountain, Overcoat Peak, and Chimney Rock. Return the same way over the summit block or from Chetwoot Lake Trail.

For the more difficult loop, follow thin Chetwoot Lake Trail right (N) from the high ridge juncture (look SE and E to Iron Cap Mountain and top of Mount Hinman). The trail soon becomes terribly steep N down a few turns (boulders, vertical meadows). Get your best and last look toward Angeline Lake with its bright cerulean water, and see Delta and Trout Lakes down valley with Glacier Peak above. Traverse faded Chetwoot Lake Trail NW across rock fields laboring up 4 super-steep tight rocky switchbacks W to a notch in the N ridge near the end of the summit loop. Trek to the TH with your ear-to-ear grin!

ELEVATION: 5066 ft; vertical gain of 2250 ft

DISTANCE: Less than 4 mi up, almost 8 mi round-trip

DURATION: 2 hours up, 3–4 hours round-trip

DIFFICULTY: Strenuous (steady grade, never steep, family-friendly, switchbacks, popular, mosquitoes July into August, drop-offs, lingering snow into late July okay to cross, possible in winter with traction)

TRIP REPORT: Day hike the highest of several tiny peaks on a distinguished mountain far above the South Fork Skykomish River Valley corridor in Mount Baker-Snoqualmie National Forest with the reward-to-effort ratio greatly lopsided toward the hiker! Views rival the finest hikes within the I-90 corridor and with fewer visitors. Wildlife sightings may include deer, elk, coyotes, mountain goats, and bears. Northwest Forest Pass required, and an outhouse is present.

TRAILHEAD: Jennifer Dunn TH. From Seattle, take I-5 N to exit 171 onto WA-522 E (Bothell) for 24 mi, exit right merging onto US-2 E (Wenatchee) in Monroe for 37.25 mi, and turn left on FR-6066 (yellow sign, milepost 52) up 6.75 mi to the TH (gravel, one-lane, watch for oncoming traffic, potholes, improved after 2.5 mi, 2WD okay). There is pull-in parking on the right or on the sides, with 15 to 20 spots, as the drivable road ends.

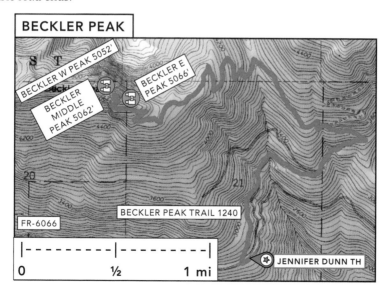

BECKLER PEAK

BECKLER W PEAK 5052'

BECKLER MIDDLE PEAK 5062'

BECKLER E PEAK 5066'

BECKLER PEAK TRAIL 1240

FR-6066

JENNIFER DUNN TH

0   ½   1 mi

Baring Mountain and others beyond the more precipitous pinnacles of Beckler Peak.

From Portland, take I-5 N to exit 154B (Renton) onto I-405 N for 21 mi to exit 23, onto WA-522 E (Woodinville) 14 mi, exit right merging onto US-2 E, and follow as on previous page (75 mi, 2 hours from Seattle; 250 mi, 4–4½ hours from Portland).

ROUTE: Walk past the kiosk/sign (self-register for Wilderness Permit) heading left (NNE) from the fork on wide Beckler Peak Trail 1240 almost 1.25 mi easily (woods, small creeks). The trail becomes steeper NE to the first switchback. Then ascend NW (larger hemlocks, cedar, fir) with 2 easier turns steepening briefly through a small clearing (rocky, wildflowers, see over clear-cut to Malachite Peak and others). Reenter the old-growth forest, moving up a turn over Harlan Saddle (almost 3900 ft, 2 mi up), then hike W more than 0.75 mi with 6 switchbacks steeper to the E ridge of Beckler Peak. Cruise SW up the tree-covered ridge with a pleasant grade (narrowing, trail-finding with snow coverage tricky but not difficult).

Ascend 9 switchbacks (some stone steps, S of ridgeline at times) W then N to the summit. You'll gain the crest again through the thinning woods (almost 3.5 mi up, views) as Trail 1240 will become steeper after switchback 5 into 6 (back onto rocky ridge crest near an overlook). Step 15–30 ft off-trail from the switchback right (E, 4980 ft) to see Glacier Peak far N of nearby Mount Fernow, panning left to the Monte Cristo Group, Vesper, Sperry, and Del Campo Peaks, Three Fingers, and more! The final turns take you up a few feet to the narrowing top (don't play King-of-the-Mountain with mountain goats) where there's only room for one at a time to be safe. There are plenty of picnic spots nearby and excellent 360-degree panoramas (very few trees), but there are also major drop-offs and cliffs surrounding (careful with children). Look NW over the other, much rockier Beckler Peaks to Baring Mountain, Mount Index, Merchant and Gunn Peaks, and Eagle Rock! And check out the view S to Cathedral Rock, Mount Daniel, Mount Hinman, Iron Cap Mountain, Summit Chief Mountain, Overcoat Peak, Chimney Rock, Lemah Mountain, and Chikamin Peak!

ELEVATION: 5540 ft; vertical gain of 2600 ft total (including Sunrise Mountain)

DISTANCE: More than 3.75 mi to Scorpion Mountain, almost 8 mi round-trip

DURATION: 2 hours one way, 3–4 hours round-trip

DIFFICULTY: Very challenging (ups/downs, very steep at times, lack of switchbacks, not popular, bonus summit, smooth tread, biting flies and mosquitoes July into August, lingering snow into late July okay to cross without gear, possible in winter with snowshoes, GPS device helpful)

TRIP REPORT: Don't let the absence of huge elevation gain fool you. This arachnid's got some sting! Try July to October for wildflowers and superb vistas for most of the day hiking along Johnson Ridge to Sunrise and Scorpion Mountains within Wild Sky Wilderness. No fee or restroom.

TRAILHEAD: Johnson Ridge TH. From Seattle, take I-5 N to exit 171 onto WA-522 E (Bothell) for 24 mi, and exit right, merging onto US-2 E (Wenatchee) in Monroe for 34.75 mi. Fork left on Beckler Rd/FR-65 (milepost 49) for 6.75 mi, turn sharp right on FR-6520 (shot-up sign, gravel, one-lane, 2WD okay) for 2.75 mi, keep left (FR-6520) for 4.25 mi, and reach the end with limited parking of a dozen spots.

From Portland, take I-5 N to exit 154B (Renton) onto I-405 N for 21 mi to exit 23, onto WA-522 E (Woodinville) 14 mi, exit right merging onto US-2 E, and follow as above (80 mi, 2 hours from Seattle; 255 mi, 4½–5 hours from Portland).

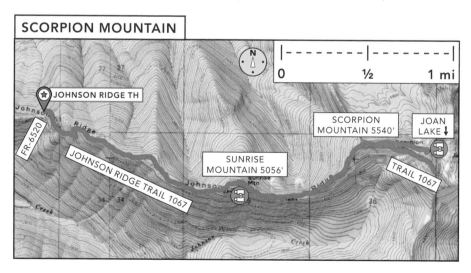

SCORPION MOUNTAIN

From Scorpion Mountain over avalanche lilies to Captain Point and Mount Fernow.

ROUTE: Begin from the end of the road to the right (no sign) through high brush 50 ft up (passing signage, self-register for Wilderness Permit) as Johnson Ridge Trail 1067 becomes clearer SE (steadily steep, rocky) before you ascend the hike's only true switchback (sadly) at more than 0.25 mi from the TH. After a sweeping turn and another 0.25 mi, follow the narrower route through tall trees (sun penetrating canopy) as the wider ridge defines itself. Continue SE steeply up the tree-covered ridge before easing (1.5 mi from TH, see Glacier Peak), then grind steeper E. The trail becomes very steep again for the final feet NE topping Sunrise Mountain. Step right off-trail 10 ft to a tiny obvious open space with sweeping views!

Hike down Johnson Ridge (Trail 1067) SE very steeply from Sunrise Mountain almost 0.5 mi to the indiscernible saddle between summits continuing E (brief steep ups/downs, trees) another 0.25 mi. Clamber NE 0.5 mi very steeply (overgrown) through small open meadows (simple to cross with lingering snow through July, wildflowers), steepening to the high ridge (3.25 mi from TH). It's 0.5 mi farther to the summit juncture as you undulate E narrowly, heading much steeper up grassy meadows (best views yet) before moving easier through open terrain SE to the unsigned fork (5450 ft). Trail 1067 continues more than 0.5 mi right (SE then NE steeply) almost 500 ft down to Joan Lake.

Keep left (E) on Johnson Ridge a couple hundred yards up Scorpion Mountain Trail (wildflower-covered) to the nearby rounded and mostly treeless top of Scorpion Mountain (Joan Lake below). The path resumes SE briefly down to meet Johnson Ridge Trail. There are incredible views from the summit that span S between Captain Point and Mount Fernow to Mount Daniel and Mount Hinman, and several others, including Mount Rainier. Look SW to Beckler Peak, W to Baring Mountain and others, and N to Evergreen Mountain, the Monte Cristo Group, Sloan Peak, Benchmark Mountain, and a holy host of others!

74 | DECEPTION LAKES TO SURPRISE MOUNTAIN

ELEVATION: 5053 ft at Deception Lakes, 6330 ft on Surprise Mountain; vertical gains of around 2500 ft and 3800 ft, respectively

DISTANCE: 4.5 mi to primary viewpoint at Deception Lakes, 9 mi round-trip; 6.25 mi up, 12.5 mi round-trip for summit (including lakes)

DURATION: 2–3 hours to lakes; 4–5 hours to summit, 7–9 hours round-trip total

DIFFICULTY: Very challenging (very steep ups/downs, rustic but solid trails, overgrown at times, narrow, more difficult when wet and muddy, GPS device recommended)

TRIP REPORT: Less crowded access to Surprise Mountain exists from its back door, driving deeper within Deception Creek valley to an obscure TH for decent drivers with AWD or a high-clearance vehicle. Some stop at the gorgeous underrated Deception Lakes area, but Surprise Gap or Mountain beckons with crazy views of Surprise and Glaciers Lakes as well as Glacier Peak, Mount Daniel, and others. This day trip is not to be taken lightly but is perfect for seasoned hikers. Northwest Forest Pass required, and there is no restroom.

DECEPTION LAKES TO SURPRISE MOUNTAIN

FR-6830   TRAIL 1059.1   GLACIER/SURPRISE LAKES

DECEPTION CREEK CUT-OFF TH

DECEPTION CREEK TRAIL 1059

SURPRISE MOUNTAIN 6330'

SURPRISE GAP 5800'

TRAIL 1063

SURPRISE MOUNTAIN TRAIL 1063

PCT 2000

DECEPTION CREEK

TRAIL 1059.2

DECEPTION LAKES 5053'

PCT 2000

0   ½   1 mi

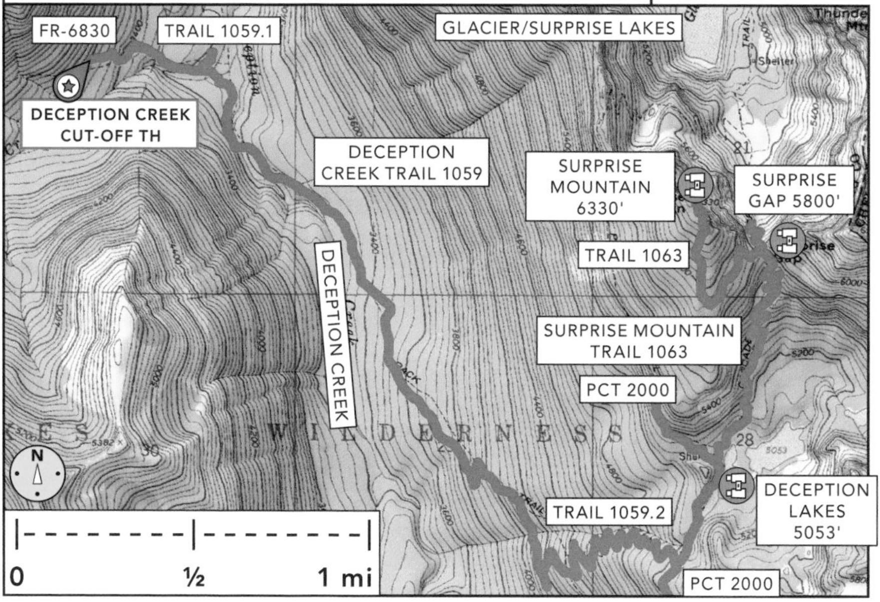

TRAILHEAD: Deception Creek Cut-Off TH. See Rock Lake to Tarn 5245 on page 220 for directions 3.5 mi to an unsigned fork on Foss River Rd NE. Stay left (opposite FR-68) on narrow FR-6830 (small old post) more than 11 mi, winding up to the only semi-confusing fork. Keep left (opposite FR-310, small old post) on FR-6830 (no sign) around 6.5 mi more (large potholes, one-lane, drop-offs) to reach the signed TH with tiny pullouts at left. Because of the narrow road, to be safe you should drive less than 0.25 mi more to the turnaround at the end and park there (without blocking) or near the TH.

From Portland, take I-5 N to exit 154B (Renton) onto I-405 N for 21 mi to exit 23, onto WA-522 E (Woodinville) 14 mi, exit right merging onto US-2 E, and follow as above (90 mi, 2½ hours from Seattle; 260 mi, 5 hours from Portland).

ROUTE: Descend Deception Creek Cut-Off (spur) Trail 1059.1 (self-register for Wilderness Permit, overgrown, narrow, old-growth trees), winding E super-steeply 0.5 mi or so to the first of many signed junctures. Proceed right (SSE, toward Crest Trail 2000) on Deception Creek Trail 1059 (much easier briefly, overgrown a few feet, past little camps), working 20 ft over Fisher Creek using logs or rocks where possible to the solid trail above the embankment (just W of Deception Creek). Soon after, move right (S, past small sign noting ford left) a few feet with another sign pointing correctly toward a footlog as you work steeply 100 ft down left (E) of a big fallen tree through some brush (Trail 1059) to the logs. Head over them 40 ft or so cautiously (see large cairn on another log near steep embankment across Deception Creek). Climb a few feet to the trail passing another small sign (on mossy felled tree) showing the footlog option (almost 1 mi from TH).

Glacier and Surprise Lakes to Glacier Peak with rugged Thunder Mountain to the right from Surprise Gap!

Hike Deception Creek Trail SE 2 mi (few ups/downs, roots okay, mossy flora). The trail becomes steeper past some fairly hefty Douglas fir, cedar, and hemlock with 2 quick switchbacks before the first of two major creek crossings (emanating from Deception Lakes above). Move over the adjacent (narrower, rocky) scenic second creek then up briefly to a signed intersection (more than 3 mi from TH). Turn left up Deception Creek Spur Trail 1059.2 pretty steeply; there are 18 switchbacks E through the forest (less undergrowth) to the next signed juncture on another switchback. Walk left (NE) onto PCT 2000 easier for 0.25 mi (across a rock field, past huge boulders) and over a solid creek approaching the lake outlet. Look toward clear green water through a few trees (technically Daisy Lake), continuing 0.25 mi to nearby Deception Lakes where there's a decent flat area at right with large boulders serving as the primary viewpoint. See across the shallow blue-green waters to the local mountains (and Surprise Gap) and the rocky W face of nearby Mac Peak! Explore spurs happily and return, or continue.

For Surprise Gap (1 mi away) and the mountaintop from the primary lake viewpoint, walk NE for 50 ft, passing a signed juncture (PCT at left, NNW 1.75 mi steeply to tree-choked Pieper Pass) NNE onto Surprise Mountain Trail 1063 (old sign a few feet farther for Deception Lakes Horse Camp confirming proper trail), skipping lakeside spurs to adjoining lake. Ascend log steps along the steady rocky path up a turn before hiking N through narrow meadows (one bordering large boulder field) and up 8 steeper switchbacks (rutted, narrow) N to the gap/saddle (5800 ft). Look N to Glacier Lake and Glacier Peak (Thunder Mountain right) in a picture-perfect postcard! Trees obscure views in other directions as you see Trail 1063 heading both straight (N) down the rocky gully to the PCT and also to the summit.

Continue from the small clearing in the gap left (SW) up the climber's trail very steeply (2 quick rocky rutted switchbacks) before the trail undulates through meadows and then climbs N much steeper again. The path narrows (rutted, fewer trees), reaching the 6-ft-tall metal post (from historic lookout) on the apex. Be cautious on the loose fine gravel near the cliff edge (drop-offs). You'll be able to see N between Spark Plug and Thunder Mountains to Glacier Peak above Glacier and Surprise Lakes; and to the SW are glaciated Mount Daniel and Mount Hinman with Cathedral Rock spotted between trees! Enjoy other surprises before the long descent down then up to the TH.

ELEVATION: 5550 ft at Minotaur Lake, 6376 ft on Labyrinth Mountain; vertical gains of 1800 ft and 2625 ft (including lake), respectively

DISTANCE: 1.5 mi to lake, 4 mi round-trip; 2.5 mi to summit, 5.5 mi round-trip

DURATION: 1 hour to lake; 2 hours to summit, 4–5 hours round-trip

DIFFICULTY: Strenuous (steep at times, roots, rocks, well traveled, faint but solid trails, bugs until late August, GPS device recommended when snow covered)

TRIP REPORT: This precious day hike N of Stevens Pass brings visitors to inspirational Minotaur Lake within a large rocky cirque under Labyrinth Mountain with options to stroll a few feet for a top-notch look to colorful Theseus Lake or continue for mind-boggling views from the summit! No fee or restroom.

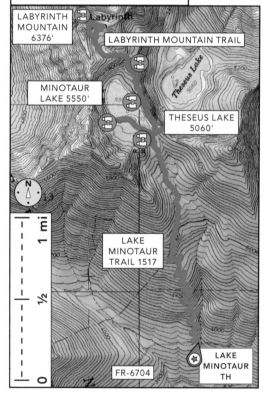

MINOTAUR LAKE TO LABYRINTH MOUNTAIN

LABYRINTH MOUNTAIN 6376'

Labyrinth

LABYRINTH MOUNTAIN TRAIL

MINOTAUR LAKE 5550'

Theseus Lake

THESEUS LAKE 5060'

LAKE MINOTAUR TRAIL 1517

N

1 mi

½

0

FR-6704

LAKE MINOTAUR TH

TRAILHEAD: Lake Minotaur TH. From Seattle, take I-5 N to exit 171 onto WA-522 E (Bothell) for 24 mi, exit right merging onto US-2 E (Wenatchee) in Monroe for 53 mi, and turn left (3.75 mi E of Stevens Pass as highway becomes divided, no signal, very brief turning lane, use caution crossing US-2 W) onto Smith-Brooke Rd (FR-6700, gravel, narrow, AWD preferred) for 4.75 mi, curve sharply left (FR-6700) 1.75 mi. Then fork left 0.75 mi on one-lane FR-6704 to reach the end with limited parking on the sides.

From Portland, take I-5 N to exit 154B (Renton) onto I-405 N

Theseus Lake and Lake Minotaur look radiant from Labyrinth Mountain toward Mount Howard in North Cascades from the Henry M. Jackson Wilderness!

for 21 mi to exit 23, onto WA-522 E (Woodinville) 14 mi, exit right merging onto US-2 E, and follow as on previous page (95 mi, 2½ hours from Seattle; 265 mi, 4½–5 hours from Portland).

ROUTE: Hike very steeply 0.5 mi NNW on Lake Minotaur Trail 1517 (signed, self-register for Wilderness Permit) up a shoulder with good tread, tight turns, and about 16 switchbacks to 4400 ft (thick woods, no views). Continue super-steeply up more S-turns steeply before traversing NNE right (E, 5100 ft) of the shoulder. Hike steeper NNW through narrow heather meadows (1 mi from TH), then move easier left (W) of a little tarn within a flatter meadow (views ahead) 100 yards shy of the lake. Move up before leveling through short trees to the outlet of subalpine Minotaur Lake at its narrow SE end (major eye candy)! A spur works left (NW) 0.25 mi with fantastic angles (and campsites), but for now head right (NE then N, respect restoration areas) over the outlet on the main path 100 yards up through a smattering of evergreens (Theseus Lake Trail moves down right, NE, and another path follows Minotaur Lake NW) to the official end of Trail 1517 at a nondistinctive rocky area on the headwall between basins (5600 ft, E of Minotaur Lake, drop-offs). You'll have exceptional views down the cliffs to brightly painted Theseus Lake (also dotted with islands), looking out N to Wenatchee Ridge above the Little Wenatchee River valley!

For the summit, continue onto Labyrinth Mountain Trail (no sign) along the rise as you see both lakes in one scrumptious shot from the boulder-laden path near the second small rock pile. Soon descend steeply and briefly to a little saddle before you hike up (N) away from Minotaur Lake through trees quite sharply then NW into a very steep meadow (white boulders, scrub). Follow the undefined wider shoulder W (easier, fewer trees, sometimes brushy, rutted, see Lake Wenatchee ESE) up past heather, wildflowers (or huckleberries), and tiny mossy creeks to an unsigned fork within the charming high alpine basin (6150 ft, 0.5 mi above headwall/rise).

Both summit routes on the mini loop reach the top in almost 0.25 mi, with the main trail left (SW then N) being easier, but both are recommended. For the slightly more challenging scramble first (counterclockwise loop, Class 2), traverse right (N then NE) on the climber's trail to a minor saddle on the high ridge with other pinnacles along the ridge right (NE) and a nice view from Glacier Peak to Mount Stuart. Hike left (W) steeply up the rocky paths on or just left (S) of Labyrinth Mountain's E ridge with a couple turns and some very easy bouldering the final 30 ft or so to the peak (bailout option moves left, W a few feet then right to top). See USGS benchmarks from 1963 with a slightly inaccurate peak height (6360 ft), perhaps meant for the subsummit just SW. The panorama is miraculous, with Mount Rainier in the distance beyond Mount Daniel and Mount Hinman, both lakes below and Lake Wenatchee, and Rock Mountain, Mount Howard, and Mount Mastiff on Nason Ridge in between. Baring Mountain and others are W, panning NW to the Monte Cristo Group, Sloan Peak, and Mount Baker.

Loop down by heading S on Labyrinth Mountain Trail along the connecting high ridge momentarily. Then follow the rocky trail left (S) from the saddle between high points (before larger boulders) a few feet down to a faint fork. The spur leading right (W) heads 75 ft up looser boulders to the tiny subsummit with similar views. Continue S down the very steep but manageable solid rock and earth trail (unless lingering snow into late July hides the route) as you head left from a switchback easier a few feet to the end of the brief summit loop. Hike right (SE) pleasantly 0.75 mi to the outlet at Minotaur Lake.

Mount Index into placid water from Lake Serene (hike 69, page 217).

NORTHERN CASCADES–NORTH CASCADES NATIONAL PARK

North Cascades
Scenic Highway

Washington P
Overlook

ELEVATION: 5324 ft; vertical gain of 2200 ft

DISTANCE: 2.75 mi up, almost 6 mi round-trip

DURATION: 2 hours up, 3–4 hours round-trip

DIFFICULTY: Strenuous (jam-packed, scree, steep sections, brief steep bouldering with solid rock near summit, Class 2, traction with snow)

TRIP REPORT: Don't let the litter, lack of solitude, bad trail etiquette by people blaring music and not yielding to uphill hikers, or poor TH conditions within Mount Pilchuck State Park stop you from doing this respectable hike with outstanding views of big volcanoes plus Three Fingers Mountain, Sloan Peak, Puget Sound, the Olympics, and more! July to October is preferred, although it's possible in winter with proper gear and experience. Avoid summer weekends if humanly possible. Northwest Forest Pass required, and an outhouse is present (BYOTP).

TRAILHEAD: Mount Pilchuck TH. From Seattle or Portland, take I-5 N to exit 194 (Snohomish/Wenatchee), merge onto US-2 E for 2 mi, stay left merging onto WA-204 E

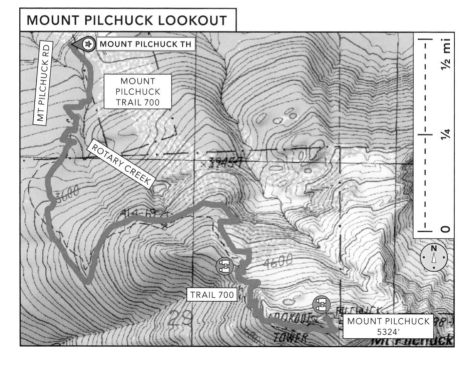

MOUNT PILCHUCK LOOKOUT

Mount Pilchuck Trail up granite slabs to the boulder-covered summit.

(Lake Stevens) for 2.25 mi, turn left on WA-9 N for 1.75 mi, then turn right on WA-92 E for 7.25 mi (traffic circles). Take the second right in a traffic circle onto WA-92 E/ Quarry Rd for 1.75 mi (with one more traffic circle) to the end in Granite Falls. Turn left from the stop sign onto Mountain Loop Hwy for 11 mi, turn right after the bridge over South Fork Stillaguamish River on Mount Pilchuck Rd for 6.75 mi (FR-42, paved first 500 ft then dusty gravel, potholes, closed 1.5 mi from MLH December 12 through April 12), and reach the end at a long parking area that fills instantly on weekends (60 mi, 1½ hours from Seattle; 240 mi, 4–5 hours from Portland).

ROUTE: See the summit from the TH and walk S up wide Mount Pilchuck Trail 700 less than 0.25 mi, forking right (SW) to stay on route through the old forest (few larger trees). Ascend many wooden steps (some bypassed) then hop over Rotary Creek and move up turns (uneven rocks and roots). Pass a couple orange posts pointing the way NE from a switchback (at 1.25 mi up) leading through a boulder field, then work S through the rock slabs (some blasted to create the trail) with a pleasant grade (see Twin Sisters, Mount Baker, Mount Shuksan). Wind S then SE up to a saddle on the NW ridge of Mount Pilchuck (2.25 mi up) with a big brown sign pointing toward the parking area.

The peak seems rather daunting from this angle where you ascend stone steps steeper E then curve right (E) around the cliffy ridge crest from the S. Climb the narrower steep rocky trail and final switchback NW to the lookout and be careful near the huge boulders surrounding the top. Ascend the solid ladder like many before you, finishing to the usually open (and informative) lookout with decks (and people camping within and nearby). Be respectful, leaving the shutters closed as it gets very windy on top, and don't break in if locked. Be cautious bouldering around the peak area if you choose to wander.

77 BATHTUB LAKES

ELEVATION: 4800 ft; vertical gain of around 2400 ft

DISTANCE: 3 mi up, around 7 mi round-trip

DURATION: 2½–3 hours up, 6–7 hours round-trip total

DIFFICULTY: Very challenging (consistently quite steep, Class 2, rocky, muddy until mid-August, tree roots, route-finding, GPS device recommended, solitude, bugs July into August, mountaineering skills and gear required with snow until late July)

TRIP REPORT: Advanced day hikers will more than enjoy this wonderful backcountry utopia at Bathtub Lakes, known as Twenty Lakes Basin, just E of overpopulated Mount Pilchuck. The snow finally disappears late July into August, revealing the route from Iodine Gulch to the subalpine basin above. Late August into September, wildflowers slowly fade (mosquitoes gone) with wild blueberries flourishing. Wildlife sightings may include mountain goats. No fee or restroom.

TRAILHEAD: Bear/Pinnacle Lake TH. See Mount Pilchuck Lookout on page 239 for directions to Granite Falls. Turn left from WA-92 E/Quarry Rd onto Mountain Loop Hwy for 14.5 mi, turn right on FR-4020 (signed, gravel, sizable potholes) for more than 2.5 mi, and fork right on FR-4021 (signed Bear Lake, one-lane, potholes, slightly overgrown, AWD preferred) for almost 3 mi to reach the signed TH at left and a wider pullout at right (65 mi, less than 2 hours from Seattle; 240 mi, 4½–5 hours from Portland).

ROUTE: Begin W on Bear Lake Trail 703 (sign denotes old numbers 661 and 703 for Pinnacle Lake Trail) up steep switchbacks and turns almost 0.25 mi to a signed juncture. Head right (W) around 100 yards to visit Bear Lake. Follow wide gravel Trail 703 to a fork. Right leads to a privy and Bear Lake briefly while if you walk left, the path would take you 50 ft directly to the sizable round lake as it becomes visible through the surrounding thick woodland (somewhat underwhelming compared to what's ahead). Many scout around lakeside brush for open areas to swim or fish.

From the main juncture, keep S on Pinnacle Lake Trail 703.1 easy a moment, crossing Bear Creek (nearly dries up in late summer) then ascend 13 switchbacks nearly 1 mi S (fairly steep, overgrown track at times) through big old-growth cedar nearing a rise. Switchback one more time onto the rise curving right (W) easier briefly, then begin climbing again (SW then W, less roots) 0.5 mi up the clear trail (703.1, sometimes muddy) before leveling. Pass a more appealing tarn just to its left, then continue down the rockier trail W briefly to its termination at Pinnacle Lake (almost 2 mi up). This subalpine glassy blue bonus is longer than wider as you see Hermans Peak just above the lake with trees on the right and the more open rocky side left holding the route to Iodine Gulch and Bathtub Lakes. For the partial bushwhack on unofficial Bathtub Lakes Trail, continue left (NW) around Pinnacle Lake over the boulder-covered outlet (Black Creek), then work 100 yards (caution nearest lake), including across a boulder field to the bottom of the lush inlet creek coming down Iodine Gulch.

It's 1.5 mi to the top of the ultra-steep gulch as you move left (W) up Bathtub Lakes Trail (faint, rocky) 0.25 mi in the narrow creek bed or just right (N) of the creek to begin as the gulch widens and levels somewhat surrounded by much larger boulders. See far up the gully right for the steep grassy hillside you'll soon ascend. Move W left (S of) a large cliff band (cairns), hiking steeply right (N) of the creek bed then right (N) before the next little cliffy area NW very steeply up Bathtub Lakes Trail. Follow the grass-, fern-, and wildflower-lined trail with less rock up the center (lumbering nearest the small side creek or just right, N) to the very top of the gully where a painted rock (4700 ft) points to the trail down Iodine Gulch.

Views and wildflowers are outstanding for the remainder less than 0.5 mi into the Bathtub Lakes basin as you round the corner, heading WNW (easier and even) down a few feet. Cross 75 ft over a scree field (rocks with painted yellow dots) then move up steeply a few feet before traversing easier past small tarns (see pinnacles of boulder-enshrouded Mount Pilchuck directly above basin) just before descending W to the first of Bathtub Lakes. There are around 10 actual lakes that reside within smaller

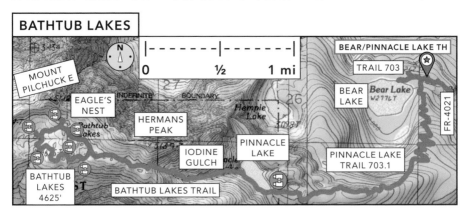

BATHTUB LAKES

Mount Pilchuck and Mount Pilchuck East near Bathtub Lakes from remote Twenty Lakes Basin.

charming rocky basins (or bathtubs) encompassing the larger basin in whole. The area is speckled with evergreens and a number of tarns of different sizes that dry up by end of summer with the lakes losing a bit of volume as well (no inlet creeks).

For the entertaining counterclockwise loop (around 1 mi), head down Bathtub Lakes Trail only a few feet, then walk up NW right (N) of the first deep blue lake (then a tiny lake) and very briefly between the next two picturesque lakes with sheer walls and broken rock (nice reflections). Either stay on the main trail WSW down 100 yards to the largest lake between a couple other lakes at the W end of the basin or bushwhack almost 100 ft N up steeply (no clear trail) to a smaller lake. From there you can see better up to the ridge directly above that spans from Mount Pilchuck to Hermans Peak (with Mount Pilchuck East and Eagle's Nest between). Moving W easily a few feet from the highest lake past a couple trees, see all three lakes farthest W in the basin before returning to the main trail and those (visible) lakes.

Explore the rocky way between the shimmering largest lake and the smaller one at right (N), then make your way down Bathtub Lakes Trail at left (S, fades over slabs) to the lowest lake (SW edge of basin). It's a captivating bathtub indeed, with a small island and the basin's only outlet creek! Either take Bathtub Lakes Trail back the primary way or bushwhack closer (loop) NE past wildflowers up the steeper hillside less than 100 yards, then walk SE to the right of a small shallow lake. Climb steeply right (S) up the open rock field very briefly, then walk easier left (E) from a minuscule hill looking down right (E) to a tarn on the rim of the basin. Hike one of the paths a bit steeper ENE down to the next sizable scenic lake (handful of trees scattered), exploring different angles including from the rocky peninsula on the S side of the water. Walk E around the lake to the next nearby deeper (easternmost) lake a bit lower within a small bowl. Enjoy the sights (once easily down) to the less rocky S shore before hiking N up to the end of the loop. Walk steeply up the grassy hill, moving very carefully left around the little cliff band just right (E) of the lake on a 2–4 ft wide rock ledge without difficulty. Pass a few large boulders, brush, and short pines 40 ft (no path) over to the visible Bathtub Lakes Trail at the end of the loop. Turn right (SE) up a few feet past tarns leaving the outrageous basin!

78 BIG FOUR ICE CAVES

ELEVATION: Almost 2000 ft; vertical gain of around 300 ft

DISTANCE: 1.25 mi one way from either TH, 2.5–3 mi round-trip

DURATION: ¾ hour one way, 1–2 hours round-trip

DIFFICULTY: Easy (gentle ascent, family-friendly, boardwalks, very popular on summer weekends, avalanche danger until late July or so)

TRIP REPORT: Permanent snowfields from persistent avalanches that fall off the vertical N face of Big Four Mountain (winter through late spring) in Mount Baker National Forest reside at the base of the intimidating mountain! Running through the snowfields are creeks that form from cascading waterfalls thousands of feet above with the end product being the mammoth snow caves of different sizes developing throughout the brief season! Northwest Forest Pass required at both THs, and restrooms are present at both THs.

TRAILHEAD: Big Four Picnic Area (preferred) or Ice Caves TH (primary). See Mount Pilchuck Lookout on page 239 for directions to Granite Falls. Turn left from WA-92 E/Quarry Rd onto Mountain Loop Hwy for almost 24.5 mi (rougher after 18 mi). Turn right on FR-4059 (Big Four Picnic Area) for less than 0.25 mi to the end (smaller lot), or follow MLH 0.5 mi farther E (Ice Caves TH), and turn right into the larger parking area (70 mi, 1½ hours from Seattle; 240 mi, 4½–5 hours from Portland).

ROUTE: Views from the preferred TH are superior to those from the primary TH. There is a brief trail that connects both THs, so a short lollipop loop is recommended to catch all the sights. It's less than 0.25 mi to the intersection for the Ice Caves from either TH. For the spur from Ice Caves TH to Big Four Picnic Area TH, take Ice Caves Loop Trail (paved) right of the restrooms NW for less than 0.25 mi (down a tiny bit) as you can practically see the other TH along the straightaway. You walk through a few trees (views) past an old cement bench near a swampy area, then cross a bridge with a great shot to Big Four Mountain just before the preferred TH.

From Big Four Picnic Area, begin in the meadow (past the picnic tables) right of the info kiosk and trail sign (pointing toward Big Four Mountain) on Big Four Mountain Trail. Note Ice Caves Loop Trail to Ice Caves TH right of the restrooms. Walk SSW over the boardwalk through the open marshy area and move S across a footbridge with great reflections of the surrounding summits including Big Four Mountain, Hall Peak, and Stillaguamish Peak across the valley. Continue briefly into the woods to the intersection with Ice Caves Loop Trail left (to Ice Caves TH).

From Ice Caves TH, take Ice Caves Loop Trail (paved) left of the restrooms and info kiosk down slightly SW into the lovely ancient forest (shots to mountains ahead). Pavement becomes boardwalk approaching the signed intersection (Big Four Mountain Picnic Area right).

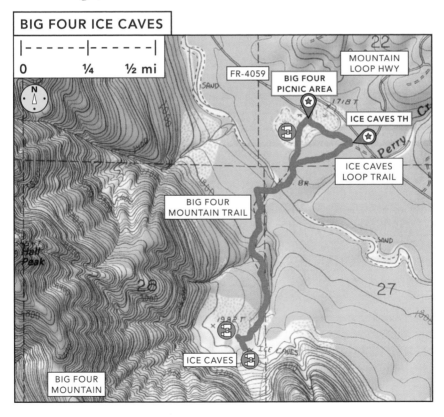

Uniquely evolving each season, Big Four Ice Caves attract locals from Granite Falls and visitors from much farther as well.

Continue left (SW) on Big Four Mountain Trail (into gravel, level) with a bit of boardwalk before crossing the South Fork Stillaguamish River (bridge closes for erosion repair at times, check ahead). Follow more boardwalk W a few feet to cross Ice Creek over a much smaller bridge, then walk SW (gravel) past a bench and mossy trees (some rather large) to a faint fork at less than 0.5 mi from either TH. Either take the boardwalk (easier) right 200 ft then up a switchback to meet the shorter spur, or take the unsigned dirt spur left 40 ft steeper then sharply left onto the main trail. Continue up S steadily parallel to Ice Creek along the log-lined trail (boardwalk, gravel). At 0.75 mi from either TH, pass another bench walking SE near the edge of the forest as Big Four Mountain towers ahead with a very long cascade traveling down the sheer face into the Ice Caves zone!

At 1 mi from either TH, Big Four Mountain Trail levels S coming out of the woods (views). Walk past high brush and wildflowers to the end of the official trail in a small rock circle. Signs warn people not to venture into the caves just as you will probably take a picture of people doing just that (continuously collapsing and with help from rockslides). Don't leave the main trail before late July or August (at your own risk). Some people continue N (steeper) in late summer or fall up the bushwhack path from the circle 200 yards or so to view additional caves, but most curious types venture directly S 100 yards from the circle over rocks through the flats (no trail, beware of falling rocks) to the base of the main caves for a bird's-eye view.

ELEVATION: 6214 ft; vertical gain of almost 4000 ft

DISTANCE: 3.75 mi up, 7.5 mi round-trip

DURATION: 4–5 hours up, 8 hours round-trip

DIFFICULTY: Very challenging (steady grade, scree, switchbacks, very steep summit block, Class 3, slight exposure on top, traction/ice axe required with snow until August)

TRIP REPORT: Here's an outright thrill of a day hike just W of Barlow Pass with gripping payoffs from Lake Elan, where some people stop, up to the peak! The view down to colorful Copper Lake with North Cascades as the backdrop is unrivaled. Northwest Forest Pass required, and an outhouse is present (BYOTP).

TRAILHEAD: Sunrise Mine TH. See Mount Pilchuck Lookout on page 239 for directions to Granite Falls. Turn left from WA-92 E/Quarry Rd onto Mountain Loop

Insane view from Vesper Peak over Copper Lake, within a deep basin under Big Four Mountain, to Three Fingers and Whitehorse Mountain!

Hwy for 27.5 mi (rougher after 18 mi), then turn right on easy-to-miss Sunrise Mine Rd (FR-4065, small brown sign, gravel, few potholes, 2WD okay, views) around 2 mi to reach the end at a small parking area (145 mi, 2 hours from Seattle; 250 mi, 4½–5 hours from Portland).

ROUTE: Begin S (signed Sunrise Mine Trail 707–Headlee Pass 2 mi, but closer to 2.5 mi) 100 yards, passing a kiosk (self-register for Wilderness Permit), then soon move across a rocky creek bed (0.5 mi from TH, S Fork Stillaguamish River) using the logs during high water. Climb steeply SW (roots, dense trees, flora, smaller creeks) then traverse more right (W, down some) 0.5 mi to the bottom of Wirtz Basin (2200 ft, see sheer rock wall opposite), continuing up as you break out of the trees on solid Trail 707 (1.5 mi from TH, rocky, cairns). Traverse SW up the right side of the basin (tiny cascades coming down rocks) around 0.5 mi, then climb 8 switchbacks SW (steeper, scattered trees), continuing the traverse SSW (open rocky slope) to a major switchback near the top of Wirtz Basin. You have your first real look at Headlee Pass up the steep narrow gully right. Ascend around 30 countable tight switchbacks with a decent grade (above steeper bottom) NW to the pass (old sign) where it's closer to 4730 ft (around 2½ hours up). Enjoy great angles of the nearby distinct mountains above Wirtz Basin, including Morning Star Peak, and for the first time see Vesper Peak!

Descend NW only around 50 ft or so in elevation from Headlee Pass on Trail 707, traversing up 0.25 mi NW (talus field, larger boulders, cairns) to a juncture. Cross Vesper Creek left (W) from the fork instead of hiking more than 100 yards N to Lake Elan (Vesper Lake, or have at it). Follow one of the steeper paths (Trail 707) a few

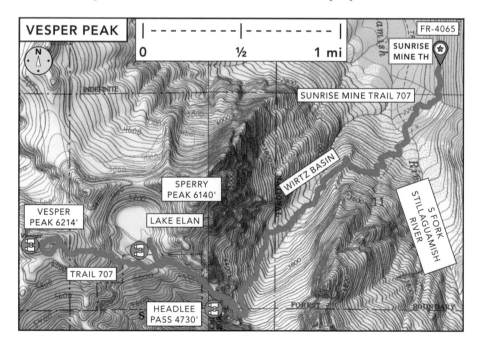

feet, passing a campsite, grasses, rocks, and smaller pines for great picnic spots and stupendous views of Sperry Peak rising sharply from Lake Elan within the boulder-filled basin. Also see the remainder of the steep route 0.5 mi to Vesper Peak.

Scramble W very steeply up turns (Trail 707, last trees) with a micro-break before the wide-open, steeply sloped rock slabs. Follow the cairned course W up the center with a touch of bouldering, approaching the jagged SE ridge. Then there's a couple quick options (less than 100 yards) to the nearby peak for a possible summit mini loop (6000 ft). Following the actual ridgeline (N a few feet) provides some exciting bouldering that yields views of Copper Lake W to the top. Left from the high ridge option is the walk-up on (Trail 707, also cairned, easier) W then NW to the peak from the S with last-second vistas that pop into your eyeholes the moment you reach the top. Descend a few feet to safer ground and enjoy the panorama from Copper Lake to Mount Baker, and Lake Elan to Sperry Peak, with Morning Star, Lewis, Del Campo, Glacier, and Monte Cristo Peaks!

80 | GOTHIC BASIN TO FOGGY LAKE

ELEVATION: 4950 ft at Gothic Lake, 5200 ft at Foggy Lake; vertical gain of around 3100 ft total

DISTANCE: 4.75 mi directly to Gothic Lake/Basin; less than 0.5 mi more directly to Foggy Lake, 11 mi or so round-trip total

DURATION: 3 hours to Gothic Lake/Basin; ½–1 hour more to Foggy Lake, 7–9 hours round-trip if wandering

DIFFICULTY: Very challenging (super-steep at times, roots, rock slabs, ups/downs not bad, long, steep switchbacks, trekking poles helpful, winter gear required with snow coverage until August)

TRIP REPORT: This exquisite day hike can be stretched into a multiday escapade while camping, but for that you must lug a heavy backpack uncomfortably up very steep terrain (probably still worth it). Many surprises await around every turn in Gothic Basin, making for an ideal brief loop below Gothic Lake before the short jaunt to stately Foggy Lake. Northwest Forest Pass required, and an outhouse is present.

TRAILHEAD: Barlow Pass TH. See Mount Pilchuck Lookout on page 239 for directions to Granite Falls. Turn left from WA-92 E/Quarry Rd onto Mountain Loop Hwy for 29 mi (rougher after 18 mi) to Barlow Pass and find a small pullout on the right before the gated trail with the signed parking lot up left (75 mi, 1½ hours from Seattle; 250 mi, 4–4½ hours from Portland).

ROUTE: From the official TH lot atop the hill on Barlow Pass, head left (E) across MLH (as it descends into gravel) 100 ft to the corner. Walk right (S) past the old green gate on Monte Cristo Trail (gravel, wide, no vehicles) that leads 4.25 mi to Monte Cristo. Note the kiosk left in a few feet as you move through the flats (big old cedar, evergreens, views), continuing S (down a tiny bit after 0.5 mi) somewhat closer to the South Fork Sauk River before reaching a signed fork for Weden Creek and Gothic Basin right (Trail 724, more than 0.75 mi from TH).

Follow narrower Trail 724 right (S); the path undulates easily through the lovely woodland (boardwalks, tiny creeks, damp forest). Then move up steeper a moment before hopping easily over West Fork Weden Creek (2 mi from TH, see little cascade and mountains above). Continue almost 0.25 mi then ascend 12 steep rocky switchbacks for 0.5 mi SW (old forest, S of Del Campo's E ridge, steeper after switchback 4). Traverse SW briefly (from 3250 ft) then climb W up 4 quick switchbacks to 3600 ft (3 mi from TH). The pitch on Trail 724 eases SW (roots, rocks, views) for 0.25 mi, crossing a rockslide within a long, wide rocky gully without difficulty (unless snow- or ice-covered, see waterfall). Continue traversing S across another narrower chasm (smaller cascade), then go down a few feet very steeply across a tiny creek and then SE up and across boulders into trees. Climb super-steeply up 4 quick switchbacks (large boulders) keeping SSW with micro-breaks in the pitch (narrow, slightly overgrown) through the woods.

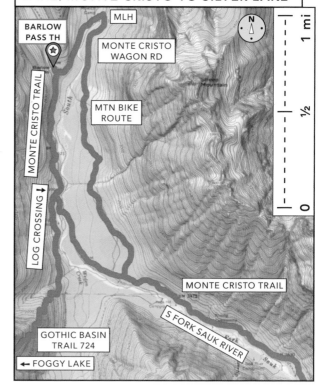

HIKES 80–81: GOTHIC BASIN TO FOGGY LAKE/MONTE CRISTO TO SILVER LAKE

See also map on page 254.

Someone fishing seems diminutive at voluminous Foggy Lake from the Barlow Pass area in North Cascades!

Rock-hop easily over a solid creek with nice cascades (4000 ft, more than 3.75 mi from TH) and see across the valley to Sheep Mountain, Foggy Peak, and Silvertip Peak.

Gothic Basin Trail becomes ultra-steep up turns and one solid switchback (large boulders) before moving S briefly and steeply up 2 quick rocky switchbacks passing another creek. The trail is level momentarily (campsites) before moving much steeper W up a rocky switchback. Head straight up a steep slab and boulders to an improved track heading S (fewer trees, more overlooks). Climb a steep switchback, cross a rocky gully (easy, wildflowers) dripping from the cliffs above, then climb another steep rocky switchback (and turn) before easing S again (more than 4.25 mi from TH). Traverse briefly then hike S steeper up the open meadow (grassy, rocky, wildflowers) with boulder steps and water running under the rock. Continue S (easier, then steeper) to mostly treeless Gothic Basin with Del Campo Peak visible up to the right. There are no welcome signs as you arrive to a small saddle juncture with myriad options and astonishing scenery in every direction (4950 ft, more than 4.5 mi from TH).

For the direct route to Gothic Lake (and Foggy Lake) on Trail 724, walk right (WSW) from the clear fork easily for only around 150 yards as the solid trail ends at the pretty lake within a rocky bowl (both sides worth exploring, swimming options) with the main route to Foggy Lake heading left (WSW) over the outlet creek (steeper) up rock slabs just S of the lake to a little saddle.

For the 0.5-mi-long lollipop loop around Gothic Basin to the slabs above Gothic Lake first, head left/straight (S) from the saddle juncture (opposite Gothic Lake, still on Gothic Basin Trail) down a bit with your first shot up right past the steep meadow and slabs to Gothic Peak's pinnacles. Walk between grass, rock, small creeks, and wildflowers past a cute little tarn with great reflections of Del Campo and pyramid-shaped Sheep Gap Mountain. A few feet farther is an even nicer tarn (bonus shot far down to Weden Lake through trees from cliff edge near outlet or scout around). Continuing over the main tarn's outlet, find paths going in several directions that all meet near Gothic Lake. Explore one path farthest W following the cliffy ledge NW close to a sweet waterfall area on Weden (or Weeden) Creek. For the primary route on Trail 724 just left (W) of the main tarn, traverse 0.25 mi up NNW through rock, dirt, and grass past smaller tarns then over solid granite slabs (cairns) to Gothic Lake.

For Foggy Lake, continue WSW above (S of) Gothic Lake on one of two paths (end of Trail 724) that traverse narrowly in the same direction 100 yards to a little saddle at the top of a rocky gully W of Gothic Lake with a sizable shallow bonus tarn opposite (SW) on Weden Creek. Gothic Basin is truly the gift that keeps giving! Two paths head NNW to Foggy Lake, one along the creek bed's E side above the bonus tarn (judiciously but simply), and the other one moving straight up the rise from the little saddle over steeper grassy ramps then past a small stand of trees steeply to the crest for easier walking (great views) as trails meet nearest the creek. Then it's only a few feet more N, traveling easily over solid boulders and rock to the rather large and round Foggy Lake with cascades audibly flowing into it. It's simple to hop left over the outlet for the best picnic locales from the flatter rock slabs with less green earth bordering the exquisite landscape. The clear blue-green water is hypnotic, especially when glassy with enormous reflections showcasing majestic Gothic and Del Campo Peaks! The lake is also just above freezing as it's only thawed a few months a year. If you have any energy left, it's possible to work right (N) on the broken climber's trail a bit tougher over boulders and scree 0.25 mi up to another small saddle viewpoint (above a narrow tarn) before returning.

Gorgeous Gothic Peak into Foggy Lake stuns all who make the effort to the upper lake!

ELEVATION: 4260 ft at the lake (5000 ft from ridge viewpoint); vertical gains of at least 2300 ft for the lake using Monte Cristo Trail (2700 ft using Monte Cristo Wagon Rd) plus 750 ft for ridge viewpoints

DISTANCE: 4.25 mi to Monte Cristo on Monte Cristo Trail (some mountain bike); less than 6 mi to Monte Cristo on Monte Cristo Wagon Rd (and MLH, most mountain bike); 2.5 mi more hiking to Silver Lake (plus 0.75 mi to ridge viewpoints), 14 mi round-trip using Monte Cristo Trail (more than 17 mi round-trip using Monte Cristo Wagon Rd) plus 2 mi round-trip for ridge viewpoints

DURATION: Less than 1 hour mountain biking either trail to Monte Cristo (1½ hours walking Monte Cristo Trail); 2 hours more hiking to Silver Lake (plus 1 hour to ridge viewpoints), 6–10 hours round-trip total

DIFFICULTY: Mix of strenuous for Silver Lake (easy from Monte Cristo Trail to Monte Cristo but river crossing over potentially wet footlog more difficult with bike, ups/downs on rockier Monte Cristo Wagon Rd, steep to lake, switchbacks, rustic, ups/downs, GPS device recommended) and very challenging for ridge viewpoints (bushwhacking, super-steep, scrambling)

TRIP REPORT: Here's one with options for day trippers of all abilities! Visit a tiny historic ghost town within a beautiful mountain valley and return (9 mi round-trip, around 500 ft vertical gain), or continue steeper up to a stunning subalpine lake directly below imposing Silvertip Peak! Adventurous hikers claw away to attain the SE ridge of that peak for enhanced vistas of the Monte Cristo Group. Camping is available near Monte Cristo as some head to Glacier Basin as well. Northwest Forest Pass required, and an outhouse is present with privies at Monte Cristo Campground and Silver Lake.

TRAILHEAD: Barlow Pass TH. See Mount Pilchuck Lookout on page 239 and Gothic Basin to Foggy Lake on page 249 for directions (75 mi, 1½ hours from Seattle; 250 mi, 4–4½ hours from Portland).

ROUTE: Most people bike-n-hike, as walking to Monte Cristo is somewhat monotonous. Although Monte Cristo Trail is briefer and much easier than Monte Cristo Wagon Rd, you would have to carry your mountain bike over logs awkwardly from the South Fork Sauk River crossing, making the route more problematic. The

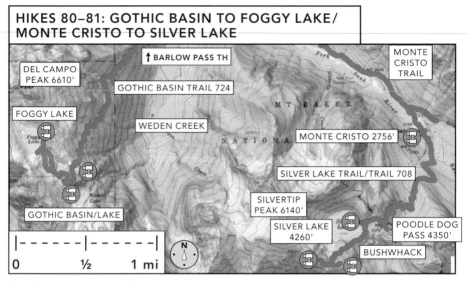

See also map on page 250.

wagon road is a great riding alternative, especially with a fat tire eMTB (respecting varying local laws). For the briefer route from the official TH lot atop the hill on Barlow Pass, head left (E) across MLH (as it descends into gravel) 100 ft to the corner. Move right (S) past the old green gate on Monte Cristo Trail (wide, kiosk left in a few feet) as you travel through the flats (big old cedar, evergreens, views). Continue S (down a tiny bit after 0.5 mi) somewhat closer to the South Fork Sauk River before passing a signed fork (right, Trail 724) less than 0.5 mi to the river crossing (non-potable water), narrowing a few feet (overgrown, rougher) to the obvious wide footlog. Be careful for less than 100 ft E negotiating other logs, then find Monte Cristo Trail widening into an old road again around 0.5 mi SE to the intersection with the wagon road.

From Barlow Pass, ride gravel MLH down almost 1 mi NE to the semi-hidden juncture right (signed Don't Pollute Lakes and Streams). Head past the brown gate (signed No Parking, Tow-Away Zone) SSW up gravel Monte Cristo Wagon Rd for 2.5 mi to meet Monte Cristo Trail. There will be several moderate ups/downs, a few with larger gravel and river rocks (rattling but short-lived), and you will cross a few bridges through the lovely mossy old forest to the end.

Continue left (SE) from the wagon trail at the unsigned intersection onto Monte Cristo Trail for 2.25 mi to the Monte Cristo Townsite sign. The trail undulates up with some river rocks to cross before you work steadily forward. Fork right opposite the signed campground spur (Glacier Basin Trail) through the woods briefly SE to the town sign. Move right over the bridge and across a smaller bridge before climbing steeper rock a couple feet to a flat open meadow (old rail yard) in Monte Cristo complete with some interpretive signage for a short-lived self-guided tour. There's a

Silver Lake and some of the Monte Cristo Group from the ridge viewpoints.

bike rack on the left behind a picnic table as you gaze up to the rugged mountains. Walk SE past the few red cabins into the next tiny meadow with a sign for the lodge, but only a very small foundation and scattered mining trinkets remain. Be aware the area was recently cleaned up, but none of the nearby creeks that feed into the South Fork Sauk River are potable even with a filter. Walk past the kiosk (noting Poodle Dog Pass Trail 708 and Silver/Twin Lakes), cross the bridge over Sunday Creek, and move through a picket fence (ignoring the other bridge crossing nearby Seventysix Creek toward Glacier Basin) to a larger partially red cabin known as the 76 building. There is a small placard on its right side (Silver Lake Trail, sharing Trail 708) with the route in a few feet to the right.

Begin S steeply up rocky Trail 708 less than 0.25 mi, following an old partially embedded water line to Sunday Flats near a faint fork (left to poor view of 373-ft cascading Sunday Falls) as you hear the creeks on both sides of you, keeping right (S) past the self-register Wilderness Permit station. Continue steeply soon up 2 quick switchbacks (of 7, roots, rocks) entering the Henry M. Jackson Wilderness after switchback 4 then easing after switchback 6 (thick ancient cedars) with nicer tread. After switchback 7 move SW (easier) through clearings across scree fields with improved views (overgrown with huckleberries in September), then walk down a bit to cross Sunday Creek (cute cascade, 1.25 mi and 1 hour from 76 building).

It's laborious to negotiate the 17 solid switchbacks that take you more than 0.75 mi SW to Poodle Dog Pass near Silver Lake. Move up (steady, steep) through switchback 10 then push through meadows (past berries), with the path becoming steeper and rockier, then super-steep after switchback 16 (views, steps) to 17 under a short cliffy area. Continue S abruptly up rocky steps (designed to prevent erosion and not to aid hikers but punish them seemingly), finishing over level ground to a Poodle Dog Pass juncture (4350 ft, privy at right). Approaching the pass, you see Glacier Falls (256 ft, at least four-tiered) NE far down in Glacier Basin under Foggy Peak and Ida Pass! Left (SE) is (sadly) abandoned Twin Lakes Trail.

Instead, walk forward 0.25 mi on Silver Lake Trail to Silver Lake, as you move right (NW) a bit then descend SW past several tarns and heather (more huckleberry), undulating past a small burn to the lake's outlet. Follow the most solid trail (past campsites/spurs) steeply down to the water and enjoy the pristine lake within a monstrous rocky cirque beneath Silvertip Peak! Silver Lake goes from green-blue to more blue-green to pure cobalt, depending on your perspective. It's possible to work right (NNW) without crossing the outlet. For more views and the difficult ridge option, cross the lake's outlet (Silver Creek) over the makeshift bridge, following the clearest path around the S side of the water (few short trees) with astounding views across the valley to Foggy and Cadet Peaks and the closer towering spires of Wilmans Peaks.

For the ridge viewpoints, follow the most pronounced trail SE of the lake left (S) onto a narrow mossy path, keeping left from forks (past a small camp). Move right through a miniature meadow (past tiny tarns), reaching a shoulder (sign for another privy) where the trail ends abruptly slightly S of the shoulder at the nearby commode (4360 ft). From there you must bushwhack 200 ft SW with no clear trail up the shoulder (thick brush, small trees), super-steeply into a clearing nearest a tarn (4450 ft, 0.25 mi from Silver Lake's outlet). Follow the flat trail a moment as it's still another 0.25 mi to the ridge. Traverse SW steeply through a meadow (small trees) briefly, then cross a boulder field (path disappears) in the same direction, finding the thin path up very steeply to a high ridge juncture.

You can proceed right (WNW) once you're on the wide ridge, past some low brush to the clear trail, walking up 100 yards or more without difficulty to a place near denser woods before turning around. The view of Silver Lake toward Sheep Mountain, and Foggy and Cadet Peaks is sublime! You should also walk left (E) from the ridge juncture off the crest to the right (S), moving effortlessly down the widening plateau past small tarns to huge scree fields beneath taller trees near the end of the high ridge (4925 ft). From there you will have unobstructed views out to the majority of the Monte Cristo Group including snow- and glacier-surrounded Columbia Peak. Also look between nearby Twin Peaks SE (Twin Lakes hidden) to Mount Daniel and Mount Hinman!

ELEVATION: 4675 ft at high point (3972 ft at lake); vertical gain of 3600 ft

DISTANCE: 4 mi one way, 8 mi round-trip (plus 1 mi round-trip for difficult optional spur across logjam to NW corner of lake)

DURATION: 3–4 hours one way, 6–8 hours round-trip

DIFFICULTY: Very challenging (switchbacks, steep ups/downs, rugged, more difficult through mid-July when wet or with snow, very popular, no signs, GPS device helpful)

TRIP REPORT: Not at all underrated is this absolutely stunning subalpine lake with a short hiking season due to lingering snow in the Henry M. Jackson Wilderness in Snoqualmie National Forest. Try late July into September for the best opportunities, with wildflowers and glossy, bright turquoise water reflected into the Monte Cristo Group. Northwest Forest Pass required, and an outhouse is present.

TRAILHEAD: Blanca Lake TH. See Beckler Peak on page 227 for directions to Beckler Rd/ FR-65 (milepost 49) for 6.5 mi and into gravel for 5.75 mi more to Jack Pass. With multiple junctions, take the second road from the left to stay on FR-65 (shared with FR-63) for 2.25 mi, turn right on narrow FR-63 for almost 2 mi, and fork left up the signed TH driveway to the small parking lot within the forest. Avoid weekends and come early (80 mi, 2 hours from Seattle; 250 mi, 4½– 5 hours from Portland).

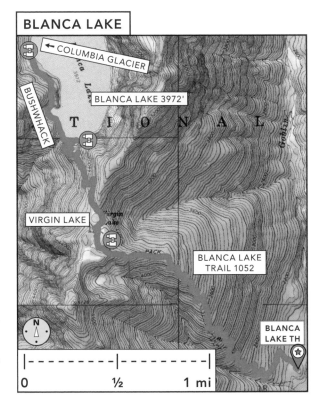

BLANCA LAKE

← COLUMBIA GLACIER

BUSHWHACK

BLANCA LAKE 3972'

T I O N A L

VIRGIN LAKE

BLANCA LAKE TRAIL 1052

BLANCA LAKE TH

N

0   ½   1 mi

Beautiful Blanca Lake from the log jam to Columbia and Monte Cristo Peaks!

ROUTE: Begin past the kiosk NW on Blanca Lake Trail 1052 (free self-issue Wilderness Permit) easily through the mossy forest (ample ferns) as you enter the Wild Sky Wilderness, then climb 30 steady switchbacks (the eighth one is technically a turn) 2.5 mi NW with very little for views (solid track, some litter). The route steepens (roots, rocks), passing a few giant old-growth hemlock, Douglas fir, and western red cedar up a tapering shoulder (overgrown at times) to around 4300 ft. Hike 0.5 mi W (easier briefly, down steps) over the lush and very narrow shoulder crest (views outward) as you work up quite steeply (ferns, huckleberry in August) with the first views of the core Monte Cristo Group and the top of Glacier Peak (through trees). Traverse 0.25 mi more moderately, leaving the shoulder right (N) through verdant subalpine meadows (fewer trees, respect restoration areas) to the apex of the hike. See Kyes, Monte Cristo, Wilmans, and Columbia Peaks to the N, Glacier Peak hugely NE, and local mountains S to Bear Mountain. Walk past a Toilet sign (and lupine in late July) then move down a steep switchback, passing tree-surrounded stagnant Virgin Lake (on a saddle) from its right (E) side.

It's almost 1 mi to the logjam at Blanca Lake as you must descend super-steeply NNW (narrow) with 2 switchbacks (and a few steps equally as steep) over many roots and rocks on the rougher section (Trail 1052). Then you are suddenly welcomed to the basin with a decent full view of Blanca Lake from a rocky opening (right off-trail) above the milky green huge lake! Climb a few more feet then descend 4 quick switchbacks NE very steeply to wildflower-lined Troublesome Creek at the logjam near Blanca Lake's outlet. Enjoy a picnic near the effervescent teal water with ideal reflections of Kyes and Monte Cristo Peaks. Many distant waterfalls are drowned out by small cascades near the outlet area, which you should also check out before the steep hike out of the basin.

The less traveled spur (opposite the creek) leads 0.5 mi to a preeminent basin vista from the NW corner of the lake. Skilled hikers cross Troublesome Creek over the logjam (when dry) nearest the chilly lake judiciously with trekking poles or ford the creek below the logjam. Follow the bushwhack path nearest the lakeshore NNW past grasses, daises, old logs, and a large boulder at the head of a scenic alcove (less than 0.25 mi from the logjam). Around the alcove, ascend 100 yards N abruptly (narrow path), working past brush over a flatter small meadow, then descend steeply as you reach large flat granite boulders on the lakeshore (wildflowers, less brush). Enjoy breathtaking views up the striking rocky basin to the shrinking Columbia Glacier and Columbia Peak. At the bottom of the glacier is a triple waterfall (twins above the lower tier).

83 | PHELPS BASIN TO SPIDER GAP

ELEVATION: 5600 ft in Phelps Basin, 7100 ft at Spider Gap; vertical gains of 2100 ft and 3600 ft (plus 300 ft with Phelps Basin), respectively

DISTANCE: 7 mi to Phelps Basin directly, 14 mi round-trip; 8.25 mi to Spider Gap, 16.5 mi round-trip (plus 1 mi round-trip with Phelps Basin)

DURATION: 3 hours to Phelps Basin; 4½ hours to Spider Gap directly, 8–9 hours round-trip for both

DIFFICULTY: Mix of strenuous for Phelps Basin (steady easy, steep briefly, popular, more than 30 simple water crossings, dry socks and trekking poles recommended) and very challenging for Spider Gap (very steep, rocky, route-finding, brief snow travel usually required, traction helpful, scrambling, GPS device recommended)

TRIP REPORT: These jewels, including Spider Meadows, lie within the heart of Glacier Peak Wilderness between two monumental ridgelines. Some hikers are satisfied with the trot to Phelps Basin, but for Spider Gap you'll need to climb a snowfield to see spectacular Lyman Lakes within another splendid basin under more majestic peaks. Try mid-July into August for wildflowers with fall colors afterward. Northwest Forest Pass required, and there is no restroom.

TRAILHEAD: Phelps Creek TH. From Seattle, take I-5 N to exit 171 onto WA-522 E (Bothell) for 24 mi, and exit right merging onto US-2 E (Wenatchee) in Monroe for almost 70 mi. Turn sharp left on WA-207 N (Coles Corner) for 4 mi, fork right on Chiwawa Loop Rd for 0.5 mi, turn right for 0.75 mi on Co Hwy 22, turn left on Chiwawa River Rd for 3.25 mi, and stay left for 5 mi on FR-62 onto FR-62/Chiwawa Valley Rd for 1.25 mi, then onto FR-6200/Chiwawa River Rd for 12.5 mi (into gravel, rough, high-clearance AWD recommended). Fork right on rougher FR-6211/Phelps Creek Trailhead Rd for 2.25 mi to the end with pull-in parking at right that fills quickly.

From Portland, take I-5 N to exit 154B (Renton) and merge onto I-405 N for 21 mi to exit 23, onto WA-522 E (Woodinville) 14 mi, exit right merging onto US-2 E, and follow as above with plenty of choice camping the final miles to the TH or along the hike (130 mi, more than 3 hours from Seattle; 300 mi, 5–6 hours from Portland).

ROUTE: Take signed Phelps Creek Trail 1511 (overgrown old mining road, free self-issue Wilderness Permit) for 0.25 mi NE across a creek then past a juncture (Carne Mountain Trail right). Cruise pleasantly through second-growth forest (past old mining remnants) along Phelps Creek through the valley for 3.25 mi N to the Leroy Creek crossing (within one of several rocky slide paths descending from Entiat Ridge above, some with creeks that cascade poetically through steep woods between trees). Then rock-hop 15 ft across a shallow part of Leroy Creek (higher runoff until late July), passing a faint signed path (right, Leroy Basin Trail) with an option to follow it 100 ft or so up to view a cool multi-tiered cascade. Resume 2 mi NW along Trail 1511 to Spider Meadows easily (fir, spruce) passing avalanche chutes through flourishing grasslands (wildflowers, streams). The route will steepen as you leave most of the trees into Spider Meadows (2 hours up, campsites).

Imposing above left (W) is Phelps Ridge with noticeably

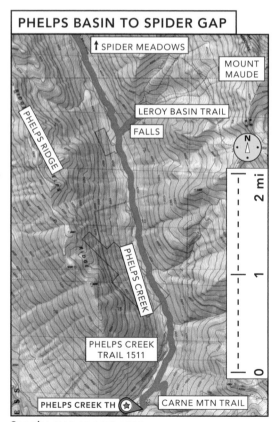

PHELPS BASIN TO SPIDER GAP

↑ SPIDER MEADOWS

MOUNT MAUDE

LEROY BASIN TRAIL

FALLS

PHELPS RIDGE

N

2 mi

1

0

PHELPS CREEK

PHELPS CREEK TRAIL 1511

PHELPS CREEK TH ⊛

CARNE MTN TRAIL

See also map on next page.

Phelps Basin under Dumbell Mountain (slightly right) would be the icing on the cake after visiting Spider Gap or a worthy destination on its own!

rusty rock leading to Red Mountain (long cascade under snowfields beneath summit), and right (E) under Phelps Ridge is a lengthy (seasonal) scenic waterfall making its way to the valley. Continue NW 1 mi easily (Trail 1511) crossing another solid creek (lingering snow into August) up through fir briefly into a lush upper meadow area (skunk cabbage, others). Hike 0.25 mi farther as you rock-hop or use logs over Phelps Creek (to the W side, more difficult until late July) climbing N to the signed intersection for Phelps Basin right (5330 ft, see final paragraph).

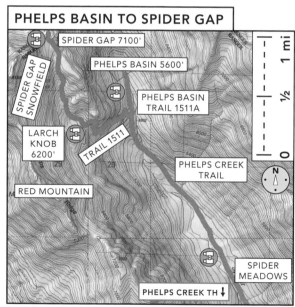

PHELPS BASIN TO SPIDER GAP

SPIDER GAP 7100'

PHELPS BASIN 5600'

SPIDER GAP SNOWFIELD

PHELPS BASIN TRAIL 1511A

LARCH KNOB 6200'

TRAIL 1511

RED MOUNTAIN

PHELPS CREEK TRAIL

SPIDER MEADOWS

PHELPS CREEK TH ↓

See also map on previous page.

Proceed left (W) from the intersection, still on Phelps Creek Trail, for 0.5 mi very steeply up around a dozen tight switchbacks to its terminus. You'll pass a boulder field with a sheer rock wall above (views NE to Dumbell Mountain then down valley), then from the top of the super-steeps you'll reach a superior small campsite on a flat overlook (left, 6200 ft, outdoor privy above), known as Larch Knob. See across the valley to Seven Fingered Jack and Mount Maude! For the gap more than 0.75 mi away, follow Spider Gap Snowfield Route (obvious) N up the rocks (see cascades glistening down cliffs) approaching the right (E) side of the dwindling snowfield (historic Spider Glacier) as you hike very steeply up the snow or just right over rocks (cautiously, few cairns). The route will steepen N without trouble up the long, narrowing gully closer to the gap as you look for a cairn on the boulders at the top/saddle. Continue past snow and boulders with no trail for 75 ft or so N (slightly right) through the rocky saddle between Dumbell and Chiwawa Mountains (East Peak) as Upper Lyman Lakes to Lyman Lake come into view in marvelous fashion. The milky blue-green waters of snow-lined Lyman Lakes contrast starkly with their high-alpine environment! From left to right, see the formidable N ridge of Chiwawa Mountain to Cloudy Pass (and Peak) with Plummer and Sitting Bull Mountains behind within the postcard shot!

For Phelps Basin from Spider Gap, it's only ½ hour down to the intersection with Phelps Basin. From there, head left (N) up Phelps Basin Trail 1511A around 0.5 mi with ease (narrows becoming overgrown briefly) into the basin. Paintbrush, aster, Queen Anne's lace, lupine, avalanche lilies, and others border the sparkling clear stream as several thin cascades fall from snowfields under declivitous walls of Dumbell Mountain to form Phelps Creek. Walk up the path (marmots nearby) within the more serene open basin as far as you wish past grasses, scree, and boulders to snowline on the creek.

84 | SAUK MOUNTAIN

ELEVATION: 5541 ft; vertical gain of around 1200 ft

DISTANCE: 2 mi up, 4.25 mi round-trip

DURATION: 2–3 hours round-trip

DIFFICULTY: Strenuous (switchbacks, steady steep grade, popular, not much shade, bugs into August, steeper and rockier to lookout site, barely Class 3 to true summit, scrambling, brief exposure, route-finding)

TRIP REPORT: Aspiring hikers and veterans alike relish this brief jaunt past wildflower-covered steep slopes to an old lookout site with great views as Mount

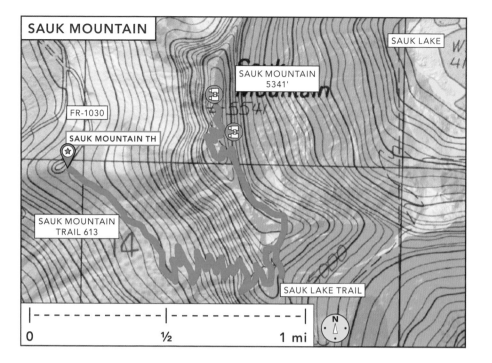

Baker looms above Sauk (pronounced Sock) Lake to the N with Mount Shuksan behind and Bacon Peak closer NE! You peer deeper E into North Cascades from Hidden Lake Peaks to Boston Peak, Sahale Mountain, and others. There is a tiny scramble to the center and highest of the few summit tops for those not afraid of heights and confident in their abilities. No fee required, and an outhouse is present.

TRAILHEAD: Sauk Mountain TH. From Seattle or Portland, take I-5 N to exit 208 (Arlington/Darrington), turn right on WA-530 E for 3.5 mi, and turn left at the signal then right immediately to stay on WA-530 E for 27 mi to Darrington. Turn left on WA-530 E for 17.75 mi to the end, turn left on WA-20 W for more than 1.5 mi, and turn right on Sauk Mountain Rd for 7.5 mi (gravel, narrow, washboard, 21 switchbacks, high clearance, AWD preferred, onto FR-1030) to reach the end at a small parking circle on a hill with great views (100 mi, more than 2 hours from Seattle; 280 mi, 4–5 hours from Portland).

ROUTE: Begin SE past the signage and aging little A-frame outhouse on Sauk Mountain Trail 613 (few trees) across the sunbaked steep hillside (see Skagit River valley), passing paintbrush, aster, penstemon, cow parsnips, daisies, valerian, lupine, and bistort while climbing 24 switchbacks E (wide, well graded, steady steep), entering trees briefly only a few times as you round the ridgeline (5200 ft, 1.5 mi up). Walk N easier briefly past a juncture (Sauk Lake Trail right), veering left (WNW) over

Sauk Mountain from the TH may be less inviting with worsening smoke from forest fires becoming the new norm. Another reason to pack an extra mask in your first-aid kit!

a ridge bump (last trees) to remain on Trail 613, traversing NW easily under scenic rocky gendarmes (along high ridge left). Watch for lingering snow beneath a rockier steeper fin, then climb 3 steep switchbacks SW to the ridge crest again, crossing to the W side. Work NE up 6 tight rocky switchbacks to the lookout site at a small flat area with only some rebar remaining (5525 ft, almost 2 mi up).

Most people return from the slightly lower perch, but for the true summit (100 yards away) hike NNW steeply (carefully) down the faint climber's trail just left (W) of the ridge a few feet then work right (NE) to a small saddle back on the ridgeline. Move to the right (E) of a tiny pillar area (easy), then climb up a very steeply sloped rock slab with decent traction 30 ft to a flatter, narrow section. Follow the 4–6 ft wide ridge path only 25 ft (severe drop-offs) to another small notch. The remainder is straightforward steeply 40 ft up a bit left (NW then E) over the wider trail to the top at a narrow but level overlook. See the entire good-looking Sauk Lake basin below (glassy blue lake and tarn) as well as the short-lived serrated high ridge in both directions from Bald to Sauk Mountains. There is another treeless summit mound N of the true summit that requires more intense scrambling. Enjoy the sights and return by the same route carefully.

ELEVATION: 6890 ft; vertical gain of 3200 ft

DISTANCE: 4 mi up, 8 mi round-trip

DURATION: 3–4 hours up, 6–7 hours round-trip

DIFFICULTY: Very challenging (steadily steep, many switchbacks, popular, fairly rocky, bugs until September, not much shade, lingering snow into August, possible in winter with traction)

TRIP REPORT: This triumphant hike on the SW edge of North Cascades National Park (best late July to September) is a great training sesh with motivating incentives! You'll ascend the wildflower-covered steep slopes of the East Fork valley with constant views up to a saddle between Hidden Lake Peaks. From there the panorama is rather intense for the remainder up to the lookout (built in 1931), which was decommissioned years ago but kept up by different groups over the decades and open to the (respectful) public. No fee or restroom.

TRAILHEAD: Hidden Lake TH. From Seattle or Portland, take I-5 N to exit 208 (Arlington/ Darrington), turn right on WA-530 E for 3.5 mi, and turn left at the signal then right immediately to stay on WA-530 E for 27 mi to Darrington. Turn left on WA-530 E for 17.75 mi to the end, turn right on WA-20 E for 8.25 mi, stay straight in Marblemount over the Skagit River onto narrowing Cascade River Rd for 9.5 mi, and fork left for 4.5 mi on FR-1540 (gravel, one-

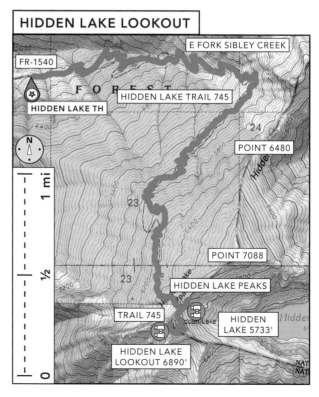

HIDDEN LAKE LOOKOUT

lane, potholes, very few pullouts, slightly overgrown, 10 switchbacks which the final few are rougher, AWD recommended). Reach the end at a small parking area or park off-road where safe (115 mi, 2½ hours from Seattle; 295 mi, 5½ hours from Portland).

ROUTE: Hike E on rustic Hidden Lake Trail 745 steadily (thick lively forest, scenic little creeks) soon up 16 switchbacks and turns (boardwalks, steps), then traverse briefly (high flora, ferns), crossing East Fork Sibley Creek easily (4300 ft, 1 mi up). Work steeper up 13 switchbacks almost 1 mi (E, very narrowly) as the terrain opens (paintbrush, heather, lupine, others) with improved vistas and decent tread sharpening across tiny streams.

Then begin the long traverse through the upper valley SW to the high saddle between Hidden Lake Peaks with one more imminent turn continuing easier (streams, mountain blueberries) as you move across the bottom of huge boulder fields under snowy Hidden Lake Peaks (with burly Mount Baker NW). Ascend 2 quick switchbacks (Trail 745, more than 2.5 mi up), hiking 0.25 mi more before you climb 14 switchbacks (S then E a tad, steeper), reaching the bottom of a rocky rise (almost 6000 ft) just right (W) of a rocky or snowy gully (see lookout far ahead perched on sheer summit). Climb 7 rocky switchbacks steeply S as the rise narrows around 20 more tight turns (small evergreens, grasses or snow with less turns) to the top of the rise. Find the route left (E)

Overwhelmed hikers with their first look from Hidden Lake to Mount Torment, Forbidden Peak, Boston Peak, Sahale Mountain, and Johannesburg Mountain!

or walk down a few feet to a wider, flat expanse with a little creek and move left (E) of the water up less than 0.25 mi on the most solid path (Trail 745, lupine, snow, steeply sloped rock), following cairns straight up adjacent huge slabs to the nearby high saddle (3.75 mi up). Voila! Glassy Hidden Lake is 800 ft below, appearing as a deep, blue infinity pool dropping off below the basin to the North Fork Cascade River valley. Hidden Lake Peaks true summit is left (NE, 7088 ft), along the adjoining ridge more than 0.5 mi up a semi-steep rocky climber's trail.

For the lookout (0.25 mi away), climb the boulders right (SSW) from the panoramic saddle very briefly and steeply (cairns), then traverse easier left (S) under the high ridge a minute (micro-spikes and ice axe with snow). Move W up 2 switchbacks and possibly a couple more little turns to the high SE ridge at some larger boulders. See The Triad above Hidden Lake past Hidden Lake Peaks with Eldorado Peak behind, following the glaciated cirque right to Klawatti Peak, Mount Torment, Forbidden Peak, Boston Peak, and Sahale Mountain. Across Cascade Pass are The Triplets, Cascade Peak, and closer Johannesburg Mountain. S past Mount Buckindy is Glacier Peak. To the SW is dominant Snowking Mountain. Turn right (NW), scrambling less than 100 yards to the lookout either by following cairns up the steeper boulders straight or by moving just left (W) a few feet with less rock and more path. At the precariously placed shelter it's first come, first served, and remember to leave the tiny lookout in better shape than you found it. There is actually a bed, a desk, chairs, a stocked bookshelf, and lots of windows to scintillating views!

86 | CASCADE PASS TO SAHALE GLACIER

ELEVATION: 5400 ft at Cascade Pass, 7600 ft at Sahale Glacier; vertical gains of 1800 ft and 4100 ft, respectively

DISTANCE: 3.75 mi to Cascade Pass, almost 8 mi round-trip; 6 mi to Sahale Glacier, around 12 mi round-trip

DURATION: 1½–2 hours to Cascade Pass, 3–4 hours round-trip; 4–5 hours to Sahale Glacier, 7–9 hours round-trip

DIFFICULTY: Mix of strenuous for Cascade Pass (gentle switchbacks, wide, popular) and very challenging for Sahale Glacier (steep at times, possible snow crossings, long, rocky, bugs through August)

TRIP REPORT: Here are two more action-packed hikes in North Cascades National Park with stunning views from the parking lot that only progress past Cascade Pass

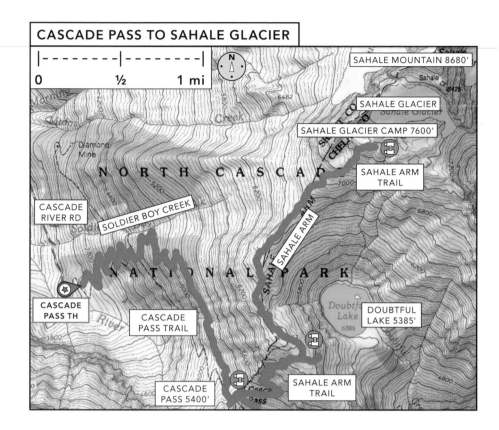

CASCADE PASS TO SAHALE GLACIER

|- - - - - - - -|- - - - - - - -|

0   ½   1 mi

N

SAHALE MOUNTAIN 8680'

SAHALE GLACIER

SAHALE GLACIER CAMP 7600'

SAHALE ARM TRAIL

CASCADE RIVER RD

SOLDIER BOY CREEK

NORTH CASCADE

Diamond Mine

SAHALE ARM

NATIONAL PARK

CASCADE PASS TH

CASCADE PASS TRAIL

Doubtful Lake

DOUBTFUL LAKE 5385'

CASCADE PASS 5400'

SAHALE ARM TRAIL

Cascade Pass

up Sahale Arm to Sahale Glacier (Camp) under Sahale Mountain. Remember trail and driving etiquette, yielding to uphill traffic at all times. (For road conditions, check: nps.gov/noca/planyourvisit/road-conditions.htm.) No pass required, and outhouses are present with privies at Cascade Pass and Sahale Glacier Camp.

TRAILHEAD: Cascade Pass TH. See Hidden Lake Lookout on page 265 for directions to Marblemount onto narrowing Cascade River Rd for 10.25 mi into gravel for 6.25 mi. Keep sharply left from a switchback to stay on Cascade River Rd (steeper, rougher, potholes, washboard, one-lane, winding, brief paved sections, AWD preferred) for less than 6.5 mi to reach the end at a relatively small and busy parking circle (125 mi, 3 hours from Seattle; 300 mi, 5–5½ hours from Portland).

ROUTE: Views are striking from the TH, looking up from right to left to Johannesburg Mountain, Cascade Peak, and The Triplets, with countless glaciers and waterfalls descending from these beauties. Take Cascade Pass Trail heading N past all the signage, then head NNE more than 2.5 mi through the handsome forest up 33 steady switchbacks (only real shade) that become a bit steeper and rockier near the top as the trees thin. Then traverse SE easier, wandering through wildflower-covered meadows (handful of small trees, views), and move 200 ft across a steeply sloped rock field (cautiously, retains snow until late July). Work through a boulder field (40 ft) continuing easily over the stone path to Cascade Pass (grasses, wildflowers, smattering of small trees). There are picnic options from the rock benches in the center of the pass or from nearby trails (respect restoration areas). One short-lived spur heads up right (S) past the Toilet post. There are outstanding views of the valley then up to Glory, Trapper, and Magic Mountains (Hurry-up Peak between), with Pelton and Mix-up Peaks even closer!

For Sahale Arm and Glacier, continue left (NE) 50 ft from the rock benches to a juncture, keeping left from the post on Sahale Arm Trail (opposite Cascade Pass Trail down into Pelton Basin toward Stehekin River valley). Cross the rock field 150 ft, then ascend the very steep hillside for 0.75 mi NE to the signed juncture on Sahale Arm for Doubtful Lake. You trudge up 18 switchbacks past glacier lilies, others, and low-to-the-ground mountain blueberries (September) through the open meadow (fewer trees) before you finally see Sahale Mountain on the traverse E (easing) nearing the arm (at 6000 ft, 1.5 mi to Sahale Glacier). Sahale Arm is literally the broad curving SW shoulder of Sahale Mountain (Sahale Peak to climbers) below the rugged SW ridge of Sahale Mountain (and nearby Boston Peak). Also see Sahale Glacier, protecting the summit on its S face.

Continue left (N) from the crossroads sign post (Doubtful Lake Trail right/straight 0.5 mi steeply to lake) on the most pronounced path (Sahale Arm Trail) up the wide shoulder for less than 100 ft as you see Doubtful Lake far below. The sparkling blue-green lake (and small island) in a large bowl with rocky slopes has several long,

A large goat poses from Sahale Glacier Camp with Doubtful Lake left of Sahale Arm and high tops from Magic to Johannesburg Mountains!

streaming cascades feeding the pool from the glaciers above. Hike 0.25 mi NW over open terrain (few stone steps) past wildflowers (August) or rusty-red ground cover (September) with tasty views past Quien Sabe Glacier and others to Forbidden Peak, Mount Torment, Eldorado Peak, The Triad, and Hidden Lake Peaks. Continue NW much steeper briefly up turns and switchbacks before easing momentarily. Climb steeper again (stone steps), rounding a somewhat tree-covered little hill on the shoulder, then make a beeline NNE in the center of Sahale Arm directly toward Sahale Mountain. Pass small tarns (dry out later in summer) as the pitch varies above the last small pines and brush (see Boston Basin NNW) along the expansive shoulder (wildflowers, grasses) where many people are perfectly happy to stop from one of several prime perches. Don't miss Mount Baker in the distance beyond The Triad–Eldorado Peak saddle or Hidden Lake between Hidden Lake Peaks!

You'll see and hear waterfalls throughout the journey. Also, listen for the occasional loud crack of distant glaciers breaking up! Sahale Arm Trail steepens then eases again following the rutted dirt path NE to the base of the moraine 0.5 mi below Sahale Glacier Camp. Climb more abruptly (rocky), soon traversing the cairned path right (NE, above tiny tarn) as the shoulder becomes less defined (tons of scree, loose rock) directly under a minuscule rock band (with white granite stripes). Resume slogging NE upward (no trail, workable options, cairns), finding super-steep paths close to the lip at the top of the moraine near a post indicating the outhouse is left and the camps are right almost 100 ft along the rocky rise. Don't get too chummy with mountain goats!

The highest established campground in North Cascades National Park is actually made of several camps built on flatter ground with simple rock walls (barely block constant penetrating winds) located at a half dozen or so locales on the hilly moraine plateau under Sahale Glacier (0.5 mi–loop option, no trails, ups/downs, bonus shot to Trapper Lake). The first camp (where most people stop) has a few areas, including the largest on top of the mound. See Spider Mountain, Hurry-up Mountain, Mount Formidable, and others to the S, as well as Doubtful Lake below. To the E across Horseshoe Basin is Buckner Mountain with Goode Mountain (Mount Goode, the highest in North Cascades National Park at 9200 ft) behind and to the right!

87 NORTH TWIN SISTER

ELEVATION: 6650 ft; vertical gain of 5500 ft total (2900 ft mountain biking from primary TH plus 2600 ft hiking from upper TH)

DISTANCE: 6.25 mi mountain biking to upper TH plus 1.5 mi hiking, around 15.5 mi round-trip total

DURATION: 1–3 hours mountain biking (or hiking) to upper TH plus 2–3 hours hiking, 6–9 hours round-trip total

DIFFICULTY: Expert only (very steep mountain biking, narrow, rocky finish, ultra-steep ridge scramble, route-finding, some exposure, gloves helpful, helmet recommended, GPS device required)

TRIP REPORT: North Twin Sister is a serious scrambler's dream because of the high Olivine content in rock known as Dunite within the jagged and rocky Twin Sisters Range (less than 10 mi SW of Mount Baker). The curiously grippy rock (dry or wet) makes the West Ridge Route a blast to free climb with great holds everywhere. The views are stunning for the entirety of the day, especially toward South Twin Sister (7004 ft). The landowner generously shares its natural resources including the renowned route. Wildlife sightings may include deer and black bear. Call 360-442-7619 for permit info (www.WYRecreationNW.com), and there is no restroom.

TRAILHEAD: North Twin Sister TH. From Seattle or Portland, take I-5 N to exit 232 and turn right on Cook Rd for 4.25 mi, taking the second exit in the second adjacent traffic circle onto Borseth St for 0.25 mi onto W Moore St for 0.75 mi (Sedro-Woolley). Turn left on WA-9 N for 15.25 mi, turn right (over South Fork Nooksack River bridge) on Mosquito Lake Rd for 8.75 mi, turn sharp right around a large gravel pile a few feet onto Middle Fork Nooksack River Rd (signpost for FR-38 in 100 yards, gravel, bumpy, 2WD okay) for 4.5 mi (keeping right at forks, cross Clearwater Creek bridge) to a juncture (FR-38 continues left). Fork right for 0.25 mi on unsigned one-lane Weyerhauser Rd 9000 down to the bridge/gate/TH. Park safely on the sides without blocking the circle as truckers use this turn-a-round on weekdays. The open gate may be locked randomly, be warned (100 mi, 2 hours from Seattle; 275 mi, up to 5 hours from Portland).

ROUTE: Begin riding over the river bridge beyond the gate on Rd 9000 (gravel) very steeply, traversing upward (SE) for 2.5 mi (ignoring side roads) to a nondescript juncture on a curve (2600 ft, barely legible Twin Sisters sign on ground). Keep right

(W then SW) onto the unnamed road for 1.5 mi (easier) through a clear cut (even down slightly), across a bridge and up to an unsigned fork (cairns). Continue left (S) 1 mi up to Dailey Prairie (see West Ridge Route on North Twin). At 5 mi from the TH, you arrive in the trees to a juncture (downed log, "100" post, 3250 ft). Bike or hike the single track left of the wider road up several turns (steep, narrow, overgrown, rocky) for 1.25 mi E to the upper TH at a firepit and small camp (4100 ft, stash and lock bike).

Follow the unsigned West Ridge Route (overgrown to start, ultra-steep, narrow) almost 0.5 mi SE to the base of the rocky W ridge in the open with a good shot of your goal. Continue SE up the ridgeline (last scrub, small trees), moving slightly right (S) of the crest as you begin climbing super-steep sections (bouldering, cairns, narrow gully) NE and E to a small landing on the ridge below a large sharp pillar (5500 ft). Scramble E straight up over rock a few feet (drop-offs), then head right (S) a bit easier around the base of the gendarme to another little saddle (cairns, Class 5 options N side, backtrack from Class 4/5 objectionable moves). Traverse barely E right (S) of the ridge over the path with narrow ramps back to the main ridge again at a 100-ft-long knife's edge segment. Move just left (N) after the knife's edge easier a moment (carefully, not too far down) en route to the boulder-filled wider ridge. Then traverse left (N) of the wall on the ridgeline (looser rock, boulders) into a huge gully as you work through the wider ridge section below the subsummit. Proceed left (E) under the subsummit easier but steeply along the boulders with the final crux in the center of the ridge before the narrow peak. Scramble 12 ft or so straight up a sloping boulder with a wide crack then amble a few feet to the airy peak. Be cautious soaking in the intense landscape! A slightly lower obelisk is only a few feet away SE on the connecting ridge to nearby South Twin. Mount Baker is all too close past the impressive Warm, Wallace, and Rankin Creek valleys, with Bellingham Bay only 20 mi W.

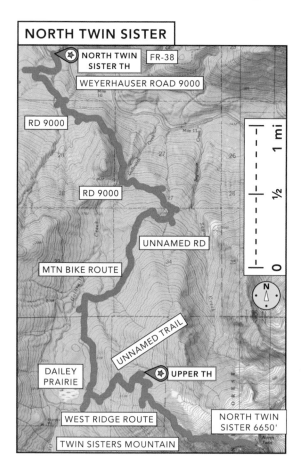

North Twin Peak approaching the West Ridge Route with several scrambling options up grippy Dunite rock for advanced hikers!

Remember on the descent to leave the wide ridge under the subsummit for the main traverse route on the N side down the rocky gully heading W to the knife's edge above the ramps. Then continue down slowly all the way to the rock field above the trees and overgrown trail, scrambling on or just S of the W ridge, as you finish the climber's trail easier but very steeply to the upper TH.

ELEVATION: 7408 ft; vertical gain of 6300 ft

DISTANCE: 9 mi up, 18 mi round-trip

DURATION: 7–8 hours up, 12–14 hours round-trip

DIFFICULTY: Expert only (extremely long and laborious as a day hike, massive vertical, quite steep, route-finding, overgrown, GPS device required, switchbacks, summer route—best July to September)

TRIP REPORT: Ruby Mountain rises unassumingly more than 6000 ft above and between Diablo and Ross Lakes within Ross Lake National Recreation Area. Views from the peak are indescribably surreal as you look down to the bright blue-jade Diablo Lake then directly N up the long and very blue (at times) Ross Lake past Desolation Peak (Jack Kerouac's old stomping grounds) and Hozomeen Mountain into Canada. Some climbers camp along the track with a proper Wilderness Permit. Wildlife sightings may include deer, elk, cougar, and black bear. No fee required, and restrooms are present.

Ruby Mountain with Ross Lake below snaking to Desolation Peak and Hozomeen Mountain from North Cascades National Park to the nearby Canadian border!

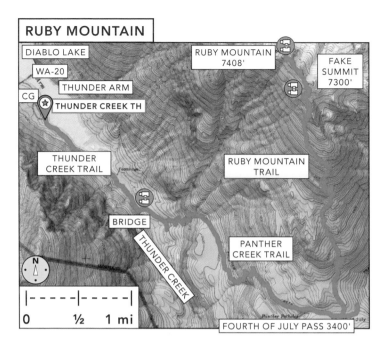

TRAILHEAD: Thunder Creek TH. See Hidden Lake Lookout on page 265 for directions, keeping left in Marblemount on WA-20 E (instead of crossing the Skagit River) for 24 mi (keep right at 21 mi, opposite Diablo Dam Rd to Diablo Lake TH/parking with beachside views across Diablo Lake to Ruby Mountain, continuing briefly to the road's end at North Cascades Environmental Learning Center). Turn right (milepost 130) just before crossing the bridge over Thunder Arm onto the nondescript TH driveway, keeping left at forks less than 0.5 mi (passing Colonial Creek Picnic Area/South Campground, restrooms, alternate parking) to the TH/kiosk farthest S (next to amphitheater), following signage (125 mi, 2½ hours from Seattle; 300 mi, 5 hours from Portland).

ROUTE: Take Thunder Creek Trail 2 mi SE (W of Diablo Lake's Thunder Arm), easily rolling through the ancient forest to a juncture. Less than 0.5 mi before the juncture you cross the beautiful blue-green Thunder Creek, working E steeper to the signage (1400 ft). Turn left (opposite Thunder Creek Trail) onto Panther Creek Trail up more than 3 mi to mostly tree-covered Fourth of July Pass. You hike the first mile steeply E up around a dozen turns and switchbacks before traversing SSE easier another mile or so (see Colonial, Snowfield, and Pinnacle Peaks above Neve/Colonial Glaciers, and also Primus and Tricouni Peaks through trees). The final mile remains steep up around 10 turns E before you head SE to Fourth of July Pass (around 3400 ft), an unremarkable flatter area (Ruby Mountain–Red Mountain saddle). Walk to the E side of the pass, past campsites (some views, swampy) then Panther Potholes (dark ponds below short cliffs), to your Ruby Mountain Trail juncture left (N, 3500 ft, unsigned, sometimes cairned). It will be after you pass the first little wooden bridge and just before (W of) the next old bridge (30 ft long, last chance for water). More than 100 ft N into the woods is a Trail Abandoned—No Longer Maintained sign.

Continue NNW up Ruby Mountain Trail (less flora, several blowdowns to navigate easily) as the primary path may be difficult to locate at times through the forest to the high ridge (3.5 mi away). Find the trail solidly again (around 5000 ft, 1.5 mi from the pass juncture) after bushwhacking up a gully through thick woods (underbrush) NNW then NE (W of developing ridge). From the more visible track you cross NE to the right (E) side of Ruby Mountain's S ridge, continuing N (decent grade then steepening abruptly) into a rockier section (brief) up the ridgeline. Climb N more than 0.5 mi for around 20 tight switchbacks through a meadow where the track becomes confusing again (almost 5800 ft, views). Leave the misleading S ridge route for the overgrown traverse path left (W, Ruby Mountain Trail) of the crest up steadily NW (thick wild blueberries in September, look SE to Elija Ridge between Stillwell and Panther Creek valleys). You hike rougher terrain briefly (to 6150 ft) before climbing 22 switchbacks 1 mi NE, then N (above tree line, see Mount Logan, Buckner Mountain, Boston Peak, Forbidden Peak, and Mount Torment) up the scree-filled wide gully to the high ridge (7200 ft).

Look to the glaciated N side of Ruby Mountain and walk the wide high ridge left (NW, no trail) 100 yards steeply to the top of a fake summit (7300 ft), as Crater Mountain then majestic Jack Mountain grab your attention to the right (NNE). Dawdle 0.25 mi NW (down a hair, then up) easily over the wide rocky high ridge to the summit at a small radio station antenna. If that bothers you, consider there were once plans for a tram from Diablo Lake with much more infrastructure (understandably), so enjoy the mostly pristine summit area with mind-blowing vistas. More glaciers can be seen at once than from most locations in the Lower 48, and that's just for starters! Not far WNW past Sourdough Mountain are Mounts Baker, Shuksan, Terror, and Prophet, and to the S is Glacier Peak beyond Klawatti, Forbidden, Boston, Sentinel, Sinister, and Dome Peaks, to name a few. Without a doubt this summit holds one of the finest panoramas within North Cascades and the Pacific Northwest!

89 | MAPLE PASS LOOP TRAIL

ELEVATION: 7000 ft near Maple Pass; vertical gain of 2300 ft

DISTANCE: 7.25 mi round-trip loop

DURATION: 4–6 hours round-trip

DIFFICULTY: Strenuous (steady grade counterclockwise, steep near Maple Pass, family-friendly, switchbacks, rocky, very popular, solid trail but borders drop-offs)

TRIP REPORT: Explore deeper into North Cascades Scenic Highway (WA-20, closed in winter from milepost 134-171) to this neighborhood that technically only grazes North Cascades National Park. Heather–Maple Pass Loop, or Maple Pass Trail, is best July (for wildflowers) into October when the larch turn from bright green to golden! Most people hike around the huge glacial cirque counterclockwise to warm up on an easier grade with solid views instead of tackling steeper switchbacks first. Some go-getters split off at Heather Pass for Lewis or Wing Lakes as optional day hikes (or camp), but completing the loop after visiting either of those would be very challenging. Rainy Lake at less than 1 mile from the TH is the easiest option (or add-on, paved, ADA-accessible) without much elevation change. Northwest Forest Pass required, and an outhouse is present.

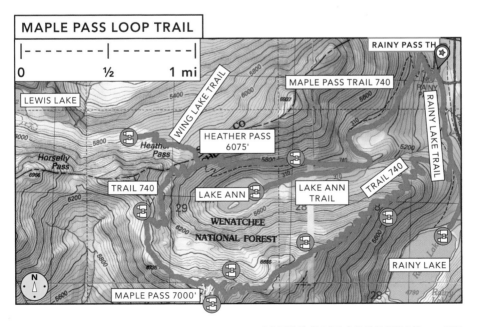

Lake Ann far below Maple Pass with a touch of both fall and winter in North Cascades!

TRAILHEAD: Rainy Pass TH. See Hidden Lake Lookout on page 265 and Ruby Mountain on page 274 for directions to Marblemount, keeping left on WA-20 E (instead of crossing the Skagit River) for 51 mi (with overlooks and viewpoints). Turn right at Rainy Pass (signed, milepost 158, FR-600, narrow driveway) for 0.25 mi through several parking areas in the trees along the circle. Backup parking exists directly across WA-20 at other THs, including for the PCT (155 mi, 3 hours from Seattle; 325 mi, 5½–7 hours from Portland).

ROUTE: Follow Lake Trail signs from the parking area to the TH kiosk (voluntary sign-in) at the start of the well-signed loop. For Rainy Lake (and clockwise loop), head left (S) on wide paved Rainy Lake Trail through the forest almost 0.5 mi down a tad (footbridges) to the juncture with Maple Pass Trail right (sign 50 ft up trail). For the lake, stay left (S, then SW) on Rainy Lake Trail for 0.5 mi effortlessly to the viewing platform at the sizable subalpine lake within a deep rocky bowl!

For the preferred counterclockwise tour from the TH, begin right (W) on Maple Pass Trail 740 through the old forest up 3 switchbacks easily (few roots, rocks), then traverse SW narrowly across a rock field (views outward, 0.75 mi up). Walk S, passing a faint juncture with Lake Ann Trail (left) 0.5 mi farther as you cross a giant rock field (fewer trees) and see the cirque and Lake Ann (with an island) below within the enormous rocky glacial punch bowl. Continue WNW steadily steeper up Trail 740 around 0.25 mi, then climb 4 quick switchbacks (wildflowers), moving W to the faint intersection on Heather Pass (2.25 mi and around 1 hour from the TH).

To see Lewis Lake from afar (also partly visible from loop, 0.5 mi round-trip add-on), walk a few feet right (N) up to the flat, open meadow on Heather Pass. Easily follow Wing Lake Trail a couple hundred yards winding NW (tiny creeks). There are great views passing a few larch on the thinning path (respect restoration areas) as it begins to descend to the sizable rock field (cairned route) that spans the narrow valley up to Wing Lake (under prominent Black Peak). From rock field's edge you can see colorful Lewis Lake and much more and with a different feel from the rest of the hike.

From the intersection at Heather Pass, continue right on Maple Pass Trail up 4 switchbacks W (view down to Lewis Lake from switchback 2), then traverse S above most trees (steep slope holds snow into July) under the high ridge. Views improve with each step (past skunk cabbage, paintbrush, penstemon) especially of Lake Ann with Cutthroat Peak and Whistler Mountain standing mightily behind as you climb steeper, bending WNW up 3 turns directly to the high ridge (less than 1 mi from Heather Pass). Past the North Cascades boundary sign, you are greeted by Corteo Peak with Frisco Mountain up the ridge just above Maple Pass! Head left (S) up the wide open ridge (0.75 mi to pass) with constant views back to Black Peak and only a brief shot to Lake Ann as you pass heather, paintbrush, and more (up and down some easily) before clambering steeper up 3 turns past a few trees to Maple Pass (3.75 mi counterclockwise from TH, 3.25 mi clockwise from TH).

Take a moment to breathe in the spectacle from different locales on the pass. Look SE up the ridge to nearby Frisco Mountain and Rainy Peak as you pan down to a small tarn well below the switchbacks on the S side of the loop. Walk up the ridge spur a few feet S for a better look W past Mount Benzarino to Goode and Storm King Mountains, with Logan, Boston, and Forbidden Peaks. Then cross the main trail moving N 200 ft more narrowly (being cautious, huge drop-offs) for a sick view of Lake Ann below with Porcupine Peak, Whistler Mountain, Cutthroat Peak, Glacier Peak, Liberty Bell Mountain, and Early Winters Spires in the background!

Continue the counterclockwise loop NE steeply down Maple Pass Trail with 4 quick switchbacks before traversing the super-steep slope (carefully) E without trouble under the ridgeline. Passing more wildflowers or red huckleberry in the fall (along with larch turning golden) you reach a viewpoint on a thin ridge section (almost 6400 ft, less than 1 mi from Maple Pass, 2.25 mi from TH directly) with only a few trees trying to obstruct otherwise great looks to parts of Rainy Lake and Lake Ann at the same time! Hike NE (down) on or near the ridge crest for 16 (of almost 40) tight switchbacks that vary in steepness, then after some tight S-turns on what would be switchback 17 you'll see part of sizable Rainy Lake in its own large rocky basin (with several cascades part of the year). You'll be able to see the blue lake better after another S-turn and 2 more switchbacks (drop-offs) with only a few trees blocking phenomenal scenery. After 38 steep switchbacks total (few roots, rocks) down Maple Pass Trail through the thickening forest, descend 1 more turn near the end to the juncture with Rainy Lake Trail. Turn left (N) on the paved interpretive track almost 0.5 mi to the TH.

ELEVATION: 6355 ft at high point (6254 ft at Blue Lake), 5620 ft from Washington Pass Overlook Trail; vertical gains of around 1000 ft and 40–175 ft, respectively

DISTANCE: 4.5 mi round-trip for Blue Lake; 0.25 mi round-trip for brief loop trail at Washington Pass

DURATION: 1 hour to Blue Lake, 2–3 hours round-trip; ¼–½ hour round-trip for Washington Pass Overlook Trail

DIFFICULTY: Moderate for Blue Lake (steady uphill, wide, family-friendly, well traveled, forested) and easy for Washington Pass Overlook Trail (mostly paved, ADA accessible, quite brief)

TRIP REPORT: Here's a two-for-one to close out, one to a crystal-clear, bright blue lake within a spectacular basin, followed by the bonus roadside stop at Washington Pass! To travel this far and not stop at the overlook (or Diablo Lake Overlook) would be unfortunate. These are best June into October. Northwest Forest Pass only required at Blue Lake TH, and vault toilets are present at both THs (and Diablo Lake Overlook).

TRAILHEAD: Blue Lake TH and Washington Pass TH. See Hidden Lake Lookout on page 265 and Maple Pass Loop Trail on page 277 for directions to Rainy Pass TH. Continue on WA-20 E (closed in winter from milepost 134-171) for more than 3.5 mi, and turn right on the signed driveway 100 yards into the small lot with overflow parking along WA-20. For Washington Pass Overlook (signed), continue almost 1 mi farther on WA-20 E, and turn left for 0.5 mi (FR-500) to reach the end at a sizable parking circle (160 mi, 3½ hours from Seattle; 330 mi, 6–7 hours from Portland).

ROUTE: From Blue Lake TH, begin NE parallel to the highway for less than 0.5 mi on Blue Lake Trail 314 (boardwalks, bridges), ascending a switchback (SSW) through the lovely old-growth forest (rocky) effortlessly for another 0.25 mi before climbing steeper turns (semi-open meadow, slightly overgrown, lupine, others) with appreciable views of the local mountains including the nearby Liberty Bell Mountain Group. Cross a tiny creek and move back into trees easier NNE 0.25 mi reaching another switchback, then hike the narrowing route SSE past a few boulders winding up steeper to a signed juncture (1.75 mi up). Head right (SW, opposite Early Winters Spires) on Trail 314, traversing the steep slope without difficulty which only becomes somewhat steeper the final feet to the outlet of Blue Lake.

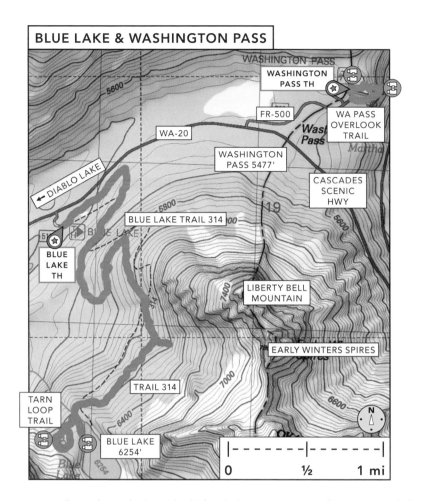

BLUE LAKE & WASHINGTON PASS

(Map labels: WASHINGTON PASS, WASHINGTON PASS TH, WA PASS OVERLOOK TRAIL, FR-500, WA-20, WASHINGTON PASS 5477', Wash Pass, Martha, CASCADES SCENIC HWY, DIABLO LAKE, BLUE LAKE TRAIL 314, BLUE LAKE, BLUE LAKE TH, LIBERTY BELL MOUNTAIN, EARLY WINTERS SPIRES, TRAIL 314, TARN LOOP TRAIL, BLUE LAKE 6254', Blue Lake, 5600, 5800, 19, 6600, 7400, 7000, 6400, 6600, 6254)

0   ½   1 mi

Inspect Blue Lake with the right (W) side being more popular as you rock-hop 10 ft over the outlet to a signed fork. The primary lakeside viewpoint is at left (S) 100 ft from an open rocky area showcasing the florescent deep-blue subalpine lake! For the charming mini loop around a couple nearby small tarns (respect restoration areas), hike right (SW) from the first lake fork a bit steeper on Tarn Loop Trail (314) then move right again (another fork, counterclockwise) past a few trees including larch (see Cutthroat Peak and Whistler Mountain) leveling around the larger tarn from its W side. Get a good view to the sheer granite comprising majestic Early Winters Spires across Blue Lake as you walk SE up a few feet then descend NE to the end of the cute loop nearest the viewpoint option. Head down to the TH giving others space.

For Washington Pass Overlook Trail (counterclockwise loop), take the signed paved path right (E) from the kiosk 100 yards through a few trees to the primary overlook on a large flat granite slab with a railing (be mindful near edges). To the right (S) hulking gigantically is Liberty Bell Mountain (across WA-20), panning left (SE) to Kangaroo Ridge with Silver Star Mountain and Vasiliki Ridge NE, and Hinkhouse Peak

Aficionados play in the early snow at the alluring Blue Lake!

directly above with Cutthroat Mountain and Whistler Mountain W. Simply sensational! Return or follow the railing left (N) as the pavement breaks up and you climb 3 steep rocky switchbacks to a little mezzanine back on the easier paved route with 360-degree views. Walk W along the laidback grade, finishing SW through the forest with a steeper turn to the TH. Return home mindfully happily, safely, with your nature battery charged! Be well!

INDEX

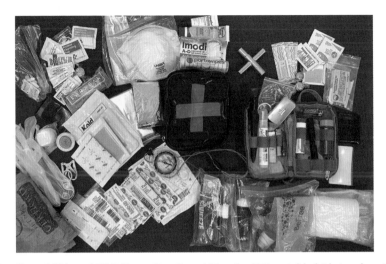

Evolving first aid kit and EDC (Every Day Carry) kit, plus TP/portable bidet and sanitizer, and choice of water filter for every hike or outing. First Aid: back-up meds (ibuprofen, acetaminophen, antihistamine, anti-nausea lozenges, anti-diarrhea pills), alcohol pads, antibiotic ointment, N-95 and other masks, lip balm, sunscreen, duct tape, snacks, pet bags, gloves, scissors, medical tape, blister pads, cold compress, emergency blankets, Steri-strips, bandages. EDC: Silcox key, mirror, emergency fishing kit, pocket knife, wire saw, deodorant, bug spray, waterproof matches and Vaseline-soaked cotton balls, flashlight, back-up meds, writing pad, tactical pen, flagging tape, magnifying glass...

Clearly I favor one name brand for each, be it backpack or hiking shoes, and always have a new pair of shoes for every season I'm breaking in, which lasts two to three years tops when hiking around 100,000 vertical feet per year! Included here: overnight pack, lightweight pack for all seasons, ultra-light pack for brief outings, smaller pack for biking, urban hiking, quick runs with minimal miles. Below: winter shoes with micro-spikes, lightweight shoes for spring/fall/winter, work horses for all seasons, spring/summer shoes, and shoes for little elevation change for spring/summer.

DEDICATION

A most heartfelt thank you goes out to our first responders in all sectors, including of course our firefighters who work very hard with Washington State Fire Fighters' Association, Washington State Council of Fire Fighters, Seattle Fire Department, National Interagency Fire Center, Washington Interagency Wildland Fire Training Academies, National Guard, National Coordination Center, State Patrol, and others, and now, especially over recent months (into years), our graciousness extends daily to our medical first responders including nurses, doctors, all hospital/clinic staff, EMTs, EMRs, health care workers, volunteers, and others in society who have worked tirelessly and fiercely under dangerous conditions risking everything to help others.

These first responders only have our well-being in mind, keeping us safe, as do volunteer trail maintenance crews including PNTA and WTA. Safe to hike and maintain or improve our health and mental fitness (more important than ever). And so I dedicate a portion of this book to all those who seek to lift their own spirits—to hike, to explore, to wonder, to contemplate, with other likeminded individuals, being thankful for what we have while breathing in the bounty of all the Pacific Northwest has to offer!

ACKNOWLEDGMENTS

Northwest Waterfall Survey, United States Geological Survey Map Database, West Margin Press—especially Jen in 2020 and my first-rate, first-class edit and design team, including Olivia, Rachel, Barbara, Sheila, Lohnes+Wright, Project Specialist Micaela, and Marketing Manager Angie! A sincere thank you also goes out to my good friends who have joined on hiking adventures, when even on the most straightforward hikes I seem to find a trail, loop, or bushwhack nobody thought of doing like that before! Friends like Erin, Yui (with Daikon-n-Murphy), Hannah, Adam, Ted, Erica, Allison, Anne, Clement, Julie, Emily, and Ernie.

Edited by Barbara Schultz
Indexed by Sheila Ryan
Overview Map by Lohnes+Wright

Library of Congress Control Number: 2020951372

ISBN 9781513267265 (paperback)
ISBN 9781513267272 (hardbound)
ISBN 9781513267289 (e-book)

Printed in China
25 24 23 22 21 1 2 3 4 5

Edited by Barbara Schultz
Indexed by Sheila Ryan
Overview Map by Lohnes+Wright

Cover photo by Don J. Scarmuzzi. Wildflower-choked meadows fed by crystal clear streams
in Paradise Park up to Mount Rainier!

Published by West Margin Press®

WEST
MARGIN
PRESS
WestMarginPress.com

WEST MARGIN PRESS
Publishing Director: Jennifer Newens
Marketing Manager: Angela Zbornik
Project Specialist: Micaela Clark
Editor: Olivia Ngai
Design & Production: Rachel Lopez Metzger

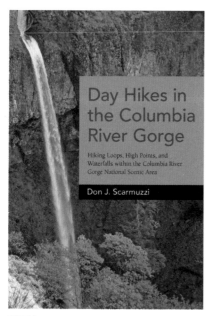
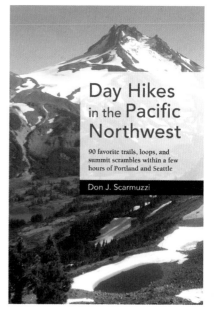